British
Buses
since
1900

Part One
1900-1945

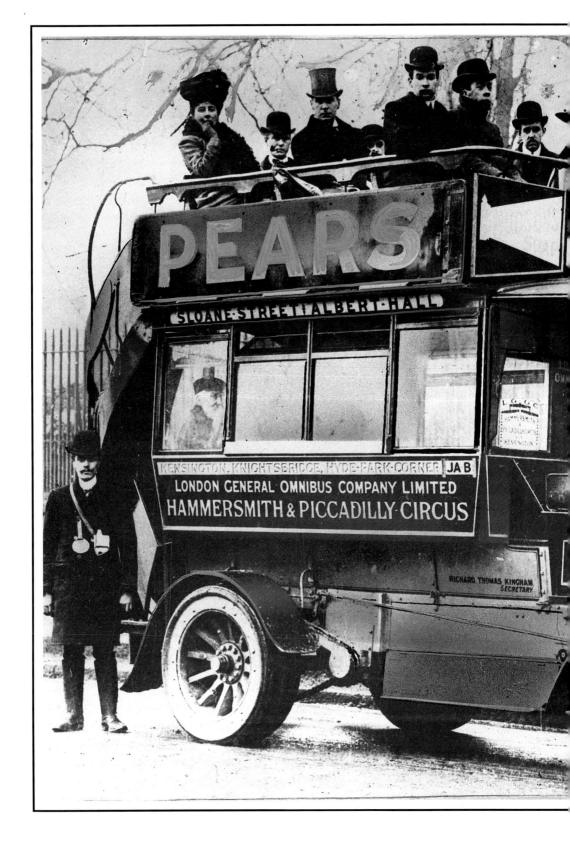

British Buses since 1900

Part One 1900-1945

John Aldridge

Ian Allan
PUBLISHING

Half title:
By the late 1920s or early 1930s most buses were reliable and durable. This 1934 Dennis Lancet *(left)* lasted until 1957, and the 1926 Leyland Lion until 1955; both are seen in their later days with Jersey Motor Traction. *Clifford Walters*

Title page:
Some early motorbuses carried adapted bodies off horsebuses, as on this 1905 Swiss Orion, one of two the LGOC put into service. *Author's Collection*

Contents — Part One

First published as:
British Buses before 1945 1995
British Buses since 1945 1995

This combined and updated edition 2000

ISBN 0 7110 2703 X

Published by Ian Allan Publishing

an imprint of Ian Allan Publishing Ltd, Terminal House, Shepperton, Surrey TW17 8AS.
Printed by Ian Allan Printing Ltd, Riverdene Business Park, Hersham, Surrey KT12 4RG.

Code: 0007/

Part Two   129

Foreword

There was a wealth of colour and variety in the buses on our roads from the turn of the century. Some 175 different makes of bus, coach or charabanc operated in the UK at some time between 1900 and 1945. Some makers produced, literally, just one vehicle. Many pioneer makers, like many pioneer bus operators, soon fell by the wayside, but others prospered and became almost household names.

At times a lack of foresight, or of advancement among the UK builders, encouraged an influx of European and North American makes. At other times the balance was redressed by British makers winning considerable export business.

In a potted history such as this, it is impossible to more than scratch the surface of what was once a large industry. Books have been written about individual makes, and even about individual models of one make. I have tried to provide interesting, but brief, portraits of some 175 makes which once ran on our roads, and also to mention some of the operators who ran them. One can only marvel at a small make such as Durham Churchill, built in penny numbers in Sheffield, achieving sales in the north of Scotland and the south of England. And how could a make with such an excellent pedigree as Milnes-Daimler, which once had the lion's share of the market, lose interest and sales just because its selling organisation found it easier or more profitable to sell cars?

Many of the early services were worked by wagonettes, which were little more than cars with extra seats. They were not able to carry enough passengers to make the services they ran profitable, and soon faded from the scene. So I have touched on them only briefly, as they never became part of the mainstream bus story.

Many of the changes that came about, as the result of technical developments or legislation, were applicable to many or most makes, and these are covered in the introduction, rather than reported and repeated under each individual make. The pictures, more than 200 of them, almost tell their own story. Incredible variety, sometimes, from one small maker; surprising uniformity from another.

John Aldridge
November 1994

The rival to the Leyland Titan was the AEC Regent, which was also designed by G. J. Rackham. The unusual 'camel's hump' in the roof was a shortlived feature to keep height down without infringing Leyland patents. These two Short Bros-bodied Regents were operated by Cornish Buses, a company later swallowed by Western National. *Ian Allan Library*

Introduction

'A vehicle without horses and without steam power... the driver of which need not be a mechanic...' wrote the *Financial Times* more than 100 years ago. It was describing a trial run in London, in 1889, of Radcliffe Ward's 'large and rather cumbrous' electric omnibus. But like so many other experiments and trials, it was to come to nothing. Certainly, by the end of the 19th century, among thinking horsebus proprietors, entrepreneurs and inventors there was the firm idea that the time was ripe for development of some kind of mechanical replacement for the horsebus. Just how uncertain it all was is exemplified by the London Steam Omnibus Co, which in 1899 changed its name to the Motor Traction Co. The company was said to have run a one-day trial of a mechanically-propelled bus between Oxford Circus and Ealing, although one report described it as an electric bus. Under its new name the company began the first regular motorbus service in London in October 1899, and that vehicle was certainly petrol-engined. The service lasted just 14 months.

The suggestion in that quotation from the *Financial Times* that the driver need not be a mechanic was not true of the early motorbus. It was not possible to recruit many drivers who had any mechanical ability, but mechanical sympathy was certainly desirable. Later, when numbers of buses were regularly at work on London's streets, one major operator employed roving mechanics to patrol the routes; when one came upon a broken-down bus he would take over, hopefully making some sort of temporary repair that would enable him to get the bus back to the depot.

Events in London in the early days were fairly well chronicled but early buses and bus services elsewhere were not always so well reported. There is also the problem as to what constituted a bus. Some of the early motor vehicles had a space behind the front seats that could be fitted with inward-looking bench seats on each side for a total of six, eight or even more people. These were known as wagonettes and were often used to provide some kind of mechanically-propelled public service.

The Edinburgh Autocar Co began what is thought to be the first licensed urban service in May 1898, using Daimler and MMC wagonettes which cost between £330 and £400. The service lasted until July 1901, when it folded with an accumulated deficit of £14,000. Heavy maintenance costs and the inability to carry sufficient passengers to generate a reasonable return contributed to the failure. There were other ventures in 1898 or 1899 at a wide spread of places, including Clacton, Falkirk, Folkestone, Herne Bay, Llandudno, Mansfield, Mablethorpe, Torquay and Tunbridge Wells. In London the South Western Motor Car Co started a Clapham Junction-Balham-Streatham service with 10-seat Daimler wagonettes in April 1901. High maintenance costs killed it off after a few months, but the service was noteworthy in having been managed by Walter Flexman French, who was later involved with East Kent, Maidstone & District and Southdown. A longer-lived London wagonette service began in September 1901 between Piccadilly Circus and Putney. This was operated by Francis John Bell, who was said to have successfully run motorbuses at Bournemouth for the previous two years. In London he used seven MMC wagonettes carrying six passengers 'inside' and two 'outside', the term 'outside' at that time being used by the Metropolitan Police to describe seats alongside the driver, outside the main saloon. The Police had juris-

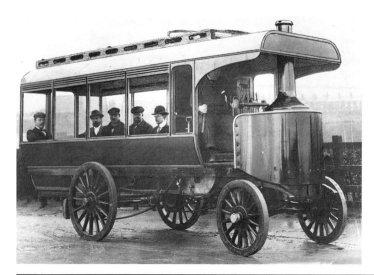

Left:
In 1900 the Dundee Motor Omnibus Co took delivery of this steam vehicle supplied by the Lancashire Steam Motor Co. The latter company was later to become Leyland. John Stirling of Hamilton is said to have arranged the sale; later he built the first Stirling and then Scott-Stirling buses. *Author's Collection*

Left:
Clarkson soon developed his steam buses into quite advanced vehicles; they boasted dynamo-driven interior lighting for example. The crew of this one, in Clarkson's own National fleet, are wearing summer uniforms. *Author's Collection*

Below:
In the early days wagonettes often operated passenger-carrying services, but limited capacity made their economics doubtful. This Wolseley-Siddeley dates from 1907. *Author's Collection*

diction over bus operations in London for many years. Bell's wagonettes had rear-entrance open bodies to which roofs and sides were added in inclement weather. Wagonettes soon faded from the scene, being replaced by more substantial (though not always more successful) vehicles. Relatively small vehicles, by the standards of the day, again reappeared in quantity in the mid-1920s. They were 14 to 16-seaters, on pneumatic tyres, when a quirk of the legislation permitted them to go faster than the more ponderous and conventional larger buses. But they were, like the wagonettes, relatively shortlived.

In the early 1900s, even the more substantial vehicles were not always successful. The Birmingham & Midland Motor Omnibus Co, better known as Midland Red, was formed in 1904 to take over and develop services begun by the Birmingham Motor Express Co in 1903. The fleet was increased, some

older vehicles being replaced, and then in late 1907 the whole fleet was withdrawn (and transferred to Deal and Warwick) and replaced with horsebuses. The company had done its best to improve the vehicles; some at least of the Milnes-Daimlers in the fleet, for example, had their original rack-and-pinion drive to the rear axle replaced by chain drive. Yet Milnes-Daimlers were arguably one of the better-designed makes.

Midland Red was not the only operator to revert to horses. Nottingham Corporation began a service in 1906 with three open-top Thornycrofts, but gave up in 1909 and substituted horsebuses on the route. That ceased in 1910, and Nottingham did not resume using motorbuses until 1920, whereas Midland Red restarted in 1912. Both Birmingham and Nottingham had efficient electric tram services, and that could be one reason for the cessation of these early motorbus

services. In contrast, political decisions had left much
of central London without trams but with a dense
network of horsebus routes and, along with the huge
and growing population and perhaps the prestige of
serving the capital, this led to many more operators
and makers attempting to serve it.

There were two main factors inhibiting the early
development of the motor vehicle in Britain. One was
the attitude of the establishment, which was generally
against the early motor vehicle. Government in
general, the church (then more powerful), magistrates
and councils saw no need or use for mechanically-
propelled vehicles. Almost the only people interested
in owning motorcars were the wealthy young, a very
small section of the community. In contrast, continental attitudes were different, particularly in France
and Germany. So, despite its engineering abilities and
talents, the UK initially possessed very few manufacturers, and most early vehicles were imported.

The other factor was the plateau of development
that the horsebus had reached. Its timber structure had
been fine-tuned to combine low weight with durability. Many of the earliest motorbuses combined high
weight with low capacity. Horsebus proprietors who
wanted change effectively wanted a vehicle that
would run an all-day service without the need for

several changes of horses. At its height the London
General Omnibus Co had a total of 1,418 horsebuses
and 17,000 horses. The companies needed stables for
the horses, enormous supplies of food and bedding,
and vets. Horsebuses usually seated a total of 26
passengers, 14 of them on the upper deck. A pair of
horses could work for some three hours before being
replaced, and an average horsebus on urban work
would run some 65 miles a day, but needed 10 horses,
plus extra spare horses to cover illness. Early motorbuses might be able to double that mileage in theory
at least, and could carry 34 passengers. Of course, the
motorbus cost more to buy, but if you take into
account the cost of 10 horses, there was not a big
difference in total costs. A rule of thumb, later, was
that three horsebuses could be replaced by two motorbuses, allowing for the slightly higher average speed
of the motorbus. But on more rural work, where daily
mileage was lower, and therefore fewer horses would
be needed, the figures were less favourable to the
motorbus.

Indirectly the railways also played an important
role in the development of the motorbus. They had
encouraged the urbanisation of the countryside and
provided a coarse passenger-carrying network across
the whole country. This, and the rising population, led
to the growth of towns and cities and the development
of tramway networks in many. By the turn of the
century, most tramways were being electrified or
were soon to be. But housing was continuing to
spread, certainly away from railway stations and
lines, and often away from the tram routes too.

Fixed rail transport of any kind is expensive to
install and needs a relatively high level of usage to

service its fixed costs. Yet there was still considerable local pressure on railways for the construction of further lines. So it is perhaps not surprising that several railway companies were very early operators of motorbuses. Some became quite big operators, with two, the Great Western and North Eastern, quickly building up sizeable fleets, seeing buses as feeders to their networks and as a way of deflecting demand for new railway lines. In the late 1920s and early 1930s the four main railways sold their vehicles and services to existing large operators (or occasionally created new operators) and then took a stake in these bus companies. By this time the railways had realised that the bus and the express coach were threatening much of their traffic.

The GWR began running two Milnes-Daimler single-deckers between Helston station and the Lizard in August 1903, and a month later the NER started a route between Beverley and Leven using new Stirling single-deckers. There were already Light Railway Orders for railways to be built to serve these places, but both companies delayed building because of the high cost and likely low returns. The GWR went on to become the best known and most successful railway bus operator with a fleet of some 300 by the late 1920s. Its first two buses, incidentally, were not new, but had been bought from Sir George Newnes, who had run them in conjunction with his Lynton & Barnstaple Railway. Within a couple of months of starting its Lizard service — in October 1903 to be

precise — the GWR had responded to an offer from Milnes-Daimler to buy 25 new bodied buses for a total cost of £19,541. It must have been the largest-ever order for motorbuses at that time and it contrasted dramatically with the position in London where, at the beginning of 1905, there were still only 20 motorbuses altogether; five of these were also Milnes-Daimlers. But during 1904 in London Thomas Tilling had ordered 24 more Milnes-Daimlers, to augment the one existing in the fleet, though when delivered, not all were used as buses. The following month, the Motor Omnibus Trust — better known as Vanguard — ordered 25 Milnes-Daimlers, with an option on a further 75. The summer of 1904 saw the GWR quick off the mark in another direction, this time with two circular tours from Penzance station. The same year also saw it start the first of several services from Slough station. By the end of 1904 the GWR had 34 motorbuses, the largest fleet in Britain.

No mention of the very early days would be complete without reference to Eastbourne Corporation. It began motorbus operations in April

1903, with a Milnes-Daimler single-decker running to Meads Village, but it was not the first municipal operator. That honour goes to Southampton, which began with an MMC Granville on trial in 1900, and in 1901 put a 12-seater Daimler wagonette into regular service. But that operation was subsequently abandoned, leaving Eastbourne as the earliest municipal operator that has continued unbroken up to the present day. Another early motorbus operator still operating today — albeit under a different name — was the Bristol Tramways & Carriage Co, which started with 12 open-top Thornycroft double-deckers in January 1906, and went on to add Fiat double-deckers and an Arrol-Johnston single-decker to its fleet in the same year. Two years later Bristol started building its own buses on an experimental basis, before going into full production in 1913.

The spur to virtually all development of the motor vehicle in the UK was, of course, the 1896 Highways Act, which abolished most of the infamous provisions of the 1865 Locomotives Act, including the need for a man with a red flag to walk in front of a mechanically-propelled vehicle. The Act of 1896 is still commemorated by the annual London-Brighton veteran car run, in which the newest vehicles date from 1904. Anyone who has seen it will have been amazed at the huge variations in shape, size and mechanism of the cars. So it was with the early motorbus. However, by 1905 a more or less standard shape and form of urban bus had emerged. The first example was said to have been a Milnes-Daimler double-decker with the engine at the front over the front axle, driver behind it, a straight frame and a rear entrance, rear staircase open-top body with a total seating capacity of 34. It was exhibited at the Crystal Palace Motor Car Show in 1904.

But it was to be some years before that relatively simple layout was developed into a reliable and economic vehicle. Chassis frames sagged, axles broke, rigid attachment of engines and gearboxes to the chassis frames resulted in thousands of breakages of bearer arms, and the individual machining of most parts meant that replacement parts rarely fitted. Use of common mild steel for parts that had to be machined and heat-treated caused endless problems; even gears were often made of mild steel which was just case-hardened. These mechanical uncertainties and frailties meant that, at least for urban use, only a double-decker was likely to make money for its operator, and even that was problematical. Lack of profit certainly drove the three major London bus operators to merge in 1908, when the London General, London Road Car and Vanguard fleets all came under one ownership, that of the London General. Between them they owned 885 of the 1,066 motorbuses running in London. There might have been no trams in central London, but there was a new competitor in the shape of the tube railways, which by this time were also loss-making.

Development of the bus in London, then, was slow at best, and its growth slower than elsewhere; horse-buses outnumbered motorbuses in London until 31 October 1910, when there were exactly 1,142 of each type licensed. Even in those days London's traffic was heavy and congested, and frequent stops and starts were hard on primitive and heavy vehicles. London was not alone among capital cities in being apparently backward; Berlin had no motorbuses in 1904.

The merger of the three major London bus operators did not initially help the finances. A special board meeting of the LGOC in 1909 described the great numbers of breakdowns and large sums spent on maintenance as 'enormous and disquieting' and talked of bringing in 'some well-known engineer... say the chief engineer of one of the leading railway companies'. That would have been a strange decision, since such a man would have been an expert on steam propulsion. Perhaps this is how the LGOC's own engineer, Frank Searle, persuaded the company to use the former Vanguard overhaul works at Walthamstow to build its own prototypes. Known as the 'X'-type, it cribbed shamelessly from the best features from the 28 types of vehicle in the existing fleet. Contemporary writers unkindly referred to it as the 'Daimler-Wolseley-Straker type'. After 61 had been built, the LGOC went on to design its famous 'B'-type. Unwittingly the 'B'-type benefited from a decision of the Metropolitan Police to reduce the maximum unladen weight of a bus from the current 5 tons to just 3^1/2 tons. That sent every bus maker with aspirations to sell vehicles for London back to the drawing board. Nobody had military use in mind when the 'B'-type was designed, but it, and mildly modified variants, were to prove of enormous worth in World War 1 — as lorries as well as buses.

The 'B'-type was not alone in this. One of the oldest manufacturers was Leyland, which had begun in 1896 as the Lancashire Steam Motor Co. It produced petrol-engined buses for London in 1905 and also produced huge numbers of vehicles for use in World War 1. Thornycroft was another pioneer maker to produce in quantity for the war effort. The concentration on military vehicles by some of the bus builders led to the brief entry into the market of a few manufacturers who had previously made only goods vehicles, though there was virtually no difference between a chassis for passenger carrying or one for goods.

A different approach to the vexed problems of clutch and transmission and high maintenance costs was taken by Thomas Tilling. Its engineer and manager, Percy Frost Smith, thought difficulties with the gearbox were the main snag, and these were both mechanical and human, the latter being the difficulty in finding suitable drivers who could handle the vehicles proficiently. Drivers were usually selected from horsebus or horse dray drivers, because of their

experience of driving in traffic, but sympathy with, or feeling for, animals did not often translate into mechanical sympathy.

Tilling's first experiment went on the road in 1908, using a Hallford chassis with petrol-electric equipment devised by W. A. Stevens, a Maidstone motor engineer. Known as the SB&S bus, and called 'Queenie' by the crews because of its smoothness, its petrol engine drove a dynamo which fed the current to two electric motors, one driving each rear wheel. An improved version was sold as the Hallford-Stevens, but Tilling took none. Instead, Frost Smith designed the Tilling-Stevens TTA1, which first appeared in 1911. This time the petrol engine and dc generator powered one electric motor which drove a live rear axle. Constraints on Tilling's London operation encouraged it to expand elsewhere, and in 1912 it transferred production of TTA1s to Maidstone, under the aegis of a new company, Tilling-Stevens, in which it had a shareholding. The design soon proved attractive to other operators, Midland Red being the first customer. The battery-electric was another type of electric bus often in the news in the early days, with companies being set up to run fleets of them. But none was really capable of a full day's work economically, and some that were demonstrated never actually ran in service.

The third means of propulsion for motorbuses was

Top:
First results of the LGOC's efforts to build a more reliable vehicle were the 60 'X'-types. They were followed by the famous 'B'-type, the first standardised bus to be built anywhere. *Author's Collection*

Above:
Operator Thomas Tilling was also unhappy with existing commercially-available designs, and wanted a vehicle that was easier to drive. The result was the Tilling TTA1 petrol-electric. *Ian Allan Library*

Left:
AEC and the LGOC were quick to introduce a new design after the end of World War 1. Their 'K'-type of 1919 placed the driver alongside the engine, thus creating room for more passengers. The vehicle also achieved a record low weight per passenger, which has never been bettered. *Author's Collection*

Below left:
Ex-War Department chassis, or chassis built to a similar specification, were bought by numerous operators. This RAF-type Leyland went into service in 1922 with Barnsley & District, the forerunner of Yorkshire Traction. Its Strachan & Brown body had a roller top roof, which could be opened in favourable weather, as shown. *Author's Collection*

Below:
Improvements in the pneumatic tyre offered not only a better ride and less skidding, but also the ability to cover greater distances. They helped particularly the development of the double-decker. Tyre makers worked hard to improve their products and show them to operators. This 22-seat Daimler charabanc was used on demonstrations in 1920, solid tyres often being substituted part way through to underline the improvement brought about by the pneumatic tyres. *Author's Collection*

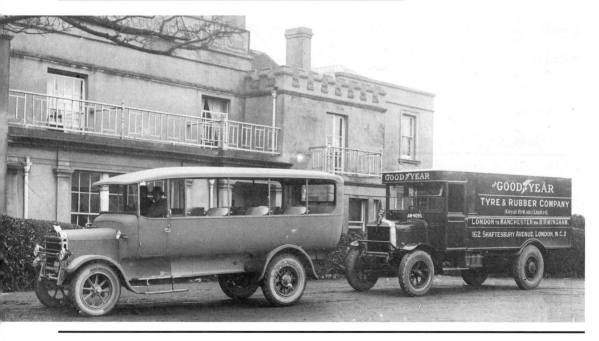

Above:
London General's 'NS' of 1923 was designed with a low chassis frame to take a covered-top body, but it took four years to gain permission to run a fleet in this form. *Author's Collection*

Right:
The chassis of an 'NS' rescued for preservation (and still on solid tyres) shows the dramatic curve of the chassis frame and the angled engine. *Author's Collection*

steam, though that too was to prove a blind alley. The very first Leyland bus was probably a steam-driven single-decker supplied to the Dundee Motor Omnibus Co in 1900, and Thornycroft put a steam double-decker on to a Hammersmith-Oxford Circus service of the London Road Car Co in March 1902. It had steel tyres, a converted horsebus body and a canopy above the upper deck, no doubt to keep the soot and sparks off passengers' heads. But it ran for only two months. The Thornycroft was coal or coke-fired, whereas most subsequent steam buses ran on paraffin. Several makers produced steam buses in the earliest days but there were only two types built in quantity that were of significance: Clarkson and Darracq-Serpollet. Metropolitan Steam Bus began operating in London during 1907, and by 1911 it had more than 50 of the latter double-deckers running. However, before the end of 1912 it had come to an agreement with the LGOC and replaced them all with 'B'-type buses. Its action was prompted no doubt by the bankruptcy of the French maker. A few of the buses and some others

of that make, plus a York-built Gardner-Serpollet, all worked for some years, probably until the mid-1920s, on the Isle of Wight for Ryde, Seaview & District Motor Services. But the best-known steamers were those of Thomas Clarkson. Unable to sell many, he decided to operate them himself, forming the National Steam Car Co in 1909. He built up a fleet of 173 double-deckers on London work; the last was withdrawn in 1919 and a smaller operation of his in Chelmsford did not last much longer.

World War 1 helped develop reliable and durable vehicles, and it also trained thousands of men to drive and repair vehicles. In its aftermath, there was a huge surplus of chassis, in varying states of repair, available cheaply. Enlightened manufacturers such as

Leyland bought as many of their own make as they could and reconditioned them, so that the company's reputation should not suffer.

Many of the vehicles were bodied as buses or charabancs, and were often bought by ex-servicemen who used their war gratuities to help set themselves up in business. Towns such as Harrogate, which at the end of the war were served by two operators, within a few years found themselves with newcomers as well — six in the case of Harrogate.

One big step in bus design was the LGOC's 'K'-type double-decker, first produced in 1919. It put the driver alongside the engine, instead of behind it. This involved changes to the engine, moving all its auxiliaries to the nearside so as to leave enough space for the driver on the offside. Rather more weight was placed on the front axle, but the bus seated 46, instead of the 34 of older designs. Part of the gain in capacity came from a modest relaxation of the width limit, which permitted forward-facing seats instead of all inward-facing ones on the lower deck. This forward-control layout, as it came to be called, eventually became standard on heavy-duty bus chassis, although not all makers followed quickly. The 'K'-type was also noteworthy in having the lowest unladen weight per passenger of any bus. A further development in London was the 'S'-type, with 54 seats in double-deck form; it needed a relaxation in the weight regulations before it became legal.

More significant was the LGOC's 'NS'-type, built of course by AEC. The company was anxious to fit covered tops to its double-deckers, since in inclement weather many would not use the upper deck. Most electric trams had had roofs for some years. So the chassis of the 'NS' was not straight-framed, with springs and axles simply hung below, but curved steeply downwards immediately behind the engine and front wheels, arched itself over the rear axle and finally lowered itself even closer to the ground to give a step height of little more than 12in (300mm). More important was the lowered centre of gravity, which the company hoped would make the covered top

acceptable to the Metropolitan Police. Eventually it did, but not before over 1,700 open-top 'NSs' had entered service. Approval for covered-top 'NSs' came in 1926. Ironically, Birmingham Corporation had gained approval for covered-top bodies in 1924 on high-frame AEC 504 chassis — the provincial version of the 'S'-type.

The achievement of the 'NS' was not merely in designing a satisfactory low chassis frame; mechanical components had to be altered or improved as well. For example, the relatively primitive lubrication system of the engine had to be made to cope with its angled mounting, which was necessary to line it up with the rear axle. For the first time, a bus chassis was significantly different from that of a goods vehicle.

For operators and manufacturers the most significant development in the 1920s was the pneumatic tyre, which gradually became a practical (and economic) proposition on larger buses and coaches. Increasing use of pneumatics coincided with a big surge in imported chassis, mainly from the USA. Its enormous domestic market offered economies of scale which permitted sales to the UK at low prices. Chassis often had six-cylinder engines and gave buses and coaches which could often out-perform established UK makes. But US supplies were ultimately strangled by imposition of import duties in the late 1920s and these in turn led to the establishment of the Bedford marque in the UK.

Above:
There were, of course, single-deck and six-wheel versions of both the Titan and the Regent from their respective manufacturers. The Leyland Tiger pictured here in 1930 was operated by Arthur Christy of Bolton on a service between that town and Gretna Green. *Author's Collection*

The coach market developed substantially in the 1920s, and became highly competitive. Small operators' purchasing decisions were often made on the cheapness of the hire purchase payments offered, rather than the durability of the vehicle.

Six-wheelers enjoyed an initial success in the mid to late 1920s, mainly because of doubts over the reliability of pneumatic tyres; Guy and Karrier did particularly well in this field. However, as tyres improved, the added complexity and weight went against the layout, and in the early to mid-1930s only operators who wanted relatively high capacity vehicles bought them; six-wheelers offered an extra few feet in length.

If there was a single event that changed the face of the bus industry it was the introduction of the Leyland Titan double-decker. This was designed by G. J. Rackham and was unveiled in 1927. Its low frame height, use of pneumatic tyres of reasonable size, coupled with a patented upper-deck layout with dropped gangway, gave a low overall height that allowed widespread use of double-deckers outside towns and cities for the first time. In themselves most features of the Titan, such as the six-cylinder engines or four-wheel brakes, were not new, but the total combination was. This was one reason for the Titan's success, while Gilford's more revolutionary double-decker a few years later was an utter failure. The Titan was just one of a family of double and single-deck models whose main attributes were to be copied by virtually every successful chassis builder in the 1930s.

New legislation was shortly to make its mark on the industry. Construction & Use Regulations laid down lengths, widths, gangway widths, seat spacing, tilt tests and also ended the more extreme rebuilds of vehicles such as those practised by the Barton Brothers. A licensing system for routes and timings introduced at the same time gave established operators protection. Together these measures killed off most of the remaining imports of small chassis, and several UK makers as well. But the licensing system, despite some unfairness, provided security for operators and that allowed them to make large-scale investments in new vehicles. The bus industry became one of relative prosperity at a time when the country as a whole was still depressed. The availability of qualified and skilled engineers at relatively low salaries launched the bus industry on a path of rapid improvement. Oil (or diesel) engines came in during the early 1930s. Early models were often found wanting, but within a few years they had been developed as successful and reliable, and were far more economical to run than petrol engines.

These modern, durable designs permitted large-scale replacement of many tram systems. 'Buy a Titan and bury a tram' said the famous Leyland advert. For political, economic and other reasons many trams were little changed from their form in the early 1900s, and Titans, AEC Regents and Daimler double-deckers were well able to replace them. Such sales again improved the total volume from these makers and this not only added to the economies of scale they enjoyed but also allowed further funds to be used for more research and development, which again put them ahead of smaller makers such as Thornycroft.

From the early 1930s there were trials with alternative engine positions. Of these, the AEC 'Q'-type achieved the highest volume of sales (which, even so, totalled just 348 chassis), and Leyland and the London Passenger Transport Board later in the decade developed the underfloor-engined single-decker (of which 88 were built). Midland Red produced four prototypes with rear engines, subsequently rebuilding them to an underfloor-engined layout; and AEC produced an underfloor-engined prototype for Canada in 1939.

Leyland also tried the rear engine position and, after trials with one prototype, went on to build 48 smaller single-deckers of this type for the LPTB. Maudslay had reasonable success with a set-back front axle design which still retained a vertical engine at the front, but provided room for up to 40 seats.

The outbreak of World War 2 first slowed and then halted PSV production. Subsequently makers were allowed to complete building vehicles on which work had already begun; these were known as 'unfrozen'

vehicles. New production was resumed under Government control and utility vehicles were produced. Single-deckers came solely from Bedford (the OWB, which was petrol-engined) and double-deckers initially from Guy (a surprising choice) and subsequently from Daimler and Bristol as well. Designs were basic with no use of chrome, aluminium or other materials in short supply. The same restrictions and others as well were applied to bodybuilders, with opening windows being limited to one per side per deck and, later, wooden slatted seats only being permitted. Strangely, the same restrictions did not always apply to vehicles that were rebodied, and at least one bodybuilder was allowed to go on using its standard metal frame body design. However, very poor timber framing was the worst feature of most utility bodies, and that was something beyond the control of the bodybuilders.

Three factors brought about the need for unfrozen

Above:
G. J. Rackham took a poor view of six-wheelers, considering them unnecessary, dated and unlikely to sell in quantity. However, mainly because of LGOC's enthusiasm for the type, AEC was to supply the operator with well over 1,400 chassis in just three years. This is the prototype double-deck AEC Renown when new. *Author's Collection*

Right:
Guy and Karrier had been pioneers of six-wheelers. Great claims were made for the advantages of six-wheel vehicles, and in the early days of giant pneumatic tyres, they might have had some merit. In front of Karrier's first of the type is posed comedian Wee Georgie Wood (far right) and others of a similar build. *Geoff Lumb Collection*

Guy had been first to complete a six-wheel double-decker. These five were supplied to Great Yarmouth Corporation in 1929, by which time their overall height, high lower-deck floor level and other features made them somewhat dated against AEC Renowns and Leyland Titanics. *Author's Collection*

Above right:
Legislation brought in to specify maximum dimensions and certain basic design parameters meant the end of ingenious rebuilding of the kind carried out by the Barton brothers. This Morris 1-ton chassis has been lengthened and gained an extra axle to enable it to seat 24. Barton also rebuilt and extended many Lancia chassis. *Author's Collection*

and utility vehicles. Older vehicles were continuing to wear out, some operators had vehicles destroyed in air raids, and the number of passengers carried had increased enormously as factories turned to war production and more factories — often in rural areas inaccessible by any other means — were specially built. However, wartime allocation of new vehicles (and indeed, spare parts as well) was under a Government bureaucracy, with its own interpretation of need. Particularly in its early days, this bureaucracy seemed quite unable to take account of operators' existing fleet composition. Operator A, with Leylands, might get two AECs, while operator B, with mainly AECs, would get three Leylands — all unfrozen examples, of course. Even worse was allocation of bodybuilder, with seven identical chassis for one operator, for example, carrying three different makes of body.

Another example of wartime stringency was Government plans for most operators to use 'producer gas' fuel for a proportion of their fleets. Petrol-engined vehicles were more suited for this conversion, which generally involved towing a two-wheel trailer. Coke or anthracite was burnt in the trailer to produce the gas. Considerable numbers of these trailers were manufactured, but operators were, not surprisingly, reluctant to use them. Those who did found power output was very low, so hilly routes were out of the question. Engine life was also reduced. London found it had to move stops to the far side of bridges over railways, as restarting on a rising gradient with a full load could prove impossible. Luckily, fuel supplies began to improve — all liquid fuel was imported in those days — and many trailers were scrapped without being used.

In the later part of the war some manufacturers and bodybuilders were permitted to develop and build prototypes of planned postwar designs. Later the austerity specification was modified; upholstered seats, more opening windows, polished aluminium radiator shells and other features all returned.

Wartime buses may not have appeared particularly attractive, but they were reliable and ran high mileages with the minimum of attention. Many utilities, and indeed many 1930s vehicles, often rebodied, survived in active service into the middle and late 1950s, while some lasted into the early 1960s. In 45 years the British bus industry had come a long way.

Left:
The new breed of relatively lively, low buses meant the end of older vehicles, though many World War 1 designs had lasted well. This former War Department Daimler 'Y'-type of Potteries had had its wheelbase extended, and was not withdrawn until 1930. *Ian Allan Library*

Below:
Makers lost no opportunity to promote their products. To coincide with the announcement of the Regent in October 1929, AEC's first prototype made a 12hr non-stop 500-mile continuous run round the Brooklands race track. It averaged 41mph and speeds were said to have reached 50mph at times. AEC went on to deliver over 1,000 chassis in the first year of production. *Author's Collection*

Left:
AEC was the first UK commercial vehicle maker to install a moving track on which chassis were built. But another much smaller company to track build was Gilford, pictured here. Its models enjoyed enormous success, mainly with smaller operators, but later these sold out to larger companies (or just faded away) and a subsequent obsession in developing a revolutionary low-floor double-decker (which proved unsaleable) ultimately killed the company. *Author's Collection*

Above:
AEC did not rest on its laurels. Late in 1932 a prototype side-engined bus with single wheels all round and virtually all floorspace given over to passenger accommodation appeared on the streets of London. It was the first of the 'Q'-type. *Author's Collection*

Right:
Double-deck variants of the 'Q' were also built. They offered an unrivalled front-entrance layout that would have been ideal for one-man operation, except that there was no requirement for it; 20 or (later) 26 seats were the most permitted on a one-man operated bus for many years. *Ian Allan Library*

Below:
A major development in the early 1930s was that of the oil (or diesel, or compression ignition) engine. Here at AEC's special Oil Engine Show at Southall in November 1930 are members of the Municipal Tramways & Transport Association. Among the vehicles they are inspecting is (left) one of the first three Regents (the LGOC 'ST'-type) to be fitted with the AEC-Acro 8.1 litre oil engine, the first to be offered commercially. However, it was not until AEC called in Ricardo to help with a redesign that the engine became reliable. *Author's Collection*

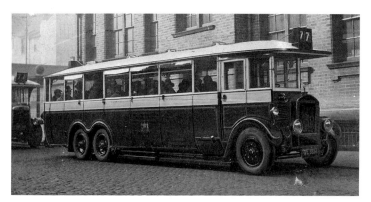

Left:
Mercedes-Benz was an undoubted pioneer of the oil engine and Sheffield Corporation put this Karrier six-wheeler into service in 1930 with a Mercedes diesel under the bonnet. It was probably much more reliable (and more econom-ical) than it had ever been with a Karrier engine. *Author's Collection*

Above:
A surprising move saw Tilling divest itself of Tilling-Stevens, which reformed as TSM. For a few years the new company did well with conventional petrol-engined models, but began to lose out after Tilling bought Bristol. This TSM with Strachan body was a 'one off' purchase by Aldershot & District early in 1932. It had been exhibited at the 1931 motor show in the oper-ator's colours. *Ian Allan Library*

Left:
Daimler built up a considerable business with municipal operators in the 1930s, much of it with the help of the legendary Gardner engine. It still built cars as well. This is the new passenger vehicle bay at the factory, complete with bus chassis, that came into use in 1934. *Ian Allan Library*

Above:
Not all the successes of the 1930s were with heavier diesel-engined chassis. Bedford sold nothing but light, mass produced, petrol-engined chassis in large numbers. The Duple-bodied coach was the most popular version; this is one new to Southern National in 1939. It seated 25. *J. Taylor*

Right:
With Tilling Group backing, Bristol established itself as a major builder in the 1930s, making increasing use of Gardner diesel engines. A mid-1930s JO5G of United Automobile Services is guided through a tight corner in Hawes, North Yorkshire. *Author*

Right:
Interest in alternative engine positions continued, even if AEC's 'Q' had not sold well. L. G. Wyndham Shire, Midland Red's chief engineer, designed and built four rear-engined PSVs in 1935-36. These had petrol engines and entrances ahead of the front axle. Here Wyndham Shire stands by one of the bus versions. *Ian Allan Library*

Right:
Next to move the engine position was Maudslay. This is the 1937 Commercial Motor Show exhibit, the SF40, later renamed the Magna. About 100 were built between 1935 and 1939, with Maudslay petrol or Gardner diesel vertical engines and a set-back front axle that allowed 40 seats. *Author's Collection*

Above:
Tilling-Stevens' Successor of 1937 had a three-axle chassis with independent rear suspension. Its eight-cylinder 7.45 litre diesel engine was a horizontally-opposed unit of flat or underfloor layout, had twin fuel pumps and drove through a seven-speed preselector gearbox. Two chassis were built and one bodied (by Duple, as illustrated) but no operator ever ran one; probably Tilling-Stevens lacked the resources to develop the design. *Author's Collection*

Above:
Less successful was the other LPTB-Leyland, a small rear-engined bus. Teething troubles and the onset of war (when larger, not smaller buses were needed) gave all 49 vehicles a chequered career. They had a vertical engine with the radiator behind it. A bodied example is pictured on page 27. *Author's Collection*

Right:
There could be fewer greater contrasts with Leyland's success than that of Maudslay, struggling along and selling chassis mainly in single figures. Thus Neath & Cardiff Luxury Coaches represented one of the manufacturer's largest customers, buying a total of seven SF40 or Magna chassis. This is one of four with Gardner engine and striking Duple bodywork delivered in 1939. *Author's Collection*

Below:
Some operators preferred rear entrances, others front entrances on single-deckers. But both municipal and company operators in Scotland were the main enthusiasts for this style of 'cut away' rear entrance (with or without door). This SMT AEC Regal dates from 1938. In 1955 it was one of a number to lose their Alexander bodies and receive new Burlingham coach bodies. *Gavin Booth Collection*

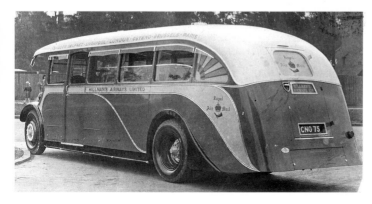

Left:
Many independent operators vanished in the early 1930s, unable to gain licences for what they were already operating. Entrepreneur Edward Hillman began coach operation in east London in 1928 and within three years had over 100 Gilfords in his fleet. Many were compulsorily acquired by the LPTB in 1934, but Hillman had also begun air services. In 1935 the link from central London to his Essex airport was provided by two of these Gilford Heras with Wycombe bodies and reinforced bullion compartments at the rear. *Author's Collection*

Left:
Some coach operators probably bought AEC 'Qs' or Maudslay SF40s for the improved appearance at the front. Bus operators also became keen on projecting a modern image. Leeds Corporation, after buying somewhat dated-looking double-deck bodywork, then took two striking full-fronted double-deckers on AEC Regent chassis. One was fitted with MCW bodywork and the other with Roe. Subsequently a new Roe body for Leeds of distinctive appearance became a regular motor show tradition. *Ian Allan Library*

Left:
London's RT type chassis of 1938 represented the peak of development of the conventional front-engined bus. Use of such a large engine — 9.6 litres — in the interest of long life and economy was new. Air brakes had been tried before (on trolleybuses) but the air-operated pre-selector gearbox was new. Flexible engine mountings, high driving position, automatic brake adjustment and chassis lubrication combined with other features to produce a design that was still ahead of its time 15 years later. Just one chassis, pictured, went outside London — to Glasgow in 1940. Its Weymann body was similar to others supplied to Glasgow. *Ian Allan Library*

Right:
Having first built one rear-engined prototype for evaluation, with a transverse petrol engine, Leyland went on in conjunction with London Transport to develop a 20-seat rear-engined version of the Cub. One prototype and 59 production versions were planned. The vertical diesel engine was mounted in line with the chassis, and gearbox and worm-driven rear axle were mounted as one unit. War intervened and only 49 were built. War also reduced the need for small buses and teething troubles were never properly solved. *Author's Collection*

Left:
Just ahead of the rear-engined Leyland came development of a full-sized underfloor-engined single-decker, again in conjunction with LT. A horizontal version of Leyland's 8.6 litre diesel engine was mounted on the offside of the chassis below floor level immediately behind the driver. Some 87 production versions followed for LT as sightseeing or Green Line coaches. The driving position on the prototype was very high (it seems to have been an LT obsession at the time) and this picture shows angles of vision being checked on the incomplete vehicle at Leyland. *Author's Collection*

Right:
The onset of war soon cut short the supply of new vehicles and many operators also lost existing vehicles requisitioned for military use. This elderly Maudslay was used as a mobile gunnery school for Merchant Navy personnel. Pupils are learning to aim at a model aircraft running on wires suspended from the outside of the bus. *Ian Allan Library*

Left:
Completed export orders that could not be shipped were diverted to some UK operators with urgent need for more vehicles. Some were of larger dimensions than legal here, and special dispensation was given to run them. The West Monmouthshire Omnibus Board received this MCW-bodied Daimler intended for Salisbury Municipality in Southern Rhodesia; it was 30ft long and 8ft wide (9.1m x 2.4m). It is seen in the postwar era. *Author's Collection*

Right:
Other home needs were partly met by 'unfrozen' vehicles. Makers were authorised to complete vehicles on which work had begun and then been stopped. Some unfrozen chassis, such as 11 Leyland Titans for LT, received utility bodywork, in this case by Park Royal. One is seen in later life as a staff bus at Hounslow. *Author*

Below:
Guy, Daimler and Bristol all eventually built utility buses, allocation of which was government-controlled. Park Royal bodywork is also fitted to this early utility Guy delivered in May 1943 to Colchester Corporation. All told, Colchester was allocated a total of 16 double-deckers between 1942 and 1945. They were of two different chassis makes and had bodywork by five different builders. *Rex Kennedy Collection*

Right:
Many single-deckers had their seats rearranged to face inwards to allow more room for standing passengers. An example is this Western National Bristol L5G of 1938, which is seen in war-torn Plymouth. Its perimeter seating will be of particular value on the busy service to Torpoint Ferry. *Ian Allan Library*

Right:
Only one utility single-deck type was made, the Bedford OWB. Three bodybuilders — Duple (which did the design), Roe and Scottish Motor Traction — constructed the bodies to an identical specification. Many large operators took none, perhaps because they did not want petrol engines, but others took a quantity. Two Belfast Corporation examples await workers from the shipyards. *Author's Collection*

Right:
Many vehicles were rebodied to replace worn-out or war-damaged bodywork. But the Scottish Bus Group replaced many single-deck bodies with new double-deck ones. This Western SMT 1937 Leyland Tiger originally had an Alexander coach body, but it, along with 45 others, was rebuilt to Titan specification and fitted with a new lowbridge utility Alexander double-deck body. *Author*

Above:
In World War 1 some operators voluntarily used town gas to overcome fuel shortages. Chapman & Sons of Eastbourne — a famous pioneering operator which ultimately sold out to Southdown — fitted this Dennis charabanc with wooden tray and inflatable bag. The equipment was probably provided by Barton Brothers, which developed similar equipment for its own fleet. *Author's Collection*

Left:
World War 2 ultimately saw the Government leaning heavily on operators to use anthracite-burning producer gas trailers to power a proportion of their fleet, and thus save scarce imported fuel. This 1940 picture shows a prototype installation developed by Eastern National and towed by a Leyland of Hicks Bros of Braintree. Each trailer used about one ton of home-produced anthracite a week. *Author's Collection*

Right:
During the war manufacturers were allowed to produce the occasional prototype of what they hoped to build when the war was over. Midland Red substantially reworked its four experimental rear-engined single-deckers; they reappeared with an underfloor-engined layout that became standard when the company resumed building its own buses. *Birmingham & Midland Museum of Transport Collection*

Above:
After the war shortages remained and operators had to cope with even greater numbers of passengers with elderly fleets. Prominent in this early postwar view at Oxford are a veteran Maudslay double-decker of Charlton on Otmoor Services and a United Counties Bristol JO5G-ECW coach of 1937. *W. T. Lambden*

Right:
Many operators solved part of their problems by having prewar chassis rebodied. Because of the poor quality of the materials used, many wartime bodies soon also needed rebuilding if not replacement. This Bristol Tramways double-decker is not a Bristol, despite its radiator, but a rebuilt wartime Guy now carrying an older body built by the operator. *Ian Allan Library*

ADC

Daimler had had a close relationship with AEC before World War 1, and this was followed by the creation of a joint company, Associated Daimler Co, in 1926, to share components but with most chassis being built at AEC, first at Walthamstow and then at its new Southall factory.

The relationship lasted only to 1928, after which the partners went their separate ways. Not all the models built under the ADC banner were new. In 1927 there was the 'LS' or London Six, a cumber-some six-wheeler (mainly a double-decker) of which most went to London General and were fitted with Daimler's six-cylinder sleeve-valve engine. More modern were a pair of forward and normal control models of modest weight, the 423 and 424, some of which had the Daimler engine. Surprisingly, they were built at Coventry, and carried no name or initials on their radiators. The most successful was the earlier forward-control 416, which had a frame almost as low as the 'NS', a new gearbox and a choice of AEC or Daimler engine. Nearly, 1,000 were sold in two-and-a-half years.

Left:
The most successful ADC chassis was the 416, available with AEC's four-cylinder 5.1 litre engine or Daimler's six-cylinder, sleeve-valve engine of just 3.5 litres. This 1927 example with Massey body went to the Isle of Man and later joined the fleet of Isle of Man Road Services. *Author's Collection*

Centre left:
Greenock & Port Glasgow Tramways had bought a batch of 'NS'-type ADC double-deckers in 1925-26, and in 1928 tried this ADC 802 for two months. None were, however, bought. The model had been hastily designed to meet competition from the new Guy and Karrier six-wheelers, but won virtually no orders. Two became AEC staff buses, one having 104 seats. They ferried staff between Walthamstow and the new AEC factory at Southall. *Ian Allan Library*

Bottom left:
This ADC 423 with United Auto body was a new chassis, built by Daimler at Coventry and fitted with Daimler's sleeve-valve, six-cylinder engine. Built for exhibition at the 1927 Commercial Motor Show, the bus was subsequently bought by Crosville to become only one of two non-Leyland full-size buses in the fleet. It is pictured at AEC's Southall works before delivery. *Ian Allan Library*

Left:
An example of AEC's 3-4-ton chassis, as built between 1915 and 1919 and here fitted with a charabanc body. This one is unusual in having a central gangway. Note the double running board. This vehicle had a Tylor engine. *Author's Collection*

Later, in 1926, there was another joint arrangement with Daimler: chassis were built (first at Walthamstow and then at AEC's new factory at Southall) as Associated Daimlers and fitted with engines by either maker. This arrangement broke up in 1928 at about the same time as the legendary G. J. Rackham was poached from Leyland — he said he couldn't stand the Lancashire weather — as chief engineer of AEC.

During World War 1 AEC had built some 8,000 'Y'-type chassis for the War Department. It was a heavier version of the 'B', with larger engine, conventional gearbox and pressed steel chassis frame (that of the 'B'-type was flitched timber). Production for civilian use continued after the war, some having Daimler sleeve-valve engines. Many were bodied as buses. New models were the 'K'-type of 1919, in which the driver was moved alongside the engine, and the later, larger 'S'-type (which still retained a flitched timber chassis). Vehicles for other than the LGOC were later known by type numbers: 301 for the 'K'; 401 for the 'S'; and, 501 for improved 'Y'-types.

A huge step forward came with the 'NS', which had a drop frame of steel, designed to lower the centre of gravity of the vehicle, and — hopefully — persuade the Metropolitan Police to allow the upper deck to be roofed. Technically it was a remarkable achievement in aligning the propshafts of an engine high above the front axle with a chassis-mounted gearbox and a low rear axle with underslung worm drive.

Major leaps in design came with G. J. Rackham, the first being a new six-cylinder overhead camshaft engine. Owing more than a passing resemblance to that which he had designed for Leyland, it went into production within months. It was fitted into the 416/426 chassis, now the Reliance model 660. It transformed the vehicle and enabled AEC to more than use up the stocks of chassis parts it already had. It sold to many coach operators who liked its smooth and quite powerful engine.

AEC

Most manufacturers begin in a small way, but the Associated Equipment Co was a separation from the vehicle building works of the London General Omnibus Co at Walthamstow and, therefore, started in June 1912 with large-scale production already under way. It was a subsidiary of the London Underground Group (like the LGOC) and no doubt the separation was intended to facilitate sales to other operators, but the full order book meant that there were none for over a year. The first major customer was United Automobile, but the outside sales were made by Daimler, with which an agreement had meanwhile been concluded. These vehicles carried Daimler on the radiator, and many had Daimler engines.

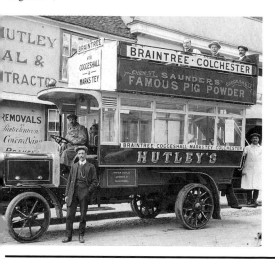

Left:
This is a very standard 'B'-type chassis of 1914, albeit operated by Arthur Hutley of Braintree, Essex. He had bought the bus from the Daimler Co of Pall Mall, London — at the start of the co-operation between the two makers. *Author's Collection*

The next step was the Regal single- and Regent double-deckers, announced in 1929. With nicely curved dropframes, these had a more compact front end than their Leyland equivalents, and the new engine. There was also a six-wheeled version, the Renown, which was disliked by Rackham but taken up enthusiastically by the LGOC to make it by far the best-selling six-wheeler on the market.

AEC was early into developing oil engines (as diesels were then usually called) and, after the usual teething problems, developed a reliable 8.8 litre engine in 1931, soon adding a 7.7 litre unit as well. Both benefited from Ricardo combustion chamber design. From 1932 AECs were offered with fluid transmission, which greatly eased urban bus driving. London standardised on it. Initially, Daimler, which had developed the fluid coupling and Wilson-type epicyclic gearbox, supplied complete units to AEC.

The creation of the London Passenger Transport Board in July 1933 to take over all local bus and coach (along with tram and trolleybus) operations in the London area brought about the total separation of AEC, though the LPTB continued to buy most of its buses and coaches from the company.

There were two other notable developments. The first was the 'Q'-type, with engine mounted behind the offside front wheel. Designed by Rackham chiefly as a double-decker, it sold mainly as a single-decker; a total of 348 chassis were built, of which only 23 were double-deckers. With an entrance ahead of the (set back) front axle, the staircase could rise neatly over the engine and front wheel. The design deserved to do better; 20 years later most of its features could be found on new underfloor-engined single-deckers.

The other development was production, from 1939, of 150 of London's 'RT'-type to meet a new specification. With larger engine (9.6 litres) and air brakes, its features too were later to be widely copied.

Above:
United Automobile was a big buyer of AECs after World War 1. These six buses with 45hp chassis were part of a 1919 order for 50. The four on the right have rudimentary double-deck bodywork of a rather basic style used by the company at the time. The chassis was the same for either.
Author's Collection

Right:
Better remembered for its coaches, Greyhound was also a bus operator. This 'NS' supplied in 1925 was similar to those running in London, though later Greyhound had pneumatic-tyred examples. Note the man perched alongside the driver. Greyhound was later taken over by Bristol Tramways. *Author's Collection*

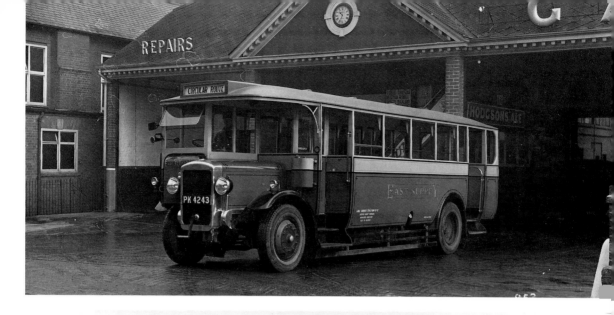

Top:
This AEC Reliance was one of the first to be fitted with the new Rackham-designed six-cylinder engine that transformed the model. It entered service with East Surrey Traction in November 1928; the new model 660 Reliance was not announced until January 1929. The bus had a Hall Lewis 32-seat dual-door body, and is seen outside the old (now demolished) Reigate garage.
Ian Allan Library

Above:
Dundee Corporation operated this AEC Regent double-decker with petrol engine and Park Royal 50-seat bus body from July 1932 until 1949. Originally a demonstrator, it was bought from AEC in October 1932.
Rex Kennedy Collection

Left:
Despite Rackham's misgivings about the concept, AEC's six-wheeled Renown sold in numbers for a few years, and there were isolated further sales in the late 1930s. The LGOC was the biggest customer, buying some 1,400. Though most were double-deckers, there were 200 single-deckers, some of which were to prove the longest-lived. Nearly half of them gained AEC 7.7 litre diesel engines from scrapped (and newer) London STLs, and some had bodywork substantially rebuilt (as here) to enable them to survive until 1952. *Tony Bunce*

Centre left:
The biggest fleet of AEC Regents was bought by London Transport. Some 2,000 of the style illustrated, with 56-seat body, AEC 7.7 litre diesel engine, fluid flywheel and pre-selector gearbox, were bought up to 1939, with the last surviving in London until 1954. This one is seen, in 1955, working for Premier Travel of Cambridge. *Author*

Below:
A production example of AEC and LT's joint design, the RT, is seen at Victoria in postwar years. The war stopped production at 150 vehicles, delivered between October 1939 and January 1942. Shortages of materials because of the war effort delayed body production in particular. *Author*

AJS

Better known for its motorcycles, A. J. Stevens & Co (1914) of Wolverhampton built PSVs for just three years — 1929-31 — at a time when sales of motorcycles were poor. There were three models, all with Coventry Climax petrol engines: the Pilot, designed as a 26-seater in either normal or forward-control layout; the forward-control 32-seat Commodore; and — finally — the Admiral which was introduced in 1931 and, therefore, had a very short production run. In October 1931 the company went into liquidation. Design of the Pilot is said to have been based on the Star Flyer, designs for which were passed on by Guy after it bought Star. All three makes were built in the same town.

Below:
A forward-control AJS Commodore is put through its paces over the *Modern Transport* test route on a wet 1930 day. A year later the company had gone. The Commodore had a Coventry Climax petrol engine. *Ian Allan Library*

Bottom:
A normal-control version AJS Admiral with Auto Cellulose body complete with two hinged doors. It was supplied to the Central Garage of Longford, Coventry. *Ian Allan Library*

Albion

Like many others, the Albion Motor Car Co began by making cars and dogcarts. However, it decided to give up cars in 1912 when it found that over two-thirds of total production was of commercial vehicles. Despite this it took until 1931 for the company name to be changed to Albion Motors. Over the years the company earned a reputation for solid, no-frills engineering exemplified perhaps by the way it still offered four-cylinder engines as an option when most others had ceased to build them. For all that, it survived the depression years when rivals such as Halley folded.

Albion began in 1899, upstairs, in 3,600sq ft of space above the Clan Line repair shops in Glasgow. It was started by Norman O. Fulton and T. Blackwood Murray, who had previously been, respectively, works manager and commercial manager at car maker Arrol-Johnston. The first vehicle was produced in 1900. By 1902 Albion was offering half-ton vans and, by 1903, had moved to much larger premises at Scotstoun, Glasgow. Larger vans soon followed and 1910 saw the introduction of the A10, a 32hp model with monobloc four-cylinder engine, chain drive and a patent engine governor and lubricator. Before World War 1 the company had built up an impressive clientele for PSVs, including Wolverhampton Corporation Tramways, David MacBrayne and the Largs, Wemyss Bay & West Coast Motor Service of Largs. Some 6,000 A10 lorries were supplied to the War Department between 1914 and 1918, and production continued into the 1920s.

New models included a 20hp 1½-tonner, while 1923 saw the introduction of the Viking for up to 18 seats, with a relatively low frame height; just one step was needed, it was said. A drop-frame range, the 26 Series, was introduced in October 1925, not that long after AEC's pioneering 'NS'. As with the earlier 24

Series a variety of wheelbases was offered. The first forward-control chassis came in 1927. It was called the Viking PM28 and used the same 30/60hp engine as the 26 Series. Scottish Motor Traction placed one order for 24 PM28s in March 1927, and by the end of 1929 had become a big Albion user, with nearly 90 of various types bought from 1926 onwards. By 1930 there were forward and normal-control Vikings, with four and six-cylinder engines, the last-named being called Viking Sixes. Vikings were phased out in 1931-32.

The Valkyrie came in at the end of 1930 with a 60bhp five-litre four-cylinder engine. It was replaced from 1933 with a 6.1 litre four-cylinder engine; by this time diesels were an option. Albion had not been particularly quick to develop its own diesels, and had, therefore, offered Beardmore, Dorman and Gardner units. These continued to be fitted after Albion had designed its own diesel. New Valkyrie models came again in 1935, with one offering a 110bhp 7.8 litre six-cylinder unit. The same petrol engine was also available in the Valiant, and soon this powerful version of the Valkyrie replaced it. Valiants were less popular, lasting from 1931 to 1936, and were forward-control chassis bigger than the Viking Six and more powerful than the Valkyrie. Yet another model running at the same time was the Victor. First designed as a 20-seater, of normal-control layout with a 42bhp 3.15 litre engine, it soon gained a 60bhp 3.62

Below:
Despite its early concentration on commercials, it took Albion a long time to change its name, as the background to the picture shows. The chassis is a normal-control, low-frame model. The relatively neat front end contrasts with that achieved on forward-control versions at the same time. *Ian Allan Library*

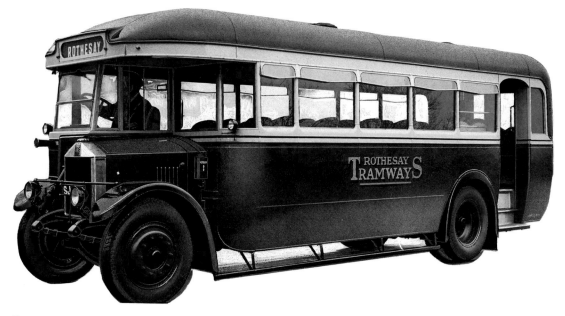

Above:
Rothesay Tramways took delivery of a batch of these Albion 30/60hp models in 1930. The 32-seat bodies featured an angled front bulkhead window on the nearside. The operator was later owned by Western SMT and still later merged into it. *Author's Collection*

Right:
No doubt the sight of all those AEC and Leyland double-deckers in service in Glasgow spurred Albion to offer a double-deck chassis. All told, Glasgow Corporation bought 130 in the years up to 1939, though Albion did not always gain a share of the annual orders. Fifteen of these Venturers, with Albion's own new 9.08 litre diesel engine and Cowieson 56-seat all-metal bodies, were delivered in 1938, alongside 85 AEC Regents. *Author's Collection*

Right:
Red & White Services was a strong Albion supporter in the 1930s, and also ran a couple of dealerships for the make. This CX11, with centre-entrance Duple body, dates from 1939. It is pictured (despite the fleetname) working for Bristol Tramways in Stroud in 1953 after an exchange of territory and vehicles with Red & White. A further exchange of territory the following year saw the bus returned to Red & White. *M. J. Mogridge*

litre unit. Further changes included forward-control models and a 65bhp 3.89 litre engine. Most were sold as coach chassis. The model lasted up to 1939 by which time 30 seats were the norm.

Albion's first venture into double-deckers came late in 1932 with the Venturer. Initially this was fitted with a 6.85 litre petrol engine or a Gardner diesel and had a seating capacity of up to 51. The 1935 Venturer could have up to 55 seats, and a larger 7.8 litre petrol engine developing 103bhp was an option as was a Gardner. The 1937 Commercial Motor Show saw the launch of the first of the CX series of models, which at last had the engine and gearbox mounted in one unit, a feature previously found only on the light Victor. Valkyrie CXs could have 6.1 litre four-cylinder or 9.1 litre six-cylinder petrol engines, Albion's own diesel, or Gardner 5LW or 6LW diesels fitted; some even had Gardner 4LWs. Venturer CXs had just Albion's 9.1 litre diesel as standard and Gardner 6LW or Albion petrol engines as options.

There was also, for a time, a high-capacity six-wheel single-decker. It was a version of the Valkyrie, with Young's Bus Service of Paisley (later to become part of Western SMT) buying 15 in 1937-38. They had cumbersome-looking Cowieson bus bodies seating 39.

All-British or ABC

George Johnston, formerly the Johnston in Arrol-Johnston, formed the All-British Car Co of Glasgow in 1906. It built and ran its own bus or buses — perhaps as many as six — in London for just a few months in 1907. They were of remarkably squat design, said to be 1ft 4in (400mm) lower than other open-top double-deckers, helped by the sunken gangway on the lower deck. A horizontal four-cylinder engine was mounted compactly over the front wheels. The chassis was said to be guaranteed for three years, and the company had an agreement (spectacularly unfulfilled) to sell 250 buses through a

sister company, the London-based All-British Chassis Bus Co.

In 1908 three ABC double-deckers went into service with Autocar of Tunbridge Wells, and one of them was still used as a spare bus in 1914.

Alldays

Alldays & Onions Pneumatic Engineering Co of Birmingham could trace its ancestry back to 1650. Some 253 years later it started building cars, followed by vans and then, in 1911, trucks with a 40hp engine. In that same year it also built the chassis for the first Railless trolleybuses. Though it never offered motorbus chassis as such, Sir William Lever (of Lever Brothers and Port Sunlight fame) began a bus service with one (plus one Star) in June 1914.

However, in World War 1, West Bridgford UDC, situated on the outskirts of Nottingham, bought a total of seven Alldays chassis. Five replaced virtually new Dennis bus chassis which had been taken over by the War Office. The Alldays were chain driven, which the War Office did not favour. Each chassis cost £595, and the first five took the registrations of the earlier Dennis quintet (a habit not uncommon in those days) as well as the latter's Dodson 32-seat double-deck bodies. The last remaining Alldays were sold by West Bridgford in 1921, one or two seeing subsequent service with another operator.

Argus

Argus was one of Germany's smaller makes and was in business for about four years. The Manx Electric Railway, on the Isle of Man, ran two of the type with charabanc bodies from 1907 until the outbreak of World War 1. The duo operated a summer service from a station on Snaefell Mountain Railway to a nearby beauty spot.

Argyll

Cars and then vans based on car chassis were the early products of this Glasgow-based company, which traded from 1902 until 1914. By 1904 there was a 15cwt (3/4 ton) model, and within a couple of years an even bigger range was available; taxis and fire appliances were subsequently added.

Left:
In terms of design this Argyll bus was a sturdy-looking product from what had been previously just a car maker. Rows of seats are raised towards the rear to improve visibility for passengers, though the mail compartment behind the driver did not permit much forward visibility for them. *Author's Collection*

Left:
This Armstrong-Whitworth, owned by Vanguard, is seen in 1908, just after it entered service with the London operator. *Author's Collection*

Arrol-Johnston

This Scottish maker began with cars and then offered a charabanc on a lengthened car chassis. Proper commercial vehicle and passenger chassis were announced in 1905 and were later followed by another PSV chassis with the driver seated alongside the engine. This had a 5.1 litre four-cylinder unit with detachable heads, whereas previous vehicles had had three-cylinder engines. Though some space was saved on the new model, the driver was positioned rather to the back of the engine, with a heavily-raked steering column reaching back to him. The model was successful in that a batch of 30 were sold to the Great Eastern Railway and fitted with conventional open-top double-deck bodies.

Not so successful were two earlier charabancs bought by the North British Railway in 1905; they broke down so often that for 1906 the summer-only service they ran was reduced so that one was spare while the other worked. Problems continued and in 1907 Arrol-Johnston undertook some kind of part exchange deal. The company took the vehicles back and refitted the bodywork to two new chassis, which proved more reliable.

The last Arrol-Johnstons were made in 1915.

Armstrong-Whitworth/Armstrong-Saurer

Sir W. G. Armstrong Whitworth & Co was a large industrial and engineering company based in Newcastle-upon-Tyne. It built its first commercial vehicles in 1906. These were bus chassis ordered by Motor Omnibus Construction of Walthamstow, a subsidiary of the London Motor Omnibus Co, which traded as Vanguard. Apparently, MOC could not take up all of its order, so those remaining were sold by Armstrong-Whitworth as lorries.

Some 25 years later Armstrong-Whitworth acquired the British manufacturing rights to the Swiss Saurer diesel-engined lorries, producing Armstrong-Saurer heavy lorries from 1931 onwards. There were also a few bodied as PSVs.

Below:
Placing the radiator behind the engine gave early Austins a distinctive appearance, shared only with Renault. This charabanc dates from about 1914. *Author's Collection*

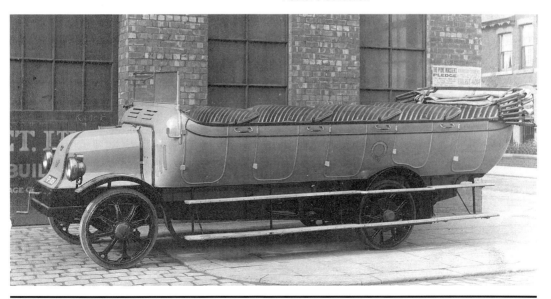

Atkinson

It was not until 1950 that Atkinson made its first purpose-designed diesel buses, but in 1924 it was said to be building a bus based on its four-ton steam wagon chassis, with upright boiler.

Austin

Austin was one of the most successful British car makers, and before World War 1 had added commercial vehicles to its range. A feature that easily distinguished them externally for some years was the coal-scuttle style bonnet: the radiator was mounted behind the engine with the fan being used to draw the air forward over the engine. Some 2,000 trucks went to the army in the war, numerous design changes being made in 1917. City of Oxford Tramways, the predecessor of City of Oxford Motor Services, bought 12 during the war, but the last had gone by the end of 1920. Austin had its own bus fleet (of Austins, of course) for transporting staff for some years.

The Russian Revolution resulted in the termination of an order placed by the murdered Czar's government, and many of these 2-3 ton models were slowly sold off until about 1922. Some, along with other ex-army Austins, were then bodied as buses and coaches. A smaller chassis, offered for a period in the early 1920s, was of more conventional design, but with the engine mounted over and forward of the front axle. Bodied as a 17-seat bus, with 'the great advantage of a four-speed gearbox' (a dig at the two-speed Ford T, no doubt), it cost £775 complete; electric light was an extra.

Subsequently the largest car chassis were occasionally bodied as small buses, but Austin did not reappear in the PSV market until 1939, when it announced the 'K' series goods and passenger models. Built in a new factory, the new semi-forward-control range had an overhead valve engine of 3,460cc, hydraulic brakes, synchromesh gearbox and an engine mounted far forward over the front axle. The whole design, even down to the shape of the radiator grille, was remarkably similar to the contemporary Bedford, and

some say only the outbreak of war prevented Bedford taking legal action. Few 'K'-types were built before production was switched to military requirements.

Auto-Mixte

For some six years this Belgian maker built petrol-electric chassis using the transmission designs of Henri Pieper, which were later also used in a Daimler bus. At least one Auto-Mixte chassis came to Britain. It was said to be the maker's first bus. Even by the standards of the day the chassis was remarkably high and bodybuilder E. &. H. Hora designed and built, in 1906, a special body for it in just eight days. It was of a two-compartment type with high front compartment with steps and entrance doorway just ahead of the rear axle; the rear compartment was at a lower level and had an open-sided but roofed back in Paris bus style.

Auto-Traction

This Belgian maker set up in 1920, originally building a road tractor with Minerva engine. Pneumatic tyres were adopted quite early, and Minerva acquired the company in 1925. That year bodybuilder Waveney of Lowestoft was offering an Auto-Traction (normal-control, of course) fitted with 30-seat coach body with side access doors to each row of seats, sliding hood and rigid side curtains, and 12V lighting for £900 complete.

BACS

The British Automobile Construction Syndicate built a 32-seat open-top double-decker with 25hp Aster engine in 1910 for the London & North Western Railway, which used it on a route between Colwyn Bay and Old Colwyn.

Baico

Baico Patents was producing chassis extensions for commercial vehicles even in the 1920s. But from 1926 it also offered the Baico Boulevard Car, a small-wheel toastrack based on the Ford 1-ton chassis and intended for slow-speed summer running along seaside promenades. The first ran at Skegness. Baico added to the Ford a chassis extension, special outriggers and 24in (0.61m) diameter wheels with solid types. It seated 28 within its 20ft (6.09m) overall length.

Barton

The Barton brothers, later Barton Transport, were successful operators who in the 1920s went in for substantial rebuilding of chassis and later built their own. For a short time the company even designed and built its own four-cylinder diesel engine with monobloc aluminium casting; these were fitted in trucks and barges as well as Barton buses.

Early chassis conversion included lengthening various makes, and one Daimler 'Y'-type gained 10ft (3m) in length to become a 60-seat single-decker.

The company's forte was conversions to six-wheelers, often of unlikely chassis. A modest small Morris would emerge as a 24 or a 26-seat six-wheeler (and be known as a Morris-Barton); 12 or 14-seat Lancias became 26-seat vehicles on three axles; whilst a whole fleet of larger Lancias (many ex-Italian Government war surplus) appeared as 39 or 40-seat six-wheelers (Lancia-Bartons), usually with Barton's Gliders as fleetname.

Production of complete chassis began in 1929 with two chassis fitted with Meadows petrol engines. In 1930 there were 10 Bartons, five with Coventry Climax petrol engines, two with Gardner diesels, two with Continental Red Seal engines and one with a Sunbeam eight-cylinder petrol engine. Gearboxes and other mechanical parts also varied from chassis to chassis. Four chassis built in 1931 were fitted with Coventry Climax (one), Leyland petrol (one), Commer petrol (one) and Blackstone diesel (one) engines. The last-named was soon discarded. The final year, 1932, saw just two chassis, one with a Commer engine the other with a Barton diesel.

Barton had pioneered diesels after being impressed by a Gardner 4L2 at a shipping exhibition. In March 1930 it put into service one of its Lancia-Bartons with a 4L2, just days ahead of Sheffield Corporation's Karrier single-decker with Mercedes-Benz diesel. One of the two Bartons with Gardner diesels built in 1930 was of particular interest as it had the five-cylinder 5L2, the forerunner of the 5LW which was to become so successful.

New construction and use regulations on lengths, overhangs and other matters brought to an end the Barton lengthening and rebuilding schemes of the 1920s, while presumably the greater efficiency of Leyland and other commercial chassis of the early 1930s dissuaded Barton from more home building.

BAT

The initials stood for British Associated Transport. The chassis were made by Harris & Hasell (1929) Ltd of Bristol, whose predecessor had sold various makes for some years. It had done particularly well with US-built Reos; after Reo set up its own sales organisation in Britain, the company then designed and assembled two models of its own. The BAT Cruiser, with six-cylinder engine, was for up to 20 seats, while the BAT Super Pullman had an eight-cylinder engine and was for up to 32 seats. Cruisers sold quite well; one was even offered as a prize to the person suggesting the best improvement to the design. Competition and depression, however, meant that BAT lasted just two years.

Bean

The makers of the Bean were originally motor component manufacturers. For eight years they also produced commercial vehicle and bus chassis before ceasing business and reforming as component makers.

Below:
BAT's Cruiser was the smaller of the two models built, but boasted a six-cylinder engine. The model sold quite well and was offered as a basis for a 20-seat body. *Ian Allan Library*

From the mid-1920s the company's pneumatic-tyred normal-control buses with about 14 seats enjoyed a degree of popularity as 'handy little vehicles' and, unusually, were available with servo-assisted front-wheel brakes. For a short time there was also a heavier, forward-control model.

Beardmore

Most familiar as a maker of London-type taxis for many years, Beardmore was a Glasgow engineering company with diverse products including boilers and, at one stage, aircraft. The same four-cylinder engine as in the taxis was offered in conventional lorry chassis of 3/4 or 1 1/2 ton in the 1920s, and a number were bodied as buses. For lighter routes the Scottish Motor Traction Co bought nine with 15-seat bodies in 1925, but kept them only four years.

Beardmore was also a pioneer in developing 'heavy oil engines' as diesels were called in the 1930s. After trying one engine in a Leyland Titan, Glasgow Corporation ordered 30 for installation in a batch of 50 Albion Venturer double-deckers delivered in 1935; the other 20 had Gardner units. However, the Beardmore engines were not reliable and production ceased. Some of the Glasgow Albions later gained Leyland engines.

Beaufort

In the early years of this century the Beaufort Motor Co of Twickenham, Middlesex, built a few motor-buses. The firm is said to have had German connections and to have been formed to sell German-built vehicles in the UK. The London General Omnibus Co tried a couple of Beauforts at an early stage while the London & District Omnibus Co had one. All three were, of course, open-top double-deckers fitted with chain drive.

Bedford

The Bedford story is a relatively simple and successful one. The American-owned manufacturer, which had been assembling Chevrolets in this country, went one step further and commenced UK production, partly to avoid import duties. It kept the model range simple, sold at competitive prices and used a talented designer. Bedford production began in 1931 and, by 1939, the company claimed that 70% of buses and coaches with less than 26 seats on British roads were Bedfords.

The first models built were goods vehicles, with two bus model derivatives with low-framed chassis following in August 1931: the WHB for 14-seat bodies and the WLB for 20-seats. The WHB had a relatively short run, being dropped in mid-1933. They were all built in the Vauxhall factory at Luton, Bedfordshire, that previously had assembled Chevrolets and recent comparisons of preserved makes from the 1930s have revealed that some Chevrolet components were used in early Bedfords.

The 1933 Motor Show saw a new 3-ton truck model unveiled. It was of semi-forward-control layout with a short bonnet and was designed by Stepney Acres. By 1935 there was a PSV derivative, the WTL. It was replaced in 1936 by the WTB, a more purpose-built chassis with a longer wheelbase. It offered space for six more seats, and its popularity soon grew, with Duple having a long and successful collaboration with

Right:
The earliest Bedford PSVs were quite small, two models generally seating 14 or 20, although lack of demand gave the smaller of the two a short life. It was, however, a useful vehicle on Scottish islands and in other rural areas. *Author's Collection*

Below:
Walter Alexander & Sons both bodied and operated this 20-seat WLB of 1934. It carries the short-lived Royal Blue Coaches fleet-name. Note the small destination display above the registration plate. *Ian Allan Library*

Above:
Bedfords really came into their own from the mid-1930s with the semi-forward-control layout which gave room for up to 26 seats. A coach version, folding roof opened, touts for trade on the front at Swanage. *Author's Collection*

Left:
This Willmott 26-seat coach body, based on a 1937 WTB chassis, was supplied to Eugene, pioneers of home perms for ladies. The coach (and three others) carried Eugene Mermaids, ladies who gave hair perming demonstrations. *Author's Collection*

Left:
The open bonnet of this 1942 OWB (described at the time as a Ministry of Supply single-decker) shows the easy accessibility of carburettor, filter, air cleaner, fuse box and dynamo. An engine-driven tyre pump was a standard fitment. *Author's Collection*

Bedford. Duple offered some nine body versions for the type. Brakes were servo-assisted.

One other major change came in the summer of 1938: an improved engine giving 72bhp against the 64bhp of the old one. The successor, unveiled in 1939, was the OB, designed for up to 29-seat bodies, with a slightly longer wheelbase but with the same engine. Just 73 were built before war intervened, though production restarted after the war. But for hard-pressed operators the Ministry of Supply authorised production from 1942 onwards of a utility version — the OWB. It was the only new single-decker available, and came only with a petrol engine. Despite this, many went to larger operators who, by that time, had standardised on diesel-engined vehicles. Mention should also be made of a factory-built seven-seater rural bus (a conversion of the 7cwt [350kg] van) which was in production from 1932 to 1939.

The OWB was the most successful chassis in production terms, with 3,398 built. In comparison there were 2,320 WTBs and 1,895 WLBs. The short (and shortlived) WHB totalled just 102. All the figures, except the OWB, include chassis built for export.

Strangely, the earliest Bedford coaches sold were based on goods chassis; Bedford generally commenced production of goods models first. Some bodybuilders and operators couldn't wait! By July 1931 Jennings of Sandbach (better known as a truck bodybuilder) was offering a 20-seater with canvas roof, while Waveney of Oulton Broad, near Lowestoft, offered a fixed-roof 20-seater. Both were probably beaten by Rainford of Lincoln, which delivered a 20-seater to a small Lincolnshire operator in August 1931. Waveney followed with a 14-seater on a proper drop frame PSV chassis at the end of that month, the first true Bedford PSV. Early in 1935 Duple and others were offering coach bodies on the new WT truck chassis introduced well before its WTB companion.

Belhaven

Belhaven built steam and petrol-engined vehicles for a number of years at Wishaw, Lanarkshire. An early Belhaven steam bus ran between Glasgow and Eaglesham for a time, and the first two buses in the fleet of Walter Alexander were Belhavens, one built in 1914 and the other in 1916. Production ceased in 1924.

Bellis & Morcom

Birmingham-based Bellis & Morcom was an established company producing mainly stationary steam engines. It built just one bus, a double-decker. The London General Omnibus Co ran the bus from the end of 1907 to the autumn of 1908 on three different routes. The bus had twin chain final drive.

Belsize

Belsize Motors of Manchester built its first commercial vehicle in 1906, after having built cars successfully since 1901. A shaft-driven three-ton truck with 28hp four-cylinder engine was introduced in 1911. This was also offered as a charabanc. Not all wartime

Below:
Belsize enjoyed brief success as a bus builder in World War 1 — when other makes were not available. British Automobile Traction, the BET subsidiary, bought a number for some of its operations. BAT buses ran under the 'British' fleetname in a number of areas before individually named subsidiaries were established. *Geoff Lumb Collection*

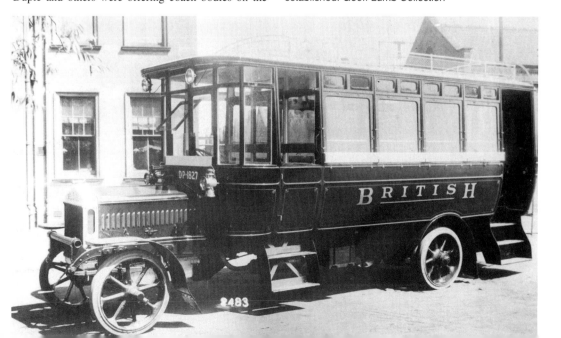

production went for military use, so British
Automobile Traction (a subsidiary of British Electric
Traction) bought a considerable number. Some of
those acquired ran in the Thames Valley, becoming
part of the fleet of Thames Valley Traction Co when
that company was formed in 1920. Scottish General
Transport, forerunner of Western SMT, ran seven, all
acquired in 1915 or 1916.

Berliet

Not many Berliets were sold in the UK, although the
maker became France's largest builder of commercial
vehicles before, more recently, being swallowed by
Renault. An early British buyer was Bristol
Tramways, which ordered three in 1907; they were
not delivered until 1909 and were open-toppers with
the driver seated far forward above the engine.

An operator of smaller, later, single-deck Berliets
was Westcliff Motor Services (later to be merged
with Eastern National), which ran six pneumatic-tyred
examples in the 1920s.

A notable feature of a new medium-sized four-
wheeler with four-cylinder engine introduced in 1924
was its brakes. 'Exceptionally large brake drums' on
the twin rear wheels were 'brought into use by the
hand lever, while the pedal brake (also of the internal-
expanding type) was drum-mounted behind the
gearbox on the second motion shaft.' There were

front brakes too, and these could, as an extra, be inter-
connected with the transmission brake. *Motor
Transport* of the time thought this feature could be of
particular value to coach owners in the hilly districts
of Wales, Scotland and the West Country, where acci-
dents due to insufficient and inefficient braking were
still all too frequent.

Berna

Sales of foreign chassis in the UK seemed to increase
in the years just before World War 1. One of the more
successful was the Swiss Berna company, although it
had a chequered career. It began exporting to Britain
in 1906, but got into difficulties. These resulted in an
English financial group, Hudson Consolidated, taking
over and continuing the business. The success of the
range improved, and in 1912 a Swiss consortium
bought the company back. An English company

handled sales in Britain, but 1914 saw a surprising development with the formation of a rival — British Berna Motor Lorries of Guildford. In the mid-1920s the normal-control chassis was offered as a 25-seat bus, 30-seat 'open coach', or even a 58-seat double-deck bus.

Bethlehem

The American steel company of this name built commercial vehicles for some 10 years with very mixed fortunes. One year saw production totalling 3,500, while a little later it had fallen to less than one a week. Some chassis were exported, and at one stage a number were assembled by the Scottish Motor Traction Co.

Blackburn

A. Blackburn & Co of Cleckheaton, Yorkshire, built 10hp two-cylinder and 20hp four-cylinder chassis for two or three years up to 1908. A number were bodied as 12-seater charabancs.

BMMO

Midland Red's path into bus manufacture began before 1923, when it built its first complete chassis. For a few years it had followed a policy of having replacement parts for the Tilling-Stevens vehicles in the fleet made to its own design by local engineering companies. Though the parts were often more expensive, the higher quality was found to be more economical in the long run.

By 1940 Midland Red had built over 2,000 chassis, of which just under half were sold to associated companies, including Ortona Motor Co and Peterborough Electric Traction (both later part of Eastern Counties), Northern General (and its sister companies), Potteries and Trent. All these chassis were known by the generic designation of SOS, which stood for Shire's Omnibus Specification. L. G. Wyndham Shire was the talented chief engineer who persuaded the company that it should build its own vehicles. Some competitors were at the time able to run rings around the company's larger, solid-tyred and ponderous buses by using small, fast lightweight buses on pneumatic tyres.

The first year of production saw three prototypes followed by 19 production models. These and the larger output in 1924 were all built on Tilling-Stevens frames, but transmission was orthodox, with four-speed gearbox. The engine was a 4.3 litre petrol unit with four cylinders and side valves. This benefited from advice by Harry Ricardo, who was later famed for his diesel expertise. The engine had high compression ratio and relatively high output. All the vehicles had pneumatic tyres. One of the hallmarks of the design was its light weight, which was helped by the maker knowing exactly what body (in style and weight) was to be put on the chassis.

From 1925 the whole chassis was of Midland Red design, and by 1926 the company had moved to forward-control models. More design changes the following year produced the 'Q'-type, on which the wheelbase was lengthened and the bonnet shortened. The cab was moved further forward, but shifting the engine and radiator slightly to the nearside improved cab space. The offset position of the radiator gave these and subsequent Midland Red vehicles an even more distinctive appearance, something that was enhanced on single-deckers by the use of destination boards instead of blinds. The changes gave the 'Q'-type a seating capacity of 37.

Right:
Many early bonneted SOS buses lost their original bodies to older chassis in 1929-30 and gained new ones of slightly lower capacity built by United Auto Services at Lowestoft. The chassis of this one had been new in 1925, and was photographed in 1949 in use as a tree cutter. *C. D. Wilkinson*

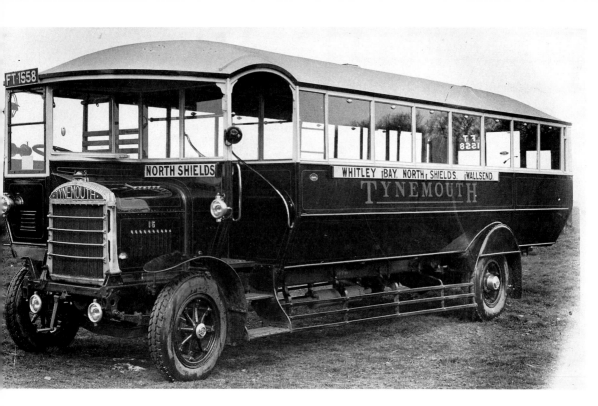

Top:
The narrow offset cab and absence of destination blind boxes gave the SOS single-deckers a unique appearance. Many went to other operators; this one is seen in later life with a subsidiary of Northern General. *Ian Allan Library*

Above:
BMMO had continued with normal-control layout for some years for charabancs. Later models had six-cylinder engines, including this 1930 QLC with Short 29-seat body seen on an extended tour of Devon, crossing the river at Kingsbridge. It was one of a batch of 18. *Author's Collection*

Developments in design came thick and fast over the next few years, with the 'QL' in 1928 with four-wheel brakes and twin rear wheels to permit a lower frame height, and the 'M' (for Madam) type in 1929 with more comfortable and fewer (34) seats to attract ladies going shopping to use the buses. Later versions were the IM4 and IM6 (the latter fitted with a six-cylinder engine), of which nearly 400 were built.

The years 1929 and 1930 saw a wealth of different types produced, and by 1934 there were four different designs of six-cylinder engine in the fleet. Strangely, there had been no double-deckers left in the fleet since 1929, but traffic growth, and maybe sheer economics, brought a prototype in 1931, followed by 50 production models in 1932-33. They eventually became known as REDDs (rear-entrance double-deckers). Another prototype, with front entrance (FEDD), came in 1933, and was followed by 50 production models in 1934. A further 135 in 1935-36 had Metro-Cammell all-metal bodies that proved remarkably durable. Surprisingly, all were petrol-engined, but the Metro-Cammell-bodied examples were converted to diesel from 1942 onwards, with a mixture of AEC 7.7 litre and BMMO's own engines being fitted. Another 150 FEDDs with diesel engines followed in 1938-39. Three had full fronts, which were later removed, but in 1942 a full-width front and concealed radiator along with restyled upper-deck front were fitted to an FEDD. It was followed by an elegant prototype postwar double-decker in 1945. This had four-bay bodywork, sliding window vents, radiused windows and full-width bonnet and concealed radiator. Its appearance set the standard for Midland Red and others for many years.

The company seemed to have mixed views on coach design. It had continued to build batches of normal-control charabancs up to 1930, the last having six-cylinder engines. It went back to normal control with a new style of touring coach in 1935, the OLR (open low Rolls-Royce). They had long bonnets and canvas roofs. More-or-less contemporary with this dated style were what might be termed the ordinary coaches, the LRRs (low Rolls-Royce) of 1934-35 which were forward-control half-cabs of rather peculiar appearance; the roof canopy was not extended over the bonnet, but the driver's cab had its windscreen and side windows at a noticeably higher level than the side windows on the rest of the coach.

Of course, the company did not get everything right first time. The first enclosed coaches (for long-distance work, not touring) were the 'XLs' (Excel) of 1929-30. However, the lightweight chassis, despite the six-cylinder engines, could not cope with the extra weight. So new chassis, the 'RR' (Rolls-Royce), were built for them, bus bodies being fitted to the 'XL' chassis. Even stranger was a batch of normal-control buses produced in 1929 for quieter routes. Their chassis were early bonneted 'SOSs', whose bodies went on surviving Tilling-Stevens buses. Fifty new normal-control 26-seat bodies were built by United at its Lowestoft, Suffolk, works — which later became ECW — and a further 33 conversions were carried out for Trent, Llandudno Blue (a company later to become part of Crosville) and Ortona. The new vehicles were designated as 'ODD'. After 1934, incidentally, Trent was the only other company to continue buying Midland Red chassis.

Coaches of a rather better appearance were the 50 SLRs (saloon low Rolls-Royce) of 1937, which were forward-control vehicles with English Electric full-fronted bodywork with concealed radiators. Surprisingly, they were built with petrol engines, but gained Leyland 7.4 litre diesel engines postwar. The first diesel-engined coaches were the ONCs of 1939, with full-fronted concealed radiator bodies by Duple. They had five-speed gearboxes.

A new range of single-deck bus introduced in 1934 was the ON (Onward) which took advantage of the recently introduced longer length limit of 27ft 6in for single-deckers and squeezed in 38 seats. Some with diesel engines followed (seating only 36) but then Midland Red designed its own 8 litre 'K' series engine, which was shorter and seating capacity was thus increased again to 38. From 1936 to 1940 the 'SON' (Saloon Onward) was standard. It also had Midland Red's 'K'-type 8 litre diesel engine. One strange feature of virtually all Midland Red's single-deck buses was the absence of roller destination blinds; the company continued to use destination boards and route number stencils.

Among the more significant vehicles were four rear-engined single-deck prototypes (three buses and one coach) built in 1935-36. These had petrol engines mounted transversely across the rear, and hydraulic throttle operation. Initially, two of the vehicles had fluid flywheels and epicyclic gearboxes. All had set-back front axles, with the entrance ahead of the axle on the three buses.

One failing discovered in operation over a period was the ingesting of dust by the engine, which caused considerable wear. However, during the war they were rebuilt by Midland Red's relatively new and innovative chief engineer, Donald Sinclair. The main change was the removal of the engine from the rear, and its replacement by a new horizontal version of the company's own 8 litre 'K'-type diesel. Experience with the buses in their new form enabled Midland Red to be the first manufacturer to put this layout into full production after 1945.

Left:
A typical mid-1930s double-decker, this FEDD dates from 1936 and has a Metro-Cammell all-metal body of a type that was to prove particularly durable. The fuel tank under the driver's seat is a typical BMMO feature. All the batch of 135 later gained AEC or BMMO diesel engines. *Ian Allan Library*

Left:
Duple bodied a batch of 25 ONC coaches in 1939. These were the first coaches built with diesel engines, and also had five-speed gearboxes. Like a previous batch of coaches built in 1937, they had full fronts and centre entrances. This one is seen in Banbury. *Author*

Brillie

Frenchman Eugene Brillie designed and had built by the Schneider company a range of commercial vehicles and buses for about four years before going bankrupt. As on other French buses, the driver was seated above the engine. The Star horsebus concern of Solomon Andrews in London began running motorbuses in 1905. The company tried a few makes before settling on the Brillie and buying 15. However, Star could not make motorbuses pay and withdrew its motorbus fleet in 1907, reverting entirely to horse traction.

Bristol

Bristol was another of the small band of early motorbus operators which found the chassis it bought to be less than satisfactory and decided as a result to built its own. The company came into being in 1874

Above right:
Bristol Tramways built and operated this design of 'composite charabanc' at Weston-super-Mare before World War 1. It could seat 20, or 22 passengers 'with centre seat' — presumably a reference to the two seats alongside the driver. *Author's Collection*

Right:
After World War 1 Bristol resumed production with the new 4-ton chassis with worm drive and 40hp Bristol engine. Kingston-upon-Hull Corporation was the buyer of this 1923 example, with body by tramcar builder Dick Kerr of Preston. *Ian Allan Library*

Below:
Bristol described its four-cylinder engined 'B'-type of 1926 as a 'light passenger model' though it was also know as the Superbus. It sold well, and widely, usually as about a 30-seater. But this was one of two built in 1930 for Stockton-on-Tees Corporation as 26-seat one-man buses. *Ian Allan Library*

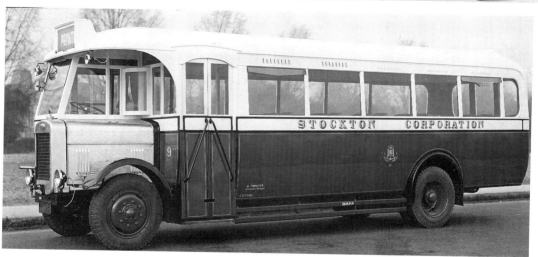

Left:
Underneath the new body and lowered radiator of this 1949 product was supposed to be the chassis of a 1930 Bristol 'B'. One of a number reconstructed by Bristol at a time when there were restrictions on supplying new buses to the home market, it probably contained a few token original parts (and the original registration number), but really was a way of obtaining more new vehicles. *Ian Allan Library*

Left:
Bristol's 'G'-type was introduced in 1932 as a double-decker, alongside 'H' and 'J' single-deckers. Initially fitted with Bristol's six-cylinder petrol engine, it was soon offered with a variety of diesel engines. Most popular was the Gardner five-cylinder, as on this 1935 example for the company's own fleet. *Ian Allan Library*

Right:
The 'K'-type double-decker of 1937 had a lower frame and other improvements. The onset of war eventually stopped production, but there were unfrozen examples. Production resumed in 1944 in utility form, initially fitted with the AEC 7.7 litre engine. Illustrated is one built for Merthyr Tydfil Corporation, which is pictured in 1963 when its Park Royal body had been somewhat rebuilt. *K. Bateman*

as the Bristol Tramways Co and in 1887 was retitled the Bristol Tramways & Carriage Co after a merger. Its horse-drawn trams were replaced by electric ones in 1895 and the company also ran horse buses and horse-drawn cabs. It began running buses in 1906 with Thornycrofts with Berliets and Fiats, soon following, but was unhappy with them; indeed the company won a legal action against the Fiat supplier.

Bristol began building its own chassis and engines in 1908, when it produced five normal-control chain-driven vehicles of type C40. These lasted until the early 1920s and were said to be an improved version of the Thornycrofts. More followed until 1911, when a slightly larger version was introduced. The Filton works where they were built was shared with sister company Bristol Aeroplane, and to give more space for building aircraft bus construction was moved to the Brislington Motor Construction Works (as it was called). By early 1915 a total of over 120 chassis had been built. First to be sold to another operator went to Imperial Tramways (Middlesbrough) in 1914, a company in which Bristol had a financial interest.

Bus chassis building ceased in 1915 and the factory turned to war work on Bristol aircraft. Building resumed in 1920, the year in which the company took a stand at the Olympia Motor Show for the first time, with a new model. This was the four-tonner, with Bristol 40hp engine, which was sold as either a bus or a truck. Bus production ended in 1927, though goods models continued for a time. All told, some 650 were built. These were bodied by outside builders as well as Bristol itself. They were sold to many operators. All bar nine were single-deck; the double-deckers went to Hull Corporation in 1923. That year saw the Bristol range widened with the introduction of the two-ton model. This was a forward-control chassis usually seating around 20. Its production ran for six years and of the 250 built over half went into the Bristol bus operating fleet.

Replacement of the four-tonner came as the 'A'-type, a low-frame heavyweight chassis that sold in small numbers mainly to municipal fleets. Much more successful was the 'B'-type or Superbus of 1926. A lightweight, with 75bhp Bristol engine, it was built until 1934 and totalled nearly 780 including 300 for Bristol's own fleet. Another big operator was United Automobile Services and several municipalities also bought the type. A similar chassis was called the 'D'-type; this had Bristol's six-cylinder JW engine.

Three new models came in 1931: the 'G'-type double-decker; and the 'H' and 'J'-type single-deckers. The 'G' and 'J' had the six-cylinder engine, the 'H' the four. These were all petrol engines, but it was not long before various diesel engines — from AEC, Beardmore, Dennis, Gardner and Leyland — were being tried. Large numbers of Gardner engines were subsequently fitted, though some Js from Bristol's own coach fleet had AEC diesel engines, while Dennis four-cylinder diesels were fitted in buses for Bristol's Gloucester subsidiary and for Eastern Counties. 'Gs' and 'Js' remained in production until 1937, by which time nearly 250 'Gs' and well over 800 'Js' had been built. 'Hs' were less popular and their production ended earlier. These high production figures reflected the 1931 incorporation of the company into the Tilling Group, and its subsequent development as a main supplier to other operators in the group, effectively filling the gap left by Tilling-Stevens and TSM. For this Bristol had to enlarge its Brislington premises.

The design of the 'Gs' and 'Js' was becoming somewhat dated, with the gearbox mounted separately amidships, while frame height was greater than most other makes. This meant that 'Gs' with low-height bodywork were rather higher than, say, a Leyland Titan with a similar body. On the other hand, the option of a five-speed gearbox on the 'J' was well ahead of other makes. The rigid mounting of the Gardner engines — particularly five-cylinder ones — on chassis built from 1936 transmitted noise and vibration through the whole vehicle, but surprisingly this feature was continued on the otherwise much more modern 'K' double-deck and 'L' single-deck chassis introduced in the latter part of 1937. By now there were no petrol engine options, and both had the 5LW as standard with the 6LW as an option. Some single-deckers for operators with easy terrain even had 4LWs. The gearbox was new, but again offered in four-speed or overdrive five-speed form.

Wartime work at Brislington consisted of production of aircraft components, armaments and other defence items, but in addition nearly 2,500 anthracite-burning trailers were built to some six different designs. These were the result of a Government initiative to reduce reliance on scarce imported fuels, and were generally used with petrol-engined buses. They consumed a home-produced fuel, but were trouble-some and reduced engine life as well. Bristol also built two 'L'-types with the gas producer built into the bodywork in a fireproof compartment at the offside rear of the vehicle. The national shortage of buses led to Bristol restarting bus production in 1944, with an austerity version of the 'K'-type. However, almost all of these were fitted with the AEC 7.7 litre engine since Gardners (as used in Guy chassis) were in very short supply.

British and Brush

The British Electric Traction Co was originally a tramway operator. However, it soon saw the potential of the motorbus, buying two Straker-Squire steam buses in 1901 and putting them to work with subsidiary Potteries Electric Traction Co. The duo did not last long, however. Another attempt at bus operation in 1904 saw PET receive three Brush-built double-deckers fitted with Mutel petrol engines, but two only lasted two years.

Above:
The Amalgamated Motor Bus Co of London had been promoted by British Automobile Development, a BET subsidiary, with the dream of running 120 motorbuses in London as replacements for 180 horse-buses. But all that transpired, between 1907 and 1908, was five of these buses of Brush manufacture. *Author's Collection*

Right:
Six of the nine Brush 'B'-types bought by BMMO between October 1906 and January 1907 moved south after the company abandoned motorbus operation, and formed the fleet of Deal & District Motor Services in 1908. They were still, however, owned by BMMO. This one was claimed to be the first front-entrance motorbus. *Ian Allan Library*

What had been BET's automobile committee became in 1905 the British Automobile Development Co, with powers of making, selling, hiring or promoting the operation of buses. Alongside BET's Brush tramcar works at Loughborough a separate assembly plant was erected. Brush built both chassis and body, some to a driver-over-engine design, with engines coming from either Peter Brotherhood or Daimler. BAD became British Automobile Traction Co in 1910.

Early buses had been badged British, but the name soon changed to Brush. The exhibit at the company's stand at what was said to be the first Commercial Motor Exhibition in 1907 was claimed to be the first bus with an all-metal body. Five Brush double-deckers were put into service by the Amalgamated Omnibus Co on a route between London's Oxford Circus and Peckham in 1907 and 1908, but all had gone by the end of 1908. Midland Red bought a number of Brush buses, and six quite new ones went to Deal & District Motor Services after Midland Red gave up motorbus operation in November 1907.

British Berna

Swiss Berna chassis had been sold in the UK for some years and, for a time, the Swiss company was owned by a British financial group. However, a surprise to many was the formation in 1914 of a rival — British Berna Motor Lorries of Guildford. The products were similar and were made in Newcastle-upon-Tyne by the engineering and casting company Henry Watson & Sons. Soon after the end of World War 1, Henry Watson & Sons announced a range of its own chassis, which were sold under its own name.

British Ensign

Beginning as Ensign Motors in southwest London in 1913, the company soon added the prefix British to its title. By 1914 it had added commercial vehicle chassis to its range. These had Tylor engines. Some chassis built after the war were fitted with Dorman engines. One British Ensign was bodied as a chara-banc by Carmichaels of Worcester for local operator Burnham. Southdown was a surprising buyer of the make, in 1915, acquiring a number along with some from other obscure manufacturers. An early buyer of Ensigns was another southeast operator, Strong's Garage & Motor Car Co of Margate, which had five.

Brockway

Brockway became one of the largest of the American truck builders and during the late 1920s a number of its chassis were imported into the UK by agent A. E. Tapper & Co. The chassis had a six-cylinder petrol engine and was of normal-control layout, with pneumatic tyres. They were suitable for bodies seating from 14 to 32 passengers.

BSA

BSA stood for Birmingham Small Arms Co, a company better known in the automotive field for its motorbikes and cars and for its ownership of Daimler. It made occasional ventures into the van market but its large car chassis were sometimes used as the basis of small buses. A notable example of this was a 12-seater BSA bus bought by Haslingden Corporation in 1919. The bus was impossibly unreliable and lasted less than a year, being replaced by an Austin 22-seater. But the BSA has a possible claim to fame as it was designed and built as a one-man bus with a front entrance alongside the driver and is said by some to be the country's first proper OMO vehicle.

Burford

Burford enjoyed considerable success with the Great Western Railway for a time, supplying over 70 small buses, some of which were later converted to GWR goods vehicles. National Omnibus & Transport was the other big customer, not altogether surprising considering that H. G. Burford was also a director. H. G. Burford had been the founder of Milnes-Daimler. In 1914 he began importing an American chassis which was sold under the Burford name. Later the chassis gained a greater British content.

By 1921 a chassis was offered with four-wheel brakes. Burford and the GWR apparently collaborated in developing semi-forward-control and forward-control models seating 16-18, an unusual feature at this time for small vehicles. Although intended for passenger carrying, most models were known by their weight capacity. Burford went into liquidation in the mid-1920s, but was bought out by its general manager who continued the business on a small scale.

Plymouth Corporation had quite a fleet of Burfords by the late 1920s, having bought two batches of 10 after an initial three. All were 'B'-type 50cwt (2½ ton or 2,540kg) bonneted 20-seaters which were one-man operated.

Bussing

This well-known and longlived German maker of buses and trucks began production in 1903, had built its first bus chassis in 1904, and, it is believed, began selling them to the UK in the same year. Certainly the rights to UK sales were acquired by an old-established Bristol engineering company in 1905, which reformed itself as Sidney Straker & Squire. Within a year the company had to move to a larger factory. The original 24hp model was followed by 34hp and 40hp models. All had chain drive and a radiator mounted low down at the front. By the time of the merger of the big three motorbus operators in London into the LGOC in 1908 there were over 350 Straker-Squires running in the capital. Straker & Squire went on to develop its own chassis designs, which are described in the entry under its name. The London Road Car Co, fleetname Vanguard, had tried a Bussing early on, before later standardising on Straker-Squires, while the LGOC had nearly 60 Bussings as well as Straker-Squires.

Many years later German-built Bussings were offered on the British market, in the shape of a normal-control 32-seater.

Caledon

Scottish Commercial Cars of Glasgow had happily handled sales of Commers for some years, only to find the supply ceasing when World War 1 broke out. The company then made the courageous decision to design and build its own vehicle. Caledon was the name chosen and production started in 1915. Dorman engines and a French design of gearbox were fitted to a very substantial chassis. Sales built up, and some of the crudities of the early chassis were eliminated. After the war the maker became the separate company, Caledon Motors, and, lured on by high sales in 1919, not only widened the range considerably, but also designed and built its own sleeve-valve engines — a costly exercise. Not many chassis with this engine were sold, though two PSV exhibits at the 1921 Olympia Show had them, together with pneumatic tyres and, in one case, electric lighting. These were quite advanced additions to what was a rather basic design.

But hard times meant that production stopped in 1922, only for it to be restarted by SCC, albeit in small numbers. Production continued haltingly until 1926 when Caledon was acquired by steam lorry builder Garretts of Leiston (Suffolk). Thereafter no more buses were made. Total Caledon production was little more than 700, with probably a modest proportion of these for passenger use, but there was at least one double-decker. However, during World War 1 there were some surprising customers, such as Southdown. Postwar adverts offered chain-driven

chassis in a number of capacities for goods as well as a 40hp chassis with live axle for passengers.

Charron

This French car maker diversified briefly into the production of a luxury single-deck 'Pullman' chassis with 30hp engine, chain drive and pneumatic tyres. The General Motor Co put some into service in London during 1908, but they do not seem to have lasted long.

Chelmsford and Clarkson

Thomas Clarkson was a Lancastrian and an inventor, who was continually innovating and improving his product — steam buses. He built and ran more than anybody else and, when that era ended, went off to design an improved steam lorry. The earliest buses were called Chelmsford, after the Essex town where they were made, but later ones carried the Clarkson name.

Several early vehicles worked in Torquay, and two Chelmsfords ran for the Sussex Motor Road Car Co between Worthing and Pulborough in 1904. Road Car, before its merger with the LGOC, built up a fleet of over 70, and in 1909 the LGOC's Frank Searle encouraged Clarkson to convert one of its De Dions to steam propulsion. However, the LGOC then began withdrawing its steam fleet so Clarkson, with the backing of friends, formed his own company, the National Steam Car Co, to take over the factory and build and run steam buses. By 1914 it had 173 in London and others in Chelmsford. All the London examples had to meet the demanding unladed weight limit of $3\frac{1}{2}$ tons brought in by the Metropolitan Police Regulations of 1909.

Unfortunately, by the end of the war, labour costs had increased considerably, there were spares problems and the fuel (naphtha or paraffin) at one stage rose 2,700% in cost. An arrangement with the LGOC saw the last withdrawn in November 1919 and National taking over LGOC's Bedford outpost. One of the most colourful aspects of London bus operation had gone.

Chevrolet

The Chevrolet Motor Co was a division of General Motors, and added one-ton commercials to its car production at the end of World War 1. The first were sold in Britain in 1923 and sales soon built up. GM

Left:
The narrow rear track of this Chevrolet bus cannot have helped stability, even if it was on pneumatic tyres. Most sold in the UK gained bodies seating about 14, though there were some seven-seaters. *Ian Allan Library*

gained control of English car maker Vauxhall in 1925 and from 1928 Vauxhall also built Chevrolet commercials at Luton. A typical transatlantic sales gimmick of the late 1920s was the new range with 3.2 litre six-cylinder 'Cast Iron Wonder' engine — 'a six for the price of a four'. Chevrolet production at Luton was phased out in 1931 as building of the new Bedford got under way; there was some carry-over of components.

Citroen

Well-known French car and commercial vehicle maker Citroen built up a range of products that might be compared with those of Morris and Morris-Commercial together. It offered normal-control chassis for PSV use in the UK for a few years up to 1933. At one time there was a $1^3/4$-ton chassis for up to 14 seats, and later a larger chassis for 20-seaters.

Clement-Bayard

It seems appropriate that the Guernsey Railway Co should have operated a 14-seat bus on this French-built chassis; the railway also ran three Brillie double-deckers. But all four were imported from England secondhand. Vans, trucks and charabancs were built by this company up to 1914, but those sold in the UK appear to have been smaller chassis, taking bodies with up to 14 seats.

Clyde

Mackay & Jardine of Wishaw, Lanarkshire, built Clyde chassis for a number of years. Both men had previously worked for Belhaven, which was also in the same locality. The products of smaller makers, such as Clyde, generally sold to smaller operators, and these were a diminishing species by the early 1930s. Despite this, the make was still listed until the late 1930s. Unusually, the company built its own gearboxes. Examples of the Clyde, which was a normal-control chassis, could be found in the Walter Alexander and Central SMT fleets. All had been acquired when smaller operators had been bought out.

Commer

This company began as Commercial Cars in 1905 and its first chassis was developed around a gearbox. The gearbox was the Lindley, a kind of pre-selector developed by an engineer who had seen the difficulties drivers had with early gearboxes, and the damage they caused to the boxes. In Lindley's design, movement of the 'gear' level positioned dog clutches, which subsequently sprang into position when the clutch was depressed. A consortium originally formed to build a prototype gearbox for test ended up designing a chassis to go with it. The combination

Above:
Commer built double-deckers from the earliest days. The picture of this well-loaded example shows the poor state of many roads, even in towns, in the earliest years of this century. *Geoff Lumb Collection*

was successful, Commercial Cars was formed and it soon moved from a small south London workshop to a new factory at Luton.

By 1907 the company was offering passenger-carrying chassis and the first double-decker followed in 1909. As well as PSV models there was also the Norfolk Convertible Country House and Estate Car, which received 'numerous testimonials from notable users'. It was an omnibus, a shooting brake or an estate lorry. For use as a shooting brake it had gun racks and cartridge lockers, while as an omnibus it could carry up to 14 passengers and about 3/4 ton (750kg) of their luggage. Sales of chassis greatly increased in the years just before World War 1, to such an extent that Dorman built engines for some vehicles to the design of Commercial Cars, and other help was provided by Hillman. An advanced passenger model, the 3P, with 'live' rear axle instead of the chain drive previously used, was about to be introduced when war broke out and so did not go on sale until 1919. Wartime production peaked at 640 four-ton trucks in 1916.

As new models were introduced in the 1920s, the Lindley gearbox was gradually phased out, ceasing to be fitted after 1926. The passenger model for 20 or 30 seats (on two different wheelbases) was the 2P, designed for pneumatic tyres on both axles. The model later gained an engine with plain bearings (as opposed to roller), becoming the 4PW, and later a forward-control version, the 4PF, was added. Pressure lubrication was another feature of the engine.

The postwar slump had hit the company hard and from 1922 it had been run by a receiver and manager. In 1926 the company was sold to Humber of

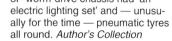

Above:
No fewer than 29 passengers could apparently be seated in this Commer demonstrator shown at the 1922 Scottish Motor Show. The 3P worm-drive chassis had 'an electric lighting set' and — unusually for the time — pneumatic tyres all round. *Author's Collection*

Left:
The operator of this Commer PLNF5, delivered in 1939, was MacDougall's Motor Excursion Tours of Oban. The vehicle's Waveney body (a make popular on Commers) had two-and-one seating. *Author's Collection*

Coventry, which changed the name to Commer Cars and then reduced prices. Passenger models with Humber engines were offered from 1927 as both four and six-wheelers, seating up to 32.

A further takeover in 1928 placed Commer as part of Rootes Securities. The next year saw the introduction of a new, light 20-seater, the Invader, which used a modified version of the Humber six-cylinder Snipe engine. The gearbox was mounted in unit with it, and had 'silent third' helical gears. A new and bigger six-cylinder engine developed at Luton and producing 105bhp was fitted in a larger new model, the Avenger, for 32-seat single-deck or 50-seat double-deck bodies. However, from the mid-1930s Commer offered only 20 or 26-seat models, the former only with normal control.

In 1939 came the new Superpoise series for a whole range of goods and passenger applications. It had in the one design 'the time-tested virtues of both normal and forward control'; in other words, it was of semi-forward control layout. Both diesel and petrol engines were offered, with a choice of wheelbases to provide from 20 to 32 seats.

Cottin Desgouttes

Shaft drive was an early feature of trucks built by French maker Cottin Desgouttes. This company was best known for its well-made, durable and attractive cars. Buses, when introduced, became popular with French municipal operators, and a few chassis with charabanc bodies of capacities between 20 and 26 operated in two Scottish independent fleets that were later taken over by Scottish Motor Traction in the mid to late 1920s.

Cremorne

Chelsea-based Cremorne built some steam vehicles between about 1903 and 1906, including cars and commercial vehicles. One c.v. chassis fitted with a horsebus body was tried in London by the Associated Omnibus Co in 1905, but found to be too lightly built. There was also a purpose-built 36-seat steam bus with kerosene-fired vertical boiler.

Critchley-Norris

Bamber Bridge is a small town just a few miles from Preston (where Atkinsons were made) and from Leyland (Leylands); for three years the town boasted its own motor manufacturer — Critchley-Norris. J. S. Critchley designed the vehicles, which were fitted (like contemporary Leylands) with Crossley petrol engines — he had previously worked for Crossley.

Across in Yorkshire, Todmorden Corporation had planned to operate trams but had been discouraged by the cost and opted for buses instead. Bus services

Above:
Widnes Corporation bought four complete double-deckers in 1909; delivery from Luton was a four-day journey, partly because they were covered-top double-deckers. They were the first covered-top double-deckers to run regularly in Great Britain. Widnes had a corrosive atmosphere from its factories, which meant that, when it rained, the resulting precipitation was mildly acidic. It is believed that this was the reason for specifying roofs. *Geoff Lumb Collection*

Below:
Despite building for only three years, Critchley-Norris managed to spread its few vehicles to a number of towns. This one, with customary admirers as well as passengers, was said to be the first motorbus in Widnes. *Geoff Lumb Collection*

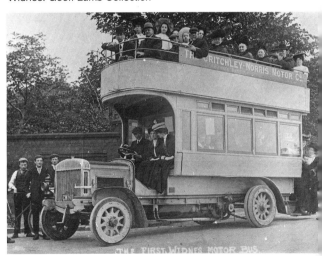

The car business was later transferred to a new company, Crossley Motors, and in 1913 it began supplying one of its models, the 20/25hp, to the Royal Flying Corps as a staff car and as an RFC tender. Thousands were manufactured and after the war many found their way to the civilian market and were rebodied as charabancs or buses, mainly for small operators (often ex-servicemen) just setting up in business. Some were remarkably longlived; four were still being run by Filkins and Ainsworth of Harefield on routes to Uxbridge and Rickmansworth when that company was compulsorily acquired by the LPTB in 1933.

Crossley resumed car building after the war, and involved itself in various other enterprises including an aircraft-building company and the joint venture company, Willys Overland Crossley, which assembled Willys cars and Willys and Manchester trucks. However, the company got into a poor financial state,

began on 1 January 1907 with one double-deck and one single-deck Critchley-Norris and two Ryknields. Two Leylands were soon added. An earlier Critchley-Norris was a charabanc bought by the Burnley Motor Pleasure Co of Burnley in 1906; it ran for a number of years.

Crompton

Electrical company Crompton was involved with two battery-electric buses. One, in 1909, was on a chassis built by Motor Omnibus Construction at Walthamstow for trials with the LGOC. It had a pair of Crompton electric motors and a motor generator. Two years later a further Crompton battery-electric double-decker featured regenerative braking and an 'electric valve' which limited the current that could be taken from the batteries. The latter is thought to be the last battery-electric double-decker built.

Crossley

Crossley Brothers of Gorton, Manchester, had been founded in 1866, and made gas and oil engines for marine and other purposes. The company added car manufacture in 1904 and had its first associations with the bus industry in 1905 when the Lancashire Steam Motor Co (later to become Leyland Motors) bought its engines for double-deckers ordered by the London Suburban Omnibus Co. Leyland was still developing its own petrol engine.

partly through dabbling in too many fields and partly because of its endemic habit of redesigning, improving (it hoped) and generally changing everything it made. This increased costs and often reduced reliability — hardly what was intended.

However, in 1928 the bus building business seemed to be doing well, so Crossley launched into this as well. By 1939 it could claim to have some 900 buses in service with 23 different municipalities. These, and a handful of independents, were the only purchasers, unfortunately. Luckily, Manchester Corporation had a policy of firm support for local industry, and not infrequently overrode the recommendations of its transport manager and the transport committee, which meant that 646 of the 900 were in the Manchester fleet. In all Manchester bought over 800 Crossleys; the next biggest was Rochdale with 80, while the corporations of Ashton-under-Lyne and Stockport were other local users.

Crossley's first purpose-built bus was the Eagle forward-control single-decker which was fitted with the 5.3 litre four-cylinder engine and was in production until 1931. The chassis was also offered from 1929 with a six-cylinder 6.8 litre engine, first as the Arrow (until Dennis, which was already using the name, objected), then as the Six and later as the Alpha. A double-deck version appeared in 1930. Initially also called the Six, it was later known as the Condor. The same year saw three Condors built with Gardner 6L2 oil engines, one for Leeds Corporation entering service in September to become the UK's first diesel double-decker.

Crossley was also developing its own diesel engine, completing the first in December 1930 to be able to win fame as the first British maker to offer a complete diesel-engine bus — Crossley also built the body. Oil engines soon gained acceptance and few further petrol Crossleys were built. Engine improvements followed in 1933, though the chassis was strangely dated in other ways, with its central accelerator pedal and right-hand gate gearchange. But the Ricardo-designed cylinder head was a decided step for the better.

A new double-deck model for 1934 was the Mancunian, appropriately named as it was developed mainly to meet a Manchester Corporation specification. The gearbox was mounted directly behind the engine. Similar changes were made to the Alpha single-decker, but batches for Manchester in 1937 and Sunderland Corporation in 1939 were the only ones made and carried the Mancunian name. Engine design changed again, with the production of a short stroke model of slightly lower output; the main aim was to try and improve bearing and crankshaft life which was (and continued to be) well below that of rival makes.

Various gearbox options were offered at times. Crossley's interest in this subject was to come to fruition after World War 2 as another technical chal-

Above:
One of the few buyers of Crossleys in the late 1930s other than Manchester, was Maidstone Corporation. This 1940 example also carried a Crossley body and was fitted with a Crossley diesel engine. *Author's Collection*

lenge not to be missed! A four-speed sliding mesh gearbox had been standard since 1928, but Bury Corporation had a pre-selector in a petrol-engined Condor in 1931 and Barrow-in-Furness Corporation took a batch of diesel-engined Condors with pre-selectors in 1932. Northampton Corporation, one of Crossley's few non-local customers (others were Aberdeen, Maidstone and Portsmouth corporations) standardised on pre-selectors. A constant-mesh gearbox was offered from the mid-1930s, while Manchester had a few Mancunians with synchromesh gearboxes. In 1936 both Manchester and Rochdale tried a bus with Freeborn four-speed semi-automatic gearbox. All this variety and experimentation might have been fine for a company building hundreds of buses every year, but when total production barely reached four figures over 12 years it must have imposed a tremendous financial burden.

There was no wartime production of Crossleys, but Manchester was able to take delivery of 70 Gardner 5LW engines in 1943 that had been intended for Daimler chassis it had on order. The Daimler chassis (and much of the factory) had been destroyed in the Blitz, but Manchester fitted the engines to Mancunians in its fleet, making them the most reliable Crossleys it ran.

CWS Bell

Retail co-operative societies used to be big users of vehicles, mainly for deliveries, but some also ran charabancs and coaches, while a select few even operated bus services. The Co-operative Wholesale Society began assembling chassis in Manchester in 1919 using patterns and designs bought from Bell Brothers. Initially 3/4, 1 and 1 1/2 ton chassis were produced, all using the same 2.5 litre engine. A Dorman-engined 1 1/2-2 ton chassis with overhead worm drive was added in 1922; some were bodied as charabancs. Five years later a larger model was added; most were bodied as 20-seat PSVs. Three years later all production ceased.

Daimler

Daimler was one of the earliest British manufacturers, but unlike most builders of PSV chassis did not make trucks (except during World War 1); its other products were cars. The name came from Gottlieb Daimler, the German from whom the company bought the British patent rights. Its early history was complicated until the formation of Daimler Motor Co (1904). Daimler had built a petrol-electric double-decker in 1908, and its subsidiary, the Gearless Motor Omnibus, produced two years later a remarkable integral double-decker — the KPL. This had an engine on each side, electric transmission, accumulators that could provide extra power, and worm drive. It was probably too complicated to be practical, and also attracted accusations of patent infringements.

In 1911 Frank Searle, of LGOC 'B'-type design fame, joined Daimler and designed a more conventional bus, the 'CC'-type, with sleeve-valve Daimler engine (as used in its cars) and an ordinary gearbox. Many were bought by British Automobile Traction, a subsidiary of the British Electric Traction Group, which had realised the limitations of the tram and was setting up bus companies.

One BET subsidiary was Metropolitan Electric Tramways, which formed the Tramways (MET) Omnibus Co in 1912. Searle sold it 100 Daimlers,

agreeing to maintain them at 3 1/2d (1.5p) a mile for three years. He then revealed this to A. H. Stanley of the Underground Group, whose LGOC bus and tube activities surrounded MET's area, and won a counter-order for 250 Daimlers. Searle then went back to MET, who outbid Stanley by agreeing to buy 350, but at a lower maintenance cost of 3d a mile. At the time it was the largest bus order ever placed.

However, Searle had not endeared himself to either side, and Stanley (later to become Lord Ashfield) negotiated with Daimler. The MET order was cut back to 226, and 124 AEC 'B'-types were added. Compensation for Daimler came by making it the sole agent for outside sales of AEC. From then on, there was considerable co-operation between the two, culminating in the unsuccessful ADC merger in the mid-1920s. Daimler also sold large numbers of its own buses up to World War 1, and was probably the largest builder after AEC.

During the war the 'Y'-type replaced the similar 'CC', and was built in quantity mainly for the military. Subsequently, the company was slow to develop new models, the double-deck 'CK' and the single-deck 'CL' and 'CM'-types differing in minor detail only from wartime models. All were still normal control although Daimler did pioneer pneumatic tyres on single-deckers, particularly charabancs.

When production under its own name restarted after the dissolution of AEC, designer Lawrence Pomeroy's first model was the CF6. This had a 5.7 litre six-cylinder engine and a radiator with the distinctive fluted top. The following year — 1930 — saw the arrival of the CG6, a much more modern chassis with wider track and lower frame. Later the same year came the CH6, which combined two separate inventions — the fluid coupling and the pre-selective epicyclic gearbox. But if the fluid transmission was modern, the sleeve-valve engine with its high consumption of lubricating oil was not.

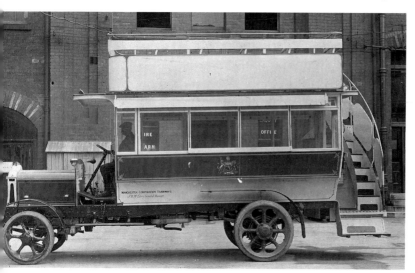

Left:
The huge MET order helped establish Daimler as a major builder, supplying many fleets. Manchester Corporation bought eight 'CCs' in 1913 and 1914, lost them to the military, but managed to obtain three 'CCs' in 1915 and five similar 'Ys' in 1916. *Author's Collection*

That was changed in 1932 with the CP6, which had a new poppet-valve 6.6 litre engine.

But with the UK economy stagnant, production was probably little more than one a week. Then, at the 1933 Commercial Vehicle Show, Daimler produced the COG5, a diesel with the Gardner 5LW seven-litre engine. Gardner economy and reliability, coupled with the ease of driving a pre-selector made the model most attractive for urban operation. Also offered was the COG6, with the 8.4 litre, six-cylinder Gardner; and the COA6, with AEC's six-cylinder diesel for which Coventry Corporation was the only (but regular) buyer.

Above:
This was Daimler's 'new silent engine developing 40hp at 1,000rpm as used by the LGOC on the London bus service where it has become famous for its silence ...'. That was Daimler's 1914 claim, and of course its sleeve-valve engine was much quieter. But in London it was fitted only in the MET buses (and an associated fleet) which were under LGOC management, and against the LGOC's 'B'-type AECs the Daimlers were in the minority.
Author's Collection

Right:
The CP6 model was a much improved vehicle all round, and Daimler had accepted the inevitable and designed a poppet-valve engine. Soon the chassis would gain the diesel engine and become far more popular. But this Cleethorpes Corporation CP6 with Willowbrook body lasted into the postwar years. Cleethorpes later merged with Grimsby Corporation.
Roy Marshall

Right:
This AEC-engined utility Daimler was one of a batch delivered to Portsmouth Corporation in 1944. All had Duple bodies, and all were fitted with new bodies (by Crossley) in 1955. Body deterioration through the use of poor quality materials was the main problem with utility buses generally. *Ian Allan Library*

Production rose rapidly. Birmingham Corporation alone took 100 chassis before the end of 1934. The model changed little over the years, except for the addition of flexible three-point mountings. There was also a COG5/40 single-decker with shorter bonnet and more upright radiator to allow bodywork for up to 40 seats.

All building ceased abruptly in 1940 after the factory was bombed. Production of diesel-engined chassis had run at about 300 a year over the previous six years. Surprisingly, the Ministry of Supply found Daimler a requisitioned factory, in Wolverhampton, and production got under way in December 1942 with the CWG5, an austerity version of the prewar model. The fluid flywheel and pre-selector gearbox were retained, perhaps because redesign would have taken too long, but no alloys were used and unladen weight was therefore heavier. By the middle of 1943 100 had been built, after which Daimler switched to the CWA6, with AEC engine, of which Daimler had also had previous experience. By mid-1945 some 630 of these had been completed, but another engine was now available — from Daimler itself. The company

had been working on its own design of 8.6 litre six-cylinder engine since about 1936 until the outbreak of war, but a prototype engine and all drawings and test records were lost when the factory was bombed. The first production chassis with the new engine was completed early in 1945, after which AEC and Daimler-engined chassis were built together. It is perhaps surprising that the Ministry of Supply permitted work on the engine to resume, and even more remarkable that Daimler was able to 'recreate' its engine at such a time. Presumably AEC and Gardner were at full capacity, and the Ministry saw that something had to be done.

Darracq-Serpollet

The Metropolitan Steam Omnibus Co, formed in 1907, built up in five years a fleet of over 50 Darracq-Serpollet steam buses — the second largest steam bus fleet in London. And yet, before the end of 1912, all had gone, to be replaced by 'B'-type petrol buses under an agreement with the LGOC. Failure followed the bankruptcy of Darracq-Serpollet, of which the operator was a subsidiary. The French company Darracq had formed Darracq-Serpollet to make steam vehicles using Serpollet's design, including the flash boiler. It had formed the Metropolitan company because it realised that this was the only way to sell steam buses; Clarkson with his buses came to the same conclusion a couple of years later. Three of the Darracq-Serpollets survived to run on the Isle of Wight until about 1923.

Below:
A. H. Creeth & Sons built up a fleet of seven steam buses of various makes by the early 1920s for their Ryde, Seaview & District Motor Services business on the Isle of Wight. This was one of three Darracq-Serpollet steam buses that had been new to the Metropolitan Steam Omnibus Co in London and was photographed in 1915. *Author's Collection*

De Dion-Bouton

'Despite its multiplicity of parts, the De Dion was among the most efficient and economical of the older type of bus before the 'B'.' according to W. J. Iden, one-time chief engineer of the LGOC. Its flitched wooden chassis frame was copied on the 'B'-type. Both London General and Vanguard ran de Dions in London, their combined fleets totalling 160 of this make. The manufacturer had a long history. It began in 1884 and finally faded away after World War 2. Double-deckers built for the French market from 1905 had a cab-over-engine layout and, of course, the De Dion axle. There were other, later, examples of De Dion in the UK and in 1928 Highland Motorways put a long-wheelbase normal control example into service. It made three runs a week in each direction between Glasgow and Inverness. It had an unusual single-deck coach body by Strachan & Brown with raised 'observation' section above the rear axle.

Delahaye

One of the oldest and longest-established French manufacturers was Delahaye, which made its first car in 1894 and added commercial vehicles to its range before 1900. Its real entry into the PSV market came in 1923 with a modest-sized vehicle fitted with pneumatic tyres, four-wheel brakes and — unusually — worm-driven back axle. A few were sold in the UK and Midland Bus Services, later to be a constituent of Western SMT, bought two in 1924. They had 20-seat bodies and survived until 1932.

Dennis

In the 1990s Dennis is virtually the only surviving British-owned bus builder, and in its long life the company has seen remarkable ups and downs. It was enormously successful in the late 1920s and early 1930s, and then slowly lost out again with a mix of

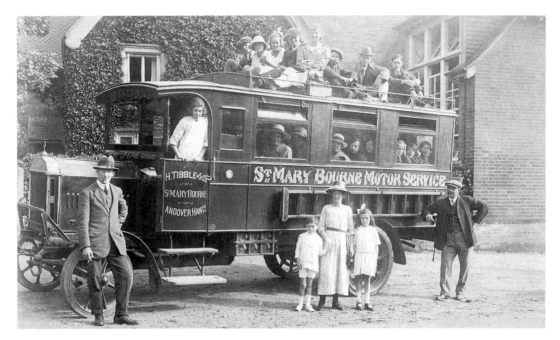

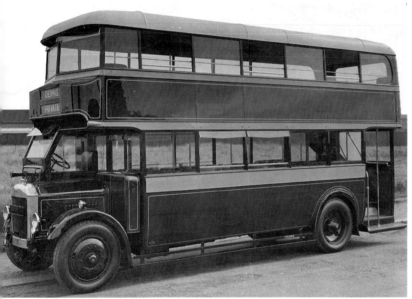

Above:
A bus body has been mounted on this War Department-type Dennis chassis. It was operated by the St Mary Bourne Motor Service, based near Andover. Photographed in 1919, it has the proprietor of the business, Mr H. Tibble, leaning on the ladder which could be unhooked to give access to the roof. The driver stands by the front wheel. *Author's Collection*

Left:
The first purpose-built double-decker was the Dennis 'H'. This example with Hall Lewis body was a show exhibit for 1928. It looks relatively smart and modern, apart from the clumsy front, but it still had a cone clutch and the upper-deck seating was longitudinal. *Ian Allan Library*

good and disappointing designs. It vacillated with its own and proprietary diesel engines long after the likes of AEC, Daimler and Leyland had settled for reliable products, and its Lance double-deckers of the mid to late 1930s suffered from chassis frame weaknesses, radiator problems and various other faults.

Despite these problems, Dennis's sales and technical successes were considerable. In the early years of the motorbus it perfected a quiet and satisfactory shaft-drive back axle; it was the first to introduce four-wheel brakes to a London bus; and it had some

of the first London buses on pneumatic tyres. Its 'E' and later 'EV'-type single-deckers sold very well in the late 1920s, as did their successor, the Lancet. But the multiplicity of smaller models of the 1930s — the Aces, Maces, Arrow Minors and Pikes — were up against enormous competition from Leyland's Cub downwards to mass-produced Bedfords, Dodges, Commers and others. Total sales of the Mace, which was a forward-control Ace, were well under 100 in four years.

The Dennis story began before 1900, with bicycles,

and quickly moved on through motorised tricycles
and larger cars to commercial vehicles by 1904. The
first bus was produced the following year, but
passenger-carrying vehicles were based on goods
chassis until 1925. A very early user of Dennis was
Provincial Tramways of Grimsby with its first 30hp
double-decker in 1906. The most enduring of
customers was the local company, Aldershot &
District Traction Co, which began buying the type
before 1914. Dennis built more of its own components than many rivals, but from 1909 fitted White
and Poppe petrol engines, later buying the company
and still later moving the production and staff to an
extended Dennis factory in Guildford.

After World War 1 Dennis offered its own bodywork for its products. A four-ton chassis announced
in 1921 was said to be ideal for double-deck bodywork. A 1924 40/50hp chassis for Nottingham had a
Short Bros 50-seat covered-top body — an early
example of a closed-top double-decker. The first PSV
specifically designed as such was the 'E'-type, with

dropped frame and forward-control layout. It had a four-cylinder engine, but later a six was an option. The companion 'F'-type, with dropped frame but normal control, was popular with coach operators. Forward-control double-deckers first appeared with the 'H'-type of 1927.

A model with a name successfully revived in recent years is the Dart. It first appeared in 1930 as a normal-control chassis with six-cylinder engine and servo-brakes. Popular with independent operators, it also became the standard small bus with the LGOC. The 1934 Ace was a compact and manoeuvrable single-decker with the engine over and forward of the front axle. It became widely used by Tilling companies such as West Yorkshire Road Car Co, Western and Southern National, and Southern Vectis. This was no doubt partly because neither Bristol nor TSM offered vehicles of this size.

Dennis-Stevens

Towards the end of World War 1 a petrol-electric chassis known as the Dennis-Stevens was introduced. Like the better-known Tilling-Stevens it incorporated the designs of W. A. Stevens, with the vehicle's petrol engine (a 40hp Dennis) being used to drive an electric motor. Radiators were badged just 'Stevens' and were larger than usual. A water pump was also fitted.

Below:
Dodge's 20-seater was of normal-control layout, but the 26-seater introduced later was of semi-forward-control. This Harrington-bodied example, dating from 1938, was built for Valliant Direct Coaches and was unusual in managing to accommodate 29 seats.
Author's Collection

Early chassis were bodied as searchlights or mobile workshops, but later ones carried bus bodies. Tram operator Cardiff Corporation bought six single-deckers as its first buses in 1920, adding six double-deckers in 1922. Ease of driving was no doubt the reason for the purchases. The Cardiff buses lasted until 1930-31, but two were then rebodied as tower wagons and these ran until 1951.

Diamond T

Trucks built by the North American maker Diamond T were sold in the UK for a number of years in the 1930s and in 1937 a normal-control chassis was also offered for PSV use with up to 25 seats.

Dodge (Britain)

American-built Dodge chassis had been imported into the UK since the early 1920s and assembled here since 1927. Dodge Bros (Britain) had been formed when imports had built up to a considerable volume and, in 1933 at Kew, Surrey, the company started to produce its own range, while continuing to use US engines and gearboxes. A 20-seat bus was first listed in 1934, with six-cylinder 23hp petrol engine, hydraulic brakes and spiral bevel rear axle. In 1937 a 26-seat model was added, and from 1938 this was the only PSV produced.

Dodge (US)

A strange purchase by Southend Corporation in 1945 was of eight North American-built normal-control Dodges, complete with bodies. They had been used in the UK by the Royal Canadian Air Force. Southend undertook rebuilding, but it was a long process and it

took until 1948 for the first to be completed and in the end only four ran as PSVs. They were rather longer than most normal-control buses in the UK and seated 28 when rebuilt.

Ducommun

This German maker built commercial vehicles with shaft drive for about three years and a number were operated in London by the Rapid Road Transport Co (fleetname Rapide) in London for a few months during 1906 until the company went out of business. The buses were sold for further use at Hastings but lasted less than a year there before that operator also went into liquidation.

Durham-Churchill and Hallamshire

The Sheffield company of Durham, Churchill & Co built Hallamshire cars and Churchills or Durham-Churchills. It completed at least one Hallamshire charabanc, with 20hp engine, and demonstrated it by running with a full load of passengers from Sheffield to Doncaster Races and return on four consecutive days in 1905. The charabanc left on its 20-mile run well after the horse-drawn conveyances, and arrived well before them.

The same year saw the start of production of Churchills or Durham-Churchills, which petered out some 20 years later, with a gap in the war years. Early models had Aster 24 or 30hp engines.

The best-known vehicle must be the roofed chara-banc bought by the Caledonian Railway. First operated on a trial basis in 1906, it was found satisfactory and purchased. After two years' work alongside a Darracq-Serpollet steam bus, the route was discontinued as uneconomic. The Durham-Churchill was then fitted with flanged wheels and, still with its open-sided body and tiered seats, ran as a rail motor between Connel Ferry and Benderloch.

At the other end of the British Isles, newly-formed Southdown Motor Services ran four Durham-Churchill charabancs on stage services in 1915 when it was very short of vehicles; they had been bought new the previous year by one of Southdown's constituents, London & South Coast Haulage Co.

Durkopp

German maker Durkopp built bus chassis from about 1902 until the late 1920s, but probably only the early models were sold in the UK. An early operator was the North Eastern Railway, which built up a fleet of 15 or more, while across the border the Glasgow & South Western Railway and the Great North of Scotland Railway both operated some. The Great Western Railway bought some, but cancelled a second order, apparently finding problems with the crankshafts and chassis frames. London horsebus proprietor Patrick Hearn had a few, whilst others ran briefly at Hastings before their operator went bankrupt.

Below:
The North Eastern Railway was a pioneer bus operator, and an early user of Durkopp chassis. The railway often built its own bodies, as on this chassis, which was one of five delivered in 1905. This, and two others, had charabanc bodies, while the remaining two had single-deck bus bodies. *Author's Collection*

Economist

Badge engineering is nothing new. Just before World War 1 Clayton & Co (Huddersfield) made Karrier Cars charabanc chassis with different radiator shells, badged 'Economist', for sale by Stagg & Robson of Selby, Yorkshire.

Edison

Several towns tried one or more Edison battery-electric buses. The earliest was Southend. The corporation bought just one, based on a US-built GMC chassis with Edison electric motors and Brush body. It ran from 1914 until 1916. The municipalities of Derby, Lancaster, South Shields, West Bromwich and York, along with Loughborough Road Car, all ran Edisons. Probably the best known were at Lancaster, which eventually had five. A booster station or recharging point was usually provided at the town centre termini. The Edisons at West Bromwich replaced four Albions that were less than a month old and which had been

commandeered by the Army. The Edisons also inherited the Albions' bodies.

Electrobus

The London Electrobus Co ran battery-powered buses in London from 1907 to 1910 and may have demonstrated vehicles earlier. The buses were assembled by the Electric Vehicle Co, West Norwood, London, and included French components. Like other pioneering operations, the buses were not profitable and all 12 were subsequently bought by the Brighton, Hove & Preston United Omnibus Co, which had also bought three new Electrobuses the previous year. It dismantled four of the ex-London buses as spares for the rest and also bought a fourth new vehicle. The last one survived until 1917.

Enfield

Originally connected with the Royal Enfield Co (of cycle and motorcycle fame), this maker built a few commercial vehicles up to about 1915. Originally based in Redditch, it later moved to Birmingham, and subsequently was acquired by Alldays & Onions. A 35hp Enfield with substantial 26-seat bus body was put into service during 1914 by the Mid Cheshire Motor Bus Co and ran for 10 years, being scrapped after North Western Road Car bought Mid Cheshire.

Fageol

American truck maker Fageol, of Oakland, California, soon discovered that the western states of the USA needed more powerful vehicles to cope with the long hills and other arduous conditions encountered there. The Fageol brothers, Frank R. and William B., collaborated with Col E. W. Hall of Hall-Scott Motor Car Co to produce their Safety Bus in 1921. Quickly renamed Safety Coach, it was of normal-control layout, but with a very low chassis frame, powerful four-cylinder Hall-Scott engine and enclosed body-

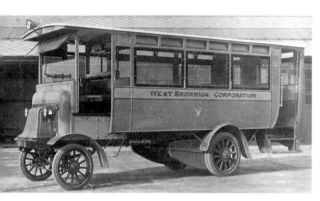

Above left:
This is one of West Bromwich Corporation's four Edisons; it was fitted with registration number and body from an Albion that had been commandeered by the Army. The Edisons cost £890 each plus £50 for adapting and fitting the bodies, which were converted to rear entrance. The chassis proved notoriously unreliable. *Ian Allan Library*

Left:
This was London's prototype Electrobus, with chassis built by Improved Electric Traction; it was fitted with BTH motors and a body by T. H. Lewis of Chalk Farm, London. In 1907-08 it was followed by a production batch of 20, with different chassis and body builders. *Author's Collection*

work seating 22, with a separate door to each row of seats. A larger model, with gangwayed body seating 29 and with a 100hp six-cylinder Hall-Scott engine, soon followed. The growing production soon had to be moved to a separate plant in Kent, Ohio.

More than 250 were built in 1923 and almost double that in 1924. The American Car & Foundry Co bought the Ohio bus factory and moved production to Detroit in 1926, bringing the Fageol brothers with it. New models were added with those after 1928 going under the 'ACF' name. But bus production also continued in a modest way at the original Oakland factory, which had not been taken over by ACF. Later, ACF was unenthusiastic about a new design of high capacity city bus with two engines, so the Fageol brothers left and formed a new company, Twin Coach Co.

A number of Safety Coaches were imported into the UK, but the Metropolitan Police refused to licence any of these low single-deckers because they had four-wheel brakes and pneumatic tyres.

Fargo

Some American Dodges were badged as 'Fargo', but in addition for a time Dodge built some Fargo-badged chassis that were not built also as Dodge. The Fargo

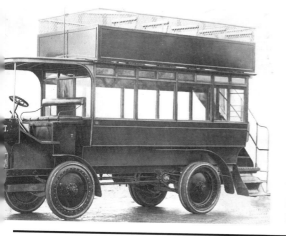

Freighter was a one-ton truck that was also offered in the UK up to 1930 as a 14-seat PSV.

Just to confuse matters further, though strictly outside the scope of this book, some British-built Dodge chassis in the 1930s were exported as Fargos.

Federal

Detroit, Michigan, was the home of the Federal Motor Truck Co, one of the more successful assemblers of commercial vehicles; every component was bought in. Some had been sold in the UK in 1914 but the make faded from the UK scene in the mid-1920s, only to reappear in 1929 with four different normal-control models. These seated between 20 and 32 and were said to have been imported from Canada; they were not available after 1930.

Federal did not produce purpose-built PSV chassis until the early 1920s, when 18 and 25-seaters were offered with six-cylinder Willys-Knight engines. Later there was a choice of Waukesha four-cylinder or Continental six-cylinder engines.

Fiat

Italian Fiat chassis were sold in the UK at various times. Some early ones were bought by pioneer bus operator Bristol Tramways, but they were not satisfactory; in 1910 Bristol won substantial damages against the supplier for vehicles which had not met the company's specification. The buses apparently found Bristol's hills too much. The North Eastern Railway, however, seemed happier, buying 18 with 29 or 34-seat charabanc bodies between 1907 and 1910.

Some surplus World War 1 Fiats were reconditioned in the UK after being brought back from conti-

Left:
A few Fiats were imported in the very early days. This 1905 24hp double-decker was described at the time as having 'forward drive' — a reference to the driver's position. *Author's Collection*

73

Left:
Although the floor height is not particularly low for what would today be termed a small bus, the two-step entrance and folding door on this Fiat are quite neat. Vehicles of this size enjoyed a — legal — speed advantage in the 1920s; if weighing under two tons they could run at 20mph, while larger buses were limited to 12mph. *Arthur Ingram Collection*

Below left:
The opposite extreme to the small wagonettes tried by some pioneer operators was this American-built Fischer battery-electric imported by the LGOC. It was too heavy and too wide ever to enter public service. *Author's Collection*

Below:
Foden's first Bandmaster chassis was bodied for the company's brass band. It had the four-cylinder Gardner LW engine. The passengers in this picture are unlikely members of the band. *Ian Allan Library*

nental battlefields by one E. B. Horne, better remembered for similarly acquired Garfords and for setting up the Gilford company.

Other Fiats were imported new in the 1920s. Biggest buyer was probably Scottish Motor Traction Co, which bought over 80 between 1921 and 1926. All were 14-seaters, mainly charabancs, but also some buses. All had been disposed of by the end of 1929.

Fischer

An American Fischer petrol-electric bus was the first motorbus bought by the LGOC. Ordered in June 1902, it was not delivered until spring 1903 and cost £450. Its petrol engine drove a generator which in turn fed two electric motors, one on each rear wheel. It was very heavy and also exceeded the permitted width of 6ft 6in (1.98m), but ran trials, fully laden, on

two nights and once during the daytime. In October 1903 the LGOC asked the suppliers to take it back and refund the price.

Foden

Foden persevered longer than most with steam-powered goods vehicles, but the early 1930s saw the company introduce diesels. Strangely, the first PSV chassis, built in 1933 and named the Bandmaster, was for carrying the famous Foden brass band. Of forward-control layout, it had the Gardner 4LW engine to the nearside of the driver but angled so that the transmission line ran diagonally across the chassis to an offset and offside housing for the worm-driven rear axle.

The Olympia Show that year saw a Burlingham-bodied Bandmaster for Green Bus Service. Foden built a small number of single-deckers with the larger Gardner 6LW, and also three double-deckers.

Ford and Fordson

Almost everybody has heard of the Ford 'T', arguably the most successful car and light commercial vehicle ever built. It and the related one-ton 'TT' were identical whether built in the US factory or in the British plant established in Trafford Park, Manchester, in 1911. The two-speed epicyclic gearbox was a particular asset in the days when few possessed driving skills or mechanical aptitude! Fords formed the basis of many — probably the majority — of the fleets of the rural operators who began in the years after World

War 1. Not only was the chassis cheap to buy and relatively reliable, but spares were widely available. The 'TT' was a lengthened 'T', but several companies offered kits to lengthen (or further lengthen) chassis, and auxiliary gearboxes were also available from some. Not all Fords were on rural routes; a number of operators used them on short urban services.

UK Ford production later moved to Dagenham and the 'AA' model replaced the 'T'. As a PSV the 'AA' was advertised as seating up to 14, whereas its 'BB' successor of 1933 could accommodate up to 20. An unusual feature was the V8 petrol engine, which was for a time offered only in PSV models and not in the basic lorries. Ford commercials were renamed Fordsons from 1933.

Among operators of the 'BB' was David Lawson, later part of the Alexander bus empire in Scotland, which bought four with 14-seat bus bodies in 1935. Another buyer that year was the Redbourn Group, which controlled a number of operators in the Thanet area of Kent. It also had four, with Duple 20-seat coach bodies. East Kent took over the company later that year and soon disposed of the Fords. Two of them, however, survived almost 20 years more with subsequent owners.

Frick

Leeds-based Dougill's Engineering built commercial vehicles under the 'Frick' name from 1904 until the company went into receivership in 1907. One, fitted with a single-deck bus body, was shown at the 1906 Agricultural Hall Show held at Islington, London. It was a 22-seater with three-cylinder 7.2 litre engine.

Another bus was said to have been exported to Egypt. A feature of the vehicles was the unusual drive, via discs, friction wheels and finally two-step chain gearing. Speed variations were obtained by rotating a wheel beneath the steering wheel.

FS Petrol Electric Equipment Co

Percy Frost Smith had been chief engineer of Thomas Tilling and involved in the design of the first petrol-electrics. Subsequently, as joint managing director of Tilling-Stevens, he designed its postwar petrol-electrics. In 1920 he resigned, set up as a consulting engineer, and designed the FS Petrol Electric. This is best described as an improved version of the Tilling-Stevens. Initially, six were assembled at Highbury, North London, using bought-in components for many parts, including Dennis units, White & Poppe petrol engines (as used by Dennis) and Kirkstall back axles.

Frost Smith put the six to work in London, but never managed to sell (or build) any more. Surprisingly, they were not very reliable, either. Before the end of 1924 the company, by now the FS Petrol Electric Omnibus Co, was bankrupt and wound up. Frost Smith died suddenly, less than a month later after a day's illness.

Garford

One of several US makes to be found in the
UK after World War 1, Garfords were, in a sense, the
forerunners of Gilford. After the war E. B. Horne had
set up in London selling former Garford military
chassis, most of which were recovered from continental battlefields. He himself often brought the
chassis back to the Holloway, London, workshops
where the chassis were stripped down and reconditioned and the engines overhauled. Some Fiats and
other makes were also handled, but of over 500 vehicles dealt with in this way most were Garfords. By
1925 E. B. Horne and his partner had decided to go
one step further and build new chassis of their own
design for PSV use — Gilfords.

Garner

Top salesman Henry Garner began selling US-built
trucks under his name in World War 1. Assembly in
Birmingham with UK-sourced components ultimately

followed. The most inter-
esting PSV was the first, the
Garner Patent Busvan of 1921. A complete vehicle, it
was aimed at country carriers. It could carry up to 20
passengers or up to 1³/4 tons (1,780kg) of goods, or a
combination. Seats faced inwards (and could be
folded up alongside the sides) and there was an
entrance alongside the driver. At the back were twin
hinged doors for loading freight.

Four years later came a proper PSV, of normal-
control layout, with a low frame and four-wheel
brakes. A 1928 announcement was of a 'high-speed
passenger chassis' for 20-seat bus or coach bodywork. Surprisingly, it had a straight chassis frame;
perhaps the company read the market correctly in
assuming that small, competing operators wanted
something fast and with a good engine.

Above:
Percy Frost Smith ran a total of six of his own design of
petrol-electrics between 1922 and 1924 in London.
However, the venture failed and he did not manage to
sell any of his design to other operators. *Author's
Collection*

Right:
The Garner Progressor chassis was designed as a de
luxe model for 20-seat bodywork. It came complete
with outriggers already fitted and had an Austin 20
engine. *Author's Collection*

In 1933 the Precursor 20-seater and Progressor were introduced. The latter was a de luxe version of the former with a strange mix of extras including chassis outriggers (ready for body attachment) and front bumper — plus a tyre pump.

However, PSV production, such as it was, faded. The company became controlled by Sentinel, later went bankrupt, and then was rescued by some ex-Chrysler employees. But no more PSVs were built.

Germain

Germain was a Belgian builder of railway equipment which, for a brief period, also constructed cars and commercial vehicles. Among the latter was a 16/20hp double-decker with the driver seated on top of the engine and with an upright steering column. The London Road Car Co took delivery of one in 1904, and two or three years later added a further 10. These were of a more conventional normal-control layout. They were apparently sufficiently troublesome to have to be returned to Belgium for rectification work.

Gilford

If the Gilford story had taken place in the 1980s it would have made compulsive viewing on a television programme about industry and business. But this was the 1920s and 1930s, when failure of vehicle makers was no novelty. However, what made the Gilford

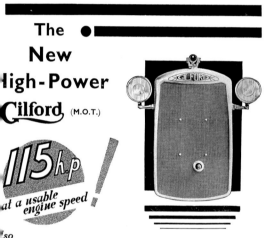

story different was the dramatic swing in fortune; it became a public company in 1929 and proceeded to pay a first-year dividend of a remarkable 33 1/3%, but two years later made a loss, subsequently sliding into bankruptcy in 1935.

The sad end to a company whose products were, generally, good can be attributed to four causes. It had sold mainly to independent operators, and they were a declining breed with the advent of proper licensing controls and takeovers by larger companies. It lost money when those small operators who survived got into financial difficulties and then defaulted on their hire purchase repayments. It had difficulty in keeping up with the continuing stream of design improvements produced by makers such as AEC and Leyland that were benefiting from large orders and the resulting economies of scale. Finally, and unique to Gilford, was the vast amount of money and effort it poured into a project to build and sell a revolutionary low-height, low-floor, front-wheel drive double-decker with opposed piston engine from Junkers.

Gilford had come into being in 1925 when E. B. Horne and V. O. Skinner decided to build their own chassis. Until then they had successfully reconditioned ex-World War 1 American Garfords (and also some Fiats). The first few chassis produced were straight-framed conventional models, with four-cylinder American-designed engines. But following quickly on the heels of AEC's 'NS' and the Maudslay, Gilford produced a drop-frame chassis with American Buda engine. This was soon followed by a similar chassis with a six-cylinder engine. This Low Line Coach (later reclassified LL) was so successful that by the end of 1927 the firm had had to move to larger premises at High Wycombe. A year later came the first forward-control chassis, the version with 16ft 6in (5m) wheelbase and 36hp American Lycoming engine — the 1660T — being a best-seller. The engine gave high torque at low speeds, Gilford saying there was no comparable UK engine.

Worthy of mention for 1928 was the following of a

popular trend towards six-wheelers, Gilford's 6WOT having the usual hydraulic-assisted brakes, on all six wheels, and a large six-cylinder American Wisconsin engine. A new smaller model for 1929 was the CP6, a low-loading chassis for up to 20 seats, or for use as a lorry. Gilford, for most of its life, reversed the usual trend, primarily making PSVs but also having some success with goods vehicles, particularly for export.

Gilford exhibited in its own right at a UK show for the first time at Olympia in 1929, displaying a new version of its successful single-deck models. The vehicles gained distinctive Gruss air springs at the front, and were offered in normal or forward-control layout. A forward-control double-decker was also available. All three had Lycoming six-cylinder side-valve engines, of slightly larger capacity than before. However, it was the single-deckers that sold. East London independent Hillmans of Romford (later compulsorily taken over by the LPTB) placed a large order and numerous other operators bought in ones and twos.

A replacement for the CP6 20-seater came in 1931. Known as the AS6, it dispensed with the Gruss air springs, had a longer wheelbase and numerous design changes. It was said to be the most reliable of all Gilfords. The other model change produced the most unreliable: it was the option of a more powerful engine, a Meadows, in the full-sized single-decker. Later the standard engine, the US Lycoming, was replaced by one built under licence by Coventry Climax, no doubt because of the punitive import duties.

Gilford was the major talking point of the 1931 Olympia Show with its revolutionary double-decker, plus a single-deck version. Enormous and talented design effort had been put into the project, but neither ever found a buyer.

A new model for the following year's Scottish Show was the Zeus, a conventional double-decker with Vulcan Juno engine. It was followed by a single-

deck version, the Hera, which luckily was much more successful. Neither had the Gruss air springs at the front, but they did have long leaf springs. Another Zeus and Hera appeared at the 1933 Olympia Show, both fitted with Tangye diesel engines. Both were one-offs; Gilford never sold any more double-deckers despite grand talk of the defeat of the Titans (Leyland) and good press reviews. Continuing economic problems meant Gilfords were no longer cheaper than, say, Leylands. At the end of 1933 Gilford announced it was selling its High Wycombe factory (with the plant's conveyor-belt chassis production facility) and moving to smaller premises on London's North Circular Road. One of the last jobs at High Wycombe was the cutting-up of the revolutionary (and unsaleable) front-wheel drive buses.

One success in 1933 was the winning of orders from W. Alexander and Western SMT for, respectively, 21 and 20 Hera chassis for use on their long-distance coach services. Unusually all 41 were fitted with reconditioned petrol engines supplied by the operators, and Meadows gearboxes and clutches. The engines had come from Leyland chassis which the two operators were fitting with new Leyland diesel engines. The chassis were built in 1934 and accounted for about 70% of that year's total production. By 1935 production was down to about one chassis a week, usually a Hera. However, Gilford persevered, introducing a lightweight model, the PF166 with four-cylinder Perkins diesel engine. Three were sold with full-front Park Royal bodies. A final fling, for the

Below:
The one and only Gilfords (HSG) chassis with its AEC engine and gas producer plant was bodied by Cowieson and bought by Highland Transport of Inverness. The plant was housed in a compartment in the rear offside of the body. *Author's Collection*

1936 London Show, was probably intended to replace the Hera. It was light and had a new design of Coventry Climax petrol engine; a diesel with four-cylinder Gardner unit was also listed but probably not built. However, not long after the show closed its doors, a receiver was appointed and Gilford was subsequently wound-up.

Gilfords (HSG)

High Speed Gas (GB) was a company formed in 1927 to experiment with producer gas as a fuel for commercial vehicles. In 1936 the company acquired the Park Royal premises of Gilford, which was in receivership, and created a new subsidiary — Gilfords (HSG) — to build experimental chassis. Subsequently, it built one bus chassis, based on a 1935 Gilford chassis that, presumably, was lying at Park Royal unsold. It was fitted with a suitably modified AEC engine and an HSG gas producer at the rear (in a separate compartment). Highland Transport of Inverness bought the bus which, apparently, covered some 20,000 miles in the next nine months at an average fuel consumption of 2lb (0.907kg) a mile.

Gloster

The long-established Gloucester Railway Carriage & Wagon had been building bodies since horse-drawn days and then, at a time when export orders had almost vanished, designed and built complete coaches. Most Gloster Gardners were for Red & White Services of Chepstow and the operator had a strong influence on the design. Of the nine built, Red & White took six.

The vehicles had six-cylinder Gardner engines mounted rigidly and five-speed gearboxes mounted flexibly, plus Kirkstall axles. Chassis frames were made by Gloucester, with reinforcing at points of high stress by close-fitting channelling instead of the usual flitch plates. Built in 1933-34, the vehicles were among the first long-distance diesel-engined coaches and could cruise at 50mph. Surprisingly, the bodies did not prove particularly durable — perhaps the rigidly-mounted Gardner engines were bad for them. Red & White fitted new Duple bodies within a few years. A subsequent large order for London Underground trains ended thoughts of building further PSV chassis.

Left:
Red & White was the major operator of Glosters. The body style was neat yet unostentatious, though structurally perhaps suspect. *Arthur Ingram Collection*

Below:
In the late 1920s General Motors was offering both GMC and Chevrolet chassis on the UK market. Pictured on the GM stand at the 1928 motor show is a Grose-bodied 20-seat GMC. *Author's Collection*

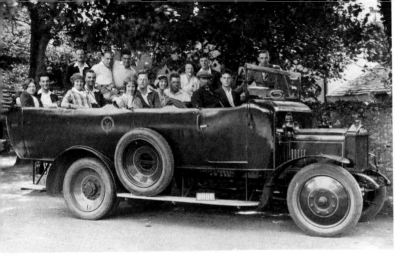

GMC

In 1911 the merging of two lorry builders already controlled by General Motors brought about the formation of General Motors Truck Co. This company became General Motors Truck & Coach division in 1925 when American Yellow Coach was merged with it. However, smaller PSVs based on truck chassis were still sold as GMCs. They were usually designed for about 20-seat bodies. A late 1920s Olympia Show saw one stand exhibiting both Chevrolet and GMC buses and coaches.

Gotfredson

One of the least-remembered makes from the 1920s is the Gotfredson, which was built in Canada. It was imported by Bonallack & Sons of London, a company later to make its name as a truck bodybuilder. The chassis were said to be speedy and have excellent hill-climbing abilities. Operators in the Eastern Counties bought a number, but others could be found elsewhere. For example, the Caledonian Omnibus Co took over a 1924 example from a two-vehicle operator, although it was scrapped in 1928. Western National acquired two from independents taken over in the late 1920s and early 1930s.

Graham Dodge and Graham

Strictly speaking, there was no such make as Graham Dodge, though some US-built chassis imported to the UK undoubtedly ran under that name. Graham Brothers of Indiana assembled truck chassis with Dodge engines from the early 1920s. Dodge itself had an interest in the company and later chassis were built in a Dodge factory. Finally, Dodge took over the company, which became its Graham Bros Division in 1928. A year later the name on the trucks also changed to Dodge. The products were typical North American designs of the period.

Granton

The Scottish Motor Engineering Co, of Granton, Edinburgh, built Granton lorry and bus chassis between 1905 and 1907, no doubt in very small numbers. The 30/40 and 45/50hp engines had four cylinders, a normal speed of 750rpm, and were said to be designed to withstand rough usage. At the 1907 Edinburgh Motor Show the company showed a 30/40hp open-top double-decker seating 36 which was said to have been built generally in accordance with Metropolitan Police Regulations. A similar bus, with a 45/50hp engine, was said to be 'doing good service' on the Edinburgh-Tollcross circular route.

Great Eastern Railway

As a result of the locomotive superintendent of the GER believing that the Milnes-Daimlers the company had bought in 1904 were expensive, 12 double-deckers were built in its own Stratford, east London,

railway workshops in 1904-5. Virtually every part was home-made, but the substantial construction of the vehicles did not ensure reliability.

GNR(I)

Buses built for itself by the Great Northern Railway Co of Ireland at its Dundalk railway works were claimed not to be mere assembly jobs, although they were fitted with Gardner 5LW diesel engines and proprietary axles and gearboxes. The railway claimed it manufactured its own chassis frames, radiators and springs as well as building the bodies. All told, 95 were constructed between 1937 and 1952. They were known as GNR-Gardners and all were forward-control single-deckers.

The first batch had David Brown gearboxes, but later ones were fitted with Leyland units, giving strength to the story that the vehicles were really Gardner-engined Leyland Lions; the GNR(I) had previously bought the Lion in petrol form.

Building its own vehicles saved payment on an import duty of 12^1/2% imposed on chassis brought in in 'knocked down' form for local assembly. Unusual features of the first batch were the dumb irons, spring brackets and other castings, all of which were of bronze as the GNR(I)'s foundry could not produce steel castings.

Greenwood & Batley

The old-established electrical engineers Greenwood & Batley designed and built a petrol-electric bus chassis in 1907. It had a French Mutel four-cylinder engine driving a generator which powered an electric motor. The motor had two separate armatures each driving a separate gear via driving shafts engaging with the cast steel road wheels.

Guy

Sidney Guy left the then successful Sunbeam Motor Co, where he had been works manager, in 1913 to set up his own company, Guy Motors, the following year. Guy began with small vehicles, notably a 1^1/2-ton truck chassis with pressed steel frame. During World War 1 the Wolverhampton factory produced armaments not vehicles and after the war there was a brief foray into the car market. Soon models for PSV use included a 30-seat charabanc and a small one-man bus. A landmark in 1924 was production of a drop-frame chassis, as pioneered by AEC only a year previously, though the Guy was of normal-control layout.

Guy, like Karrier, was quick to see the potential for six-wheelers, offering a 60-seater with pneumatic tyres and normal control in 1926. This was before it had even built a two-axle double-decker or a three-axle single-decker. Its six-wheelers were longer lived than Karriers of the same period, but not without problems. Axle and spring location, and the stresses and strains of double drive, were insufficiently understood. A forward-control six-wheel double-decker followed in 1927, the first going to the London Public Omnibus Co. It had met the stringent requirements of Scotland Yard's public carriage office, and further orders for London independents followed. Originally, the six-wheelers had Guy four-cylinder or Daimler-Knight six-cylinder sleeve-valve engines, with Guy producing its own six-cylinder engine in 1927. Guy always had an eye for publicity and around 1930 claimed its products were 'ten years in advance of the times'. Sometimes the publicity was a little short even on genuine fact, but the six-cylinder engine with its inclined side valves did offer some of the advantages of overhead valve engines without the complexity, as was claimed. Improved versions of the six-wheelers

were introduced in 1928, as were single and double-deck four-wheel models. These last were later renamed Conquest (single-deck) and Invincible (double-deck). Buyers of the six-wheelers included the corporations of Birmingham, Hull, Leicester, Middlesbrough, Morecambe, Northampton, Oldham, Reading, Salford and Wolverhampton.

The Arab name was first used in 1933 for a much revised Conquest and Invincible range, covering both single and double-deck chassis. They were probably the first UK chassis specifically designed for Gardner oil engines, and were of relatively simple layout, with the crash gearbox still mounted half-way along the chassis rather than in unit with the engine. Double-deck chassis could take either 5LW or 6LW engines, while single-deckers were offered in both normal and

Above:
Two vehicles delivered in 1929 to two fleet operators showed different thinking. That for the London & North Eastern Railway *(top)* is one of 12 forward-control ONDs seating 20, while the other *(above)* is one of 30 normal-control Conquests with 25 seats supplied to Birmingham Corporation. The latter were used as tram replacements and were soon rebuilt to forward-control. *Author's Collection (both)*

forward-control forms for 4LW or 5LW engines. However, sales were disappointing and more or less faded away completely in the mid-1930s. After that date Guy began to pick-up military contracts and perhaps was not too bothered. However, Burton-on-

Right:
There had been covered-top Guy buses since 1927, but these built in 1930 for the Cleeve Hill service of the former Cheltenham & District Light Railway were open-top, like the narrow-gauge double-deck trams they replaced. *Author's Collection*

Below:
Guy really made its name with its wartime double-deckers. This Park Royal-bodied London Guy of 1943 looks particularly austere with its angular lines and masked windows. The chassis is one of the first with projecting radiator to permit fitting of the Gardner 6LW engine (which was longer) if required. *Author's Collection*

Trent Corporation continued to support the single-deck Arab, starting with two normal-control models with Brush 26-seat bodies and 4LW engines in 1934, moving to forward-control 32-seaters in 1935, still with 4LWs, and buying more in 1940-41.

Guy was rather more successful with smaller models. Its low-cost OND and ONDF one-man buses offered between 1929 and 1931 had four-cylinder Meadows petrol engines. The F stood for forward-control. An unusual feature was the option of central or offside gear lever; the latter could be easier for one-man operation. A lengthened version was later added to the range. From 1933 until 1940 there were

four models with different wheelbases but the same 3.3 litre petrol engines. Two sizes of Wolf (for 14 and 20 passengers) were normal-control, while both Vixens (24 and 26 passengers) were forward-control. The Wolfs (or Wolves?) operated by the small municipalities of Llandudno and Colwyn Bay were well known to holidaymakers.

It was World War 2 that put Guy back into big buses. After normal bus production had ended it was realised by the Government that there was an urgent need for simple, reliable buses to help carry workers to war factories. Originally Leyland and Guy were selected to build initial batches of 500 full-size double-deckers, but it was then decided that Leyland had more important military commitments, whereas cancellation of an order for searchlight-carrying trailers meant that there would be capacity at Guy. Sidney Guy turned down the offer of use of the drawings for Bristol's 'K'-type with Gardner engine and instead redesigned the 1933 Arab. The frame was new as was the front end, but the double-plate clutch and the crash gearbox with its gear positions the reverse of normal were pure 1933 (or earlier). Bonnet and dash design were very similar to Leyland's TD7 to meet ministry requirements for standardised dimensions for bodybuilders, and the frame even had the same profile as the TD7. The chassis was relatively heavy, since use of scarce lightweight materials such as aluminium was prohibited.

Most utility Arabs had the 7 litre Gardner 5LW engine, but some operators in hilly districts were permitted the larger 6LW. The prototype was completed in March 1942 and Swindon Corporation was the first to operate the type. By December 1944, 2,000 Arab chassis had been completed. They proved reliable and longlived despite the lack of sophistication. After conditions returned to normal, Guy was able to obtain repeat business from many of its enforced users.

Halley

Once as well known and as successful as Albion, Halley went into a long and painful decline, with local rival Albion subsequently buying the empty factory and reusing some of Halley's model names. Ironically, Halley had begun in the workshop where Albion had started. George Halley was the moving force in his company, and it was his long illness contracted when in his 30s that led to his death and ultimately the collapse of his company. George Halley's Glasgow Motor Lorry Co began building steam, then petrol, lorries in the old Albion workshop from 1900. Halley's Industrial Motors was set up in 1906 and subsequently moved to purpose-built premises. By 1910 it was also building its own engines. Most chassis were for goods carrying or fire appliances, but charabancs were also built, including some with six-cylinder engines. The first two buses for the newly-formed United Automobile in 1912 were Halleys and went into service at Lowestoft driven by two Glaswegian drivers. World War 1 production of Halleys was not only of chassis, but also included axles and gearbox parts for AEC.

The early postwar years saw a misguided attempt to sell only chassis with six-cylinder engines, a brand-new engine the company had spent much time and more money developing. The chassis was the 'P'-type, a 29-35-seat bus or a 3½-ton goods vehicle. The one model policy was a disaster and, ultimately, four-cylinder engines were reintroduced. The company was relatively quick to offer the option of normal or forward control on its models. By 1925, ironically, six-cylinder engines were in vogue for coaches and charabancs, but in 1927 the bank appointed a receiver.

A new company, Halley Motors, was formed and continued building on a smaller scale, a total staff of 100 contrasting with the 1,000 once employed. The same year saw the appearance of a six-wheel PSV,

the Security Six, at the Olympia Show. It was offered in normal and forward-control forms; two of the latter were sold. The well-known Harry Ricardo helped with engine design in the late 1920s and considerable improvements resulted. The Conqueror was a new forward-control, low-frame PSV perhaps named more in hope than reality. It did, however, achieve reasonable sales; for example, Scottish General Omnibus Co, later merged with Walter Alexander, bought six.

A six-cylinder engine was offered in the Neptune, a double-decker, and in its single-deck version, the Clansman. The Neptune was offered at the time when big orders for double-deckers were in the offing from Glasgow Corporation, but the operator was more hard-headed than patriotic, with AEC and Leyland doing well, but not Halley (or Albion).

There were still users of some size: Keith & Boyle (London), which owned Orange Luxury Coaches, had quite a fleet — but it also ran Halley's London sales operation; W. & R. Dunlop's Motor Service of Greenock, later taken over by Western SMT, was faithful to the marque, buying Conquerors with Duple

bodies up to 1936. Surprisingly, the North British Locomotive Co bought Halley in 1930, perhaps seeking to diversify, but it put no money into the business. Halley gave up building in 1935, although some already-completed chassis did not enter service until the following year.

Hallford and Hallford-Stevens

J. & E. Hall of Dartford is still a well-known name in refrigeration and engineering, but for 16 years the company also built buses and trucks. The early vehicles had chain drive, four-speed gearboxes and Hall-built engines to Saurer patents. A W. Austen ran three, with double-deck bodies, between Maidstone and Chatham but could not make the route pay. By 1911 Hallfords used the company's own design of engine. Wartime production was all lorry, and vehicle production ceased in 1925.

In association with W. A. Stevens of Maidstone, Hallford also provided the chassis and engine for Hallford-Stevens petrol-electrics, a predecessor of the Tillings-Stevens.

International

International Harvester's origins are revealed by its name. From 1907 it built cars of unusual mechanical layout with large wheels, and followed with goods carrying chassis. The layout eventually became orthodox. In 1928 a batch of its Six-Speed Special chassis were built with right-hand drive for export to the UK and possibly elsewhere. They still reflected

the company's farming origins in having high ground clearance and there was a two-speed rear-axle. They were quite small vehicles and were probably used in the UK as PSV chassis for station or hotel buses. Earlier, in 1925, SMT had three 14-seaters for its North Berwick service; they ran for four years.

Total production of the Space Six in the USA for 1928-29 was 49,020, a volume that offered enormous advantages of scale. But the benefits were shortly to be lost by the imposition of import duties in the UK. Surprisingly, one Speed Six survives in the UK.

Jackson

R. Reynold Jackson & Co of Notting Hill Gate, London, made cars for a number of years. However, in 1906 the company built a bus chassis. This was fitted with a 30hp Gnome engine and a wide steel chassis frame. Engine and gearbox were supported on a sub-frame hung from the main one. The three-speed gearbox was said to be made from gunmetal.

Karrier

Clayton & Co (Huddersfield) was a family firm which began building commercial vehicles with Tylor engines in 1908. The first passenger-carrying chassis appeared in 1910. They were sold as Karrier Cars and

some 11 undertakings were named as operators in a 1912 catalogue. The following year saw a separate brochure of 'Karrier Cars for passenger services' with pictures of 16 different models including a double-decker.

Introduction of a 3-4-ton truck to meet the War Department's subsidy specification ultimately led to wartime production of such vehicles in quantity. The War Office also impressed other Karrier chassis due for delivery, including two chain-driven buses for the London & South Western Railway at Exeter; their replacements were also commandeered, but the third pair built to fulfil the order were finally delivered just before and just after Christmas 1914. A new, larger

works was built during the war, and later expanded. A new company, Karrier Motors, was formed in 1920 to take over the business. Karrier, like other makes, also rehabilitated ex-WD lorry chassis, and James Hodson, the predecessor of Ribble Motors, fitted four with open-top double-deck bodies. Over the next few years a number of new models were introduced, starting with the 'K'-type, which was a development of the wartime model. Others were the 'H'-type of 1922 for 20-26-seat bodywork, the smaller 'C'-type (1923) with Dorman engine, and the 14-seater (one-ton) 'Z'-type (1924).

A 1923 Commercial Motor Show exhibit was a 50-seater articulated vehicle, the front part being a 'K'-type tractive unit, the rear a 50-seat semi-trailer with self-steering rear axle. Unfortunately, even the limited legislation of the time did not permit its use as a PSV. A new passenger range in 1925 was the 'KL', with low-height chassis and pneumatic tyres, features which were copied by the Leyland PLSC Lion a year later. Unfortunately, Leyland seemed to have the resources or abilities to achieve a degree of reliability that eluded Karrier.

The 1925 Show saw the unveiling of the first six-wheeler, the Karrier WL6, with a platform height of only 2ft (600mm) and extravagant claims of better riding, greater safety, better braking, reduced wheel-spin, reduced tractive effort, fuel and tyre economy, and reduced maintenance costs! An even lower frame height of 1ft 9¼in (520mm) was achieved on the CL4 by cranking the main side-members of the chassis frame under the back axles. In just under seven years' production nearly 90 were sold, with either Dorman or Karrier's own engine fitted. Another six-wheeler followed at the end of 1926. This, the CL6, had the frame cranked over the rear axles. It was of a lighter build, officially for 32 passengers against the 40 of the WL6, and had a smaller Dorman engine. Production of CL6s was around 50, while WL6 (and WL6/1 with longer wheelbase) accounted for 160.

Double-deck sales reached some 40 of the three-axle WL6/2, plus another 23 DD6 or DD6/1. A Karrier sleeve-valve engine was fitted to many. The engine's distinguishing features included a separate oil cooler under the radiator and the flywheel, which was in the centre of the six-cylinder engine — in other words, between the third and fourth pistons. Karrier saw a great future for the six-wheeler and for some years had devoted much of its design efforts in this direction. Liverpool Corporation had over 80 of the type, while the corporations of Edinburgh, Oldham, Portsmouth and Salford each had 15 or 16. However, Edinburgh, having bought 14 WL6/1 single-deckers in 1927-28, found them unreliable; its last had gone by 1932. Axle and spring location and stresses and strains, particularly of double drives, were insufficiently understood, and Karrier gained a poor reputation for reliability generally. In addition, such vehicles were heavy in weight and had a high fuel consumption. By 1929 sales of six-wheelers were plummeting.

Later models were all two-axle, with four-wheel brakes ultimately becoming standard. The JKL, later renamed Chaser 4, was the most successful, and later a Chaser 6 was added for those wanting a faster vehicle. The best-known Chaser was the road/rail one built for the London, Midland & Scottish Railway. More mundane were two Chaser 6s for local operator Huddersfield Joint Omnibus Committee. These were fitted with Gardner 6LW diesel engines.

The last new passenger model was the Monitor, although few were sold. The recession, competition from AEC and Leyland, and the move to diesel engines were too much. As a result Karrier got into financial difficulties. There was an abortive plan to merge with TSM to try and survive.

In 1931 the company had 7% of the municipal bus market; two years later bus building ceased and in 1934 Rootes took it over, moving truck production to Luton the following year.

Lacoste et Battman

This French car and component maker built complete commercial vehicle chassis for a short time. London & Provincial Bus & Traction Co, whose fleetname was Arrow, ran a fleet of this make in 1906, and various other London operators tried one or two. All were of conventional layout with 34-seat open-top bodies. When Liverpool Corporation Tramways began bus operation in 1911 (by taking over a smaller operator) one of its four buses was of this make.

Lacre

Best-known as a maker of road-sweeping equipment, Lacre had a large range of models on offer by 1909 and in 1910 opened at Letchworth, Hertfordshire, what was claimed to be the first purpose-built plant in the UK for the manufacture of commercial vehicles. The first two years of World War 1 saw all production as military vehicles for Belgium, after which some chassis were bodied for passenger use. Crosville had a Lacre charabanc in 1913 and in 1916 bought some bus-bodied examples. Ultimately the operator had 10 Lacres in its fleet.

Laffly

French maker Laffly built chassis under the Laffly-Schneider name from 1922 and under the Laffly name from 1925; specific bus models were soon added.

Lambourn

Lambourn Garages, of Lambourn, Berkshire, in conjunction with Universal Power Drives, of Perivale, Middlesex, built a number of horseboxes under the Lambourn name in the late 1930s. The vehicles had a Fordson V8 petrol engine mounted low down at the rear of the chassis. In 1937 a passenger-carrying version was produced. It had a similar layout, complete with dummy Fordson radiator grille at the front and a real radiator at the rear behind the engine. Many other components, such as gearbox and clutch, were Fordson-derived. Throttle and clutch were hydraulically operated, and the remote gear control was by cable. Between-axles chassis frame height was low, just 18in (450mm).

Lancia

The old-established Italian vehicle builder Lancia first exhibited in Britain at the 1921 Olympia Show, subsequently becoming one of the more successful importers of the 1920s. The biggest operator must have been the Barton business, with 100 bought new or secondhand. Some of the Barton examples were ex-World War 1 chassis acquired from the government in Italy. Many of the Lancias became Lancia-Bartons and had greatly extended chassis. These were fitted with an additional axle, a Barton practice that was also applied to other makes.

Genuine Lancias featured in many other fleets as charabancs and had a reputation for high speeds.

Latil

The old-established French maker Latil had considerable success in the UK in the 1930s with a four-wheel drive heavy duty tractive unit built under licence by Shelvoke & Drewry. In the previous decade it had sold a few PSVs in the UK. These included, for example, a 1924 14-seat bus which operated for 10 years with Midland Bus Services and its successor, Western SMT, while the Southern National Omnibus Co also acquired a 14-seater when it took over a small operator's four-vehicle fleet in 1935.

Below:
Lancia chassis sold well in the UK in the 1920s, to a variety of operators; the Pentaiota was particularly popular as a charabanc. Barton Bros ran some Lancias in standard form and also lengthened others. Further examples were extended even more, gaining a third, trailing, axle at the same time — as shown here. The much rebuilt chassis were generally known as Lancia-Bartons. *Arthur Ingram Collection*

Leyland

Of all the bus manufacturers Leyland was undoubtedly the most successful. It built the most vehicles and successfully developed some of the most advanced designs. But it was not without hard times. The decision to buy back Government surplus World War 1 Leylands and recondition them before sale (to protect the company's reputation) almost bankrupted it and, at a later date, the bank felt obliged to put in its own manager to run the company.

If there is one legendary model it is, of course, the original Titan designed by G. J. Rackham. But after he left (and he did not stay long) Leyland kept up the momentum, constantly improving the Titan and the other models. Some pre-Titan models were very successful too, such as the Lion.

Leyland had originated as a steam vehicle builder in 1896 (having previously produced steam lawn-mowers), becoming the Lancashire Steam Motor Co, but after 11 years changed its name to Leyland Motors to reflect the greater number of petrol-engined vehicles being produced. It had been among the earlier steam builders to see the limitations of this form of propulsion and had begun to develop its own petrol engines, although initially those vehicles sold were fitted by engines of Crossley manufacture. The 'X'-type of 1907, a 3^1/$_2$ tonner for lorry or bus use, was probably the first model with an engine entirely of Leyland design.

The company was also early in offering four-speed gearboxes, with the top ratio giving direct drive. Smaller models were soon added, with smaller engines. Another range of engines followed in 1909.

Cast aluminium was used for the crankcase and other parts, and both sets of valves were on the same side.

In 1912 Leyland became the only maker to receive War Office approval for both 1^1/$_2$ and 3 tonners in its subsidy scheme. This scheme enabled buyers to receive an annual payment for buying and keeping in good condition vehicles of approved design which could be repurchased at a premium in the event of war. Although applying to goods vehicles, the scheme boosted sales generally and the chassis were the same anyway. When war broke out in 1914 not only goods vehicles were requisitioned, but also bus chassis (which were not in the scheme). Edinburgh Corporation had just bought its first three buses, but the War Department took them, and many others from elsewhere.

The models became known as subsidy models, which Leyland went on to build in huge numbers; nearly 6,000 went to the Royal Flying Corps (forerunner of the Royal Air Force) in four years. These became known as the RAF type. About half were bought back by Leyland after the war and reconditioned in a factory at Kingston, Surrey, over a five-year period. But sales of these (and other ex-WD makes) did nothing to help new chassis sales, and at

Below:
Haslingden Corporation was an early municipal bus operator, and bought this Leyland-bodied Leyland 'X'-type in 1907. The 'X' was a 3^1/$_2$ ton model and the first successful petrol-engined vehicle. It had a new four-cylinder six-litre engine with 'T' cylinder head that developed 40hp. *Author's Collection*

Above:
The 'SG' range sold in quantity as single and double-deckers in the early 1920s. The White Rose fleet of Brookes Bros of Rhyl took several; note the oil sidelights. Crosville later took over the 87-strong Brookes fleet. *Ian Allan Library*

Right:
Leyland was envious of AEC's monopoly in London, and developed a special light version of its G7 chassis to meet Metropolitan Police requirements. It was fitted with three independent brakes and a quiet four-speed gearbox. The pioneer London independent, Arthur Partridge's Chocolate Express, bought the first, in 1922, for £1,600 complete with Dodson body. He paid a deposit of £530 and the balance plus 5% interest in 12 monthly payments of £93 12s (£93.60). *Author's Collection*

Right:
Leyland's Titans, and other models that copied it, with their overall height much lower than before and a lower centre of gravity, allowed operators to run double-deckers into rural areas and on long inter-urban routes. This early Titan of Maidstone & District was photographed in Ightham, Kent, in 1936. *Author's Collection*

one stage in the early 1920s the Lancashire factory was working only four days in a fortnight. It was the bus sales that kept the company afloat, and between 1922 and 1924 these doubled each year.

A big range of new chassis, of varying sizes and capacities, had been announced fairly soon after the war ended. The 'N'-type, with 36-40hp engine and worm rear axle was the most popular for bus use, with Southdown being one big buyer. Southdown was also a buyer for the 'G'-range that quickly followed, buying more than 50 of the type over five years. The next design step, in 1922, was to move the driver alongside the engine to provide more room for passengers within a given length. Leyland called such vehicles 'side type' and added an S to the type name; thus an SG7 was a forward-control G7.

The first purpose-built bus chassis came in 1925 with five new models, all beginning with the letter 'L'. The double-deck Leviathan sold in reasonable numbers, the bonneted Lioness sold better, and the forward-control single-deck Lion sold exceptionally well; local operator Ribble bought over 180 Lions between 1926 and 1928. Chassis frame height of the 'L' models was about one foot (30cm) lower than their predecessors, largely because of a better method of attaching the axles to the frame. Most (but not the double-decker) had pneumatic tyres.

The fact that Leyland built bodies as well as chassis was of enormous benefit in developing the Titan, which was announced in 1927. Its overall height as a closed-top double-decker was about two feet (60cm) lower than the Leviathan and probably nearer three feet (90cm) lower than some other makes. The drop-frame chassis was not new, but Leyland also ran the propshaft along the nearside of the chassis (instead of along the centre line) so that the central gangway in the lower deck could be lower than the floor level under the seats, to gain a valuable inch or so. Instead of a centre gangway upstairs, seats were grouped in fours towards the nearside, with a sunken (or dropped) gangway on the offside. It intruded into the lower deck where passengers using the seats nearest the windows on the offside had to be careful to duck when entering or leaving their seats. All this produced an overall height of just 12ft 10in (3.91m). Careful body design, including use of aluminium panels, kept weight down and enabled pneumatic tyres to be used. The other big surprise with the Titan was its new six-cylinder overhead camshaft engine, with gearbox directly bolted to it. With improvements and modifications, the petrol engine was to remain in production until 1948, and it also formed the basis of the first Leyland production diesel engine. Vacuum-servo brakes were another feature of the Titan. Almost all the features of the Titan chassis were repeated on its single-deck counterpart, the Tiger, and there was also a three-axle double-decker, the Titanic, which sold in tiny numbers.

From the announcement of the first Titans the story became one of successive improvements up to the mid-1930s, after which the pace slackened a little. The most significant event was the development of Leyland's own diesel engine, initially of 8.1 litre capacity and later 8.6. It was based on the petrol engine, and that too was increased in capacity and subsequently received a top-end redesign. Take up of

petrol engines in double-deckers soon dwindled, with notable exceptions such as Bournemouth Corporation, but Ribble kept to petrol engines in single-deckers, surprisingly, and smaller coach operators generally preferred them. Final 'prewar' models of the Tiger and Titan families were not actually announced until after the outbreak of war in September 1939.

Reverting to the late 1920s, many of the Titan/Tiger improvements could also be found on new versions of the Lion and Lioness. There was a four-cylinder version of the new six-cylinder engine, and the Lion continued to sell well as a lighter alternative for other than the busiest urban bus services. These models retained the central transmission line, and so were slightly higher off the ground. Lions were redesigned in 1934, gaining a 5.7 litre diesel option, along with a more upright front end. The shorter engine permitted an extra row of seats to be fitted into the bodywork so that, ironically, the smaller-engined vehicle had the higher passenger capacity.

The Kingston works, once used for rebuilding World War 1 Leylands, was re-equipped from 1931 to build a new light range of normal-control goods and passenger chassis, the latter for 20-seat bodywork, with a new 4.4 litre petrol engine. Subsequently, forward-control models were also offered, and a 4.4 litre diesel option (later enlarged to 4.7 litres) was also available.

Leyland did not follow the AEC/Daimler path by

Right:
Leyland also had a thriving body works, which in 1935 produced this all-metal bodied Tiger demonstrator. The Tiger was the single-deck version of the Titan, and was similarly successful. Note the 'pairing' of the pillars between the side windows. The roof incorporates an opening section as well as a luggage holder. *Ian Allan Library*

Below right:
Leyland developed its own 'gearless bus' as written on the radiator of this Lion for Preston Corporation. The transmission incorporated a torque convertor and was popular for urban work for a time. It was, however, thirsty in fuel consumption terms. The Lion was a four-cylinder (petrol or diesel) version of the Tiger, and some might have thought it underpowered with a convertor. *Ian Allan Library*

Left:
The Cheetah, announced in 1935, was a lightweight designed for light bodywork and for economy. Most of its parts were a mix of Cub or Lion. The SMT group bought 300 with diesel engines and full-fronted bodywork, while Ribble took slightly more over a four-year period, all petrol-engined. This one in Alexander colours never ran for the operator; all of the intended batch were diverted to Western SMT. *Author's Collection*

Centre left:
There was a resurgence of interest in three-axle buses in the mid to late 1930s. Central SMT and Western SMT between them took 38 of these three-axle Tiger TS6Ts, while City Coach Co took some 36. City had a Wood Green-Southend stage service that was incredibly busy at summer weekends yet was limited to single-deckers — so the extra capacity was useful. *Author's Collection*

Below:
The Tiger FEC underfloor-engined chassis — note the nearside radiator. What appears to be a conventional gear lever is the selector for the pre-selector gearbox, as also found on AEC Regents and Regals supplied to London. Leyland obviously still kept an eye on America, for it described the FEC as 'the forerunner of a British transit bus'. *Author's Collection*

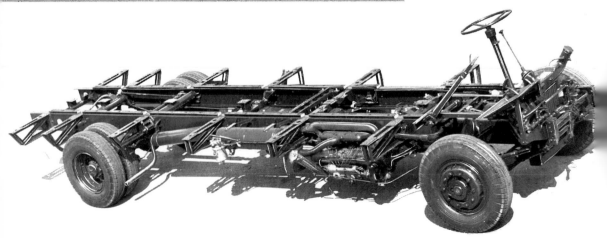

offering pre-selector gearboxes, but instead developed the torque convertor, which virtually eliminated gear changing; above about 20mph a driver just moved a lever to select direct drive. Offered from 1933 in a range of chassis, the 'gearless bus' transmission sold well, particularly to municipal operators replacing trams or those with hilly territory, or both. As an automatic transmission it was a pioneering effort, years ahead of any other. But there was a penalty in the higher fuel consumption, and sales dropped off in the late 1930s.

One new model in the mid-1930s was the Cheetah, a full-sized forward-control chassis that was a cross between a Lion and a Cub, with a light six-cylinder engine. Practically none were sold for export, which suggests that Leyland realised that performance was questionable unless the unladen weight was strictly adhered to. Even so, several hundred were sold, notably in Scotland, while Ribble was unusual in specifying petrol engines. Technically, they provided an interesting contrast with the Lion with its four-cylinder engine, which still continued in production.

War cut short another promising development — the underfloor-engined single-decker of which 88 were built for London Transport. The layout subsequently became standard for single-deckers in the UK, and was developed with LT. It reflected one of the lessons that LT had learnt with the AEC 'Q' — the desirability of keeping every mechanical part below floor level.

Leyland bus production gradually diminished in 1940, though subsequently under Government direction it completed a large number of Titans and Tigers on which construction work had started before being halted by the war.

Lifu

The copper boiler must have made a Lifu steam bus a particularly impressive — and expensive — vehicle. The name stood for Liquid Fuel Engineering Co, a company which was based at Cowes on the Isle of Wight. The company was building steam cars and trucks before 1900. A road train was used to collect and deliver parcels in and around Swindon for a syndicate which included the Midland & South Western Junction Railway; in the summer of 1898 a 20-seat car was added as a second trailer and began working between Cirencester and Fairford. The following summer the road train ran again, this time from Cirencester to Fairford, Lechlade and Faringdon. Another Lifu, a steam bus, started a Torquay-Paignton service in 1899. At that year's Agricultural Hall Motor Show, Lifu exhibited a 28-seat double-decker and a wagonette. However, the Cowes works closed in 1900.

The Scottish Motor Traction Co, having laid down a performance specification for potential suppliers, ordered two Lifus in 1905 through a Wishaw company. But after a short trial they were rejected for lack of power, presumably because they could not reach the required 12mph on the level or 3mph on a 1 in 6 gradient. They were no doubt built by another contractor under licence as the Lifu works had closed, but must have involved somebody in considerable expense. Some Belhavens were also built under Lifu patents and, ironically, SMT also tried and rejected one of these.

London General

The London General Omnibus Co began building its own buses with the 'X'-type in 1909, and continued with the famous 'B'-type in the following year. The buses were constructed at the Walthamstow overhaul works which had originally been used by Vanguard. After the Underground Group obtained control of the LGOC there was a change of policy and Walthamstow became a separate entity, the Associated Equipment Co — better known as AEC.

'High quality of parts and interchangeability' were the maxim for the 'B'-type, according to Walter Iden, who was joint designer with Frank Searle. From employing 300-400 workers in an overhaul shop

Right:
London General built its 'X'-type at Walthamstow and later went on to construct the legendary 'B'-type there. This is an early 'X'-type.
Author's Collection

A strange final episode was the decision to design and build at Chiswick six four-wheel single-deckers (type 'CB') and six six-wheel double-deckers (type 'CC'); the numbers were reduced at a late stage and only three single-deckers and four double-deckers were completed, in 1931 and 1932. By this stage the LGOC was heavily committed to AEC's new Regal, Regent and Renown types. The final Chiswick-built buses used mainly proprietary units, including Kirkstall axles and Meadows petrol engines. They later gained some AEC components, but all were withdrawn by 1940.

which also manufactured spare parts, Walthamstow went on to employ between 3,000 and 4,000. Production of new chassis ran at a regular 30 a week, but at one stage the addition of a night shift pushed the figure to 60. Some 'B'-type bodies were also built at Walthamstow.

Years later, in the mid-1920s, the LGOC's new Chiswick works assembled considerable numbers of 'NS'-type buses, the parts for which were produced by AEC at Walthamstow. Chiswick also built eight all-weather touring coaches in 1926, fitting Daimler sleeve-valve engines along with 'NS' back axles and brakes.

Lothian

Nearly 100 Lothians were built by the Scottish Motor Traction Co between 1913 and 1924. Like some other operators, SMT was not satisfied with what was commercially available at the time. A few chassis were supplied to other Scottish operators, and a number of chassis were originally built as trucks. Nearly all chassis were forward-control, unusual at that time, and took full-front bodywork. The vehicles were bodied as either single or double-deckers. The first chassis had Minerva engines and later ones had Tylor units; a chain-driven gearbox was standard.

M & D

Just one model was offered by this mid-1920s maker, a four-cylinder engined chassis suitable for 14-seat bodywork. However, it did have brakes on all four wheels. It was sold by a Birmingham company.

Below:
The Scottish Motor Traction Co assembled its own chassis for some 12 years. Known as Lothians, they used Minerva or Tylor engines. Some were sold to other operators and most were of forward-control layout. *Author's Collection*

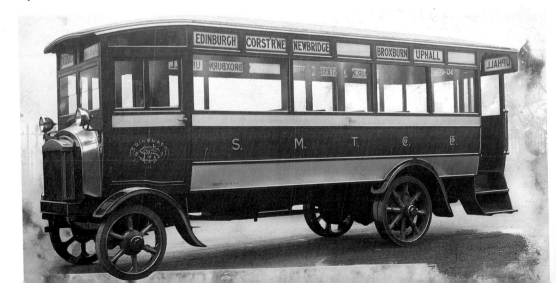

Above:
Sandgate-based Maltby's Motor Works built small numbers of charabancs for local operators in Kent for several years. This one dates from 1911. Note how the front windscreen splits horizontally and hinges forwards when the hood is down. *Author's Collection*

Maltby

Beginning as a bodybuilder, Maltby's Motor Works of Sandgate, Kent, expanded into producing complete vehicles. All were charabancs and constructed in small numbers for local operators. Production lasted for some 15 years before the company reverted to bodybuilding, mainly for cars. The earliest models had Coronet engines built in Coventry by one Walter Iden (later to become general manager and chief engineer of AEC at the same time as remaining chief engineer of the LGOC). Later Maltby charabancs were fitted with White and Poppe engines. A 40hp Maltby ordered by F. W. Wacher & Co passed straight to East Kent Road Car, having been delivered after the former company was taken over.

Manchester

In the late 1920s Willys-Overland-Crossley assembled Willys-Overlands for the British market. However, the company also made its own design of 1.25 and 1.75 ton trucks, which were of typical North American design with such features as spiral-bevel back axle and coil ignition. They were later badged as Willys-Manchester or Manchester, and the larger model was also offered as a 14-seat PSV. Seven Manchesters went into the LPTB fleet in 1933 when small operators were compulsorily acquired.

Martin

An unlikely producer of bus chassis was the Martin Cultivator Co of Stamford, Lincolnshire. It built farm tractors and trailer fire pumps, but briefly in the mid-1920s produced a fire engine and — probably — just one PSV chassis.

Maudslay

The fortunes of the Maudslay Motor Co of Coventry see-sawed in remarkable fashion. Twice, when the company was in a critical condition, it staged a comeback with advanced and innovative designs. Its pedigree was of the finest. Henry Maudslay was a pioneer of the industrial revolution. He made the first screw-cutting lathe, which made it possible for screw threads to be standardised, and he made the first micrometer which opened up developments leading to modern ideas of production engineering. His great-grandson founded the Maudslay Motor Co at the beginning of this century.

A number of 12-seat buses powered by two-cylinder overhead-valve engines of 2.4 litre were supplied to the Great Western Railway in 1905 and the same year saw a double-deck chassis with four-cylinder 6.4 litre engine with equal bore and stroke. The engine had an overhead camshaft on a hinged frame so that a valve could be changed in a claimed two minutes. One of these buses, with sliding mesh

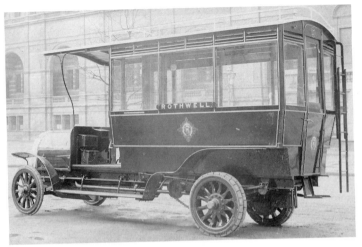

Left:
Maudslay was one of the more successful early bus builders. This 25/30hp model and a Wolseley were bought by the Midland Railway in 1908 and used to inaugurate a Desborough station-Rothwell route. The Maudslay chassis was officially a 'colonial special' and had features which had gained it an award for engine accessibility from the War Office in its 1907 trials. *Author's Collection*

Below left:
Coventry Corporation naturally supported local industry, buying numbers of Maudslays in the 1920s and early 1930s but favouring Daimler more in the late 1930s. This impressive double-decker, complete with cab doors and windscreens, dates from early 1924; later that year low-frame bus chassis were announced.
Arthur Ingram Collection

Above right:
Edinburgh-based SMT had bought Maudslays, on and off, since the earliest days. The late 1920s were good years, with 56 being bought in 1926; all had 32-seat bus bodies. This example was bodied by Vickers. Most remained in the fleet only until 1932. *Ian Allan Library*

gearbox and chain drive, inaugurated operations of the Scottish Motor Traction Co in Edinburgh in 1906.

World War 1 saw production of models to government-approved subsidy design, and Maudslays were also built by the Rover Co. Improved models came out after the war with detachable cylinder heads but without swing-over camshafts. However, times were difficult, with so many ex-War Department vehicles on the market.

Autumn 1924 saw the first dedicated PSV chassis, the four-cylinder 'ML'-type, with a low frame, a concept introduced by AEC only the previous year. Engines were mounted in a subframe with the separate gearbox inclined downwards towards the rear to give a straight transmission line to the underslung worm-driven back axle. Normal and forward-control models were offered, with six-cylinder engines added to the options in 1927. The range remained in production (with improvements) until 1936. A low-frame version of the less successful double-deck chassis came in 1925.

Particular sales successes were with the GWR and SMT, the latter buying 165 Maudslays between 1925 and 1929. Regrouping in the bus industry saw the growing Crosville Motor Services swallow Western Transport of Wrexham in 1933 and its fleet which included 16 ex-GWR Maudslays, while others of the make were amongst another part of the GWR fleet transferred to Thames Valley Traction. Events such as these meant that by the early 1930s Maudslays sold mainly to independents, with the likes of AEC, Bristol and Leyland achieving great successes with the larger operators.

Dwindling sales prompted Maudslay's other big

leap forward in design, the high capacity SF40, later named the Magna. Introduced in 1935, it had a conventional vertical engine and radiator, but the front axle was moved rearwards sufficiently to allow the entrance to be placed forward of it. Up to 40 seats could be accommodated in a bus built to the then maximum length of 27ft 6in (8.38m). Engine and gearbox were still in a subframe, now slightly flexibly mounted, and the relatively high chassis permitted a straight transmission line. Many of the units were similar to those of the 'MLs', and there was also a new conventional single-decker, the ML5, with a neater and more compact front end. It was later named Marathon; this and the Magna were offered with Maudslay's 5.43 litre petrol engine or with Gardner 4LW or 5LW diesel.

Maxwell

This American maker from Detroit had made cars for a few years, then added vans and trucks from about the end of World War 1 until 1925. The chassis were mostly car-derived, as with many other makes, with a lengthened frame and changed gear ratio. Such chassis could carry bodies for up to 14 seats. The National Motor Museum at Beaulieu has a 21hp charabanc in its collection.

McCurd

The name might sound Scottish, but W. A. McCurd was a London car dealer. In 1912 he introduced a commercial vehicle chassis which was built in his own premises, and was unusual for the time in having a worm-driven back axle. Harrogate Road Car liked the design, taking its ninth in 1919. Southdown bought a couple of McCurds in 1915, no doubt because they were of no interest to the War Office and therefore were still available.

The original factory was at Cricklewood, but production seems to have ceased for a time before recommencing from premises at Hayes in Middlesex in the mid-1920s. The company then offered a PSV chassis with four-wheel brakes. Then followed another move, to Slough, by which time the company had become McCurd Motors and offered a respectable normal-control chassis with drop frame and pneumatic tyres for up to 26 seats. McCurds at one stage certainly manufactured more of its own components than most, but by 1927 competition was just too great and production ceased.

Mercedes-Benz

Chassis built by Mercedes-Benz have never been numerous in the UK, but a limited number were sold in the late 1920s and early 1930s. One notable operation were two pioneer express services run by Pullman Roadways of Croydon; the company ran daily London-Southampton-Bournemouth and London-Torquay-Plymouth routes with a fleet of five 20-seat Mercedes-Benz luxury coaches. Both routes started from Croydon before heading to London.

Mercedes-Benz exhibits at the 1929 Olympia

Motor Show were a normal-control 20-seater with six-cylinder engine and another normal-control model for up to 32 seats. The company was early in the field with diesel engines, a Midlands operator being among the first, in September 1930, to order one for a coach.

The company rather faded from the scene after 1931, but briefly reappeared in 1938 with a forward-control model said to seat up to 44 passengers.

Milnes and Milnes-Daimler

Best known of the early motorbus builders was undoubtedly Milnes-Daimler, formed from as association between an important British tramcar builder (Milnes) and Daimler Motoren Gesellschaft of Canstatt, Wurtenburg, Germany. By 1907 the company had become by far the largest provider of motorbuses, with over 600 in service in Britain. It had started, however, with lorries made by Milnes and fitted with German Daimler engines. The first bus came in 1902; it went to Portsmouth & Gosport Motors. Later that year the Milnes-Daimler company was formed. The company later also sold Mercedes cars. One of the directors was H. G. Burford, who was later to set up his own company, which initially imported vehicles from a different continent. Once the boom in tramway building and electrification was over, the Milnes tramcar-building business went into liquidation, but luckily left Milnes-Daimler more or less unaffected. However, the company subsequently sold just chassis rather than the complete vehicles with Milnes bodies it had previously offered.

The Great Western Railway, the Great North of Scotland Railway and Eastbourne Corporation were all early operators. After the Vanguard and Road Car fleets merged with the LGOC there were over 300 Milnes-Daimlers in the combined fleet. The earliest Milnes-Daimlers had two-cylinder 20hp engines, with two change-speed (or gear) levers, and the brake and clutch were linked so that the clutch disconnected when the brakes were applied. That may have eased driving, but it probably contributed to the accident on Handcross Hill in 1906 when a Vanguard open-top double-decker on a run to Brighton ran out of control, killing eight passengers and retarding progress generally with longer distance bus services.

The Achilles' heel of what was generally a remarkably reliable bus for the time was the dead rear axle. Small pinions at the end of live drive shafts engaged with teeth cut internally around the inside of the wheel rim. It worked but was dreadfully noisy after wear and tear and dirt had taken their toll. In London the Metropolitan Police were always complaining about the noise and ordering noisy vehicles off the road.

By 1909 the company was selling Mercedes cars in some quantity, and enthusiasm for this, combined with competition from improved designs by other PSV builders, caused a big drop in bus sales. World War 1 and the German connection effectively killed the company; supply of chassis and components ceased and, in any event, few people would have wanted to buy. The company, by then named Milnes-Daimler-Mercedes, was wound up under the Trading with the Enemy (Amendment) Act in 1916.

Minerva

Based in Antwerp, Belgium, Minerva had begun with bicycles and developed through motorcycles to cars and trucks. Its first true passenger chassis were full-sized models produced in 1926, with 5.3 litre engines. Later engine size increased to 6.0 litre, but smaller PSVs seating 20 to 24 were added to the range. These were fitted with 3.6 litre engines.

When East Kent took over the Redbourn Group of coach operators in the Thanet area in 1935 it acquired nine Minervas. Some were normal-control models, others forward-control. They had been new between 1927 and 1931. Seating capacity varied from 26 to 31. All were soon sold, but few saw further service.

MOC

One of the first bus companies to build its own vehicles was the London Motor Omnibus Co, better known as Vanguard. It formed a subsidiary, Motor Omnibus Construction Ltd, which began to build double-deckers for it in 1906. MOC used Armstrong-Whitworth engines, and some Armstrong-Whitworth buses in the Vanguard fleet were also badged MOC; there was a total of 20 of these two types in the fleet. Walthamstow went on to build the 'X' and 'B'-types under LGOC control, and later became the AEC works. Not every MOC went to Vanguard; Southdown's predecessor, the Sussex Motor Road Car Co, bought one in 1908 and fitted it with what became known as Mackenzie's slipper design of charabanc body (in which each row of transverse seats was 5in (12.5cm) higher than the one in front so that the rearmost passengers were seated very high up). Mackenzie was Southdown's traffic manager for many years.

Morris-Commercial

William Morris began building commercial vehicles in 1924. Although aimed mainly at the goods vehicle market, many of the 'T', 'TX' and 'Z'-types were bought for bus use. Then, in 1930, came purpose-built chassis, starting with the six-cylinder engined Viceroy (or 'Y'-type) and the Dictator (or 'H'-type). Two years later came the meritorious, but relatively unsuccessful, double-decker, the Imperial, of which just over 80 were built in two years. Local operator Birmingham Corporation took 50 and ultimately 30 went to East Kent.

Below:
Engine, gearbox and radiator of the single-deck Dictator and the double-deck Imperial could be easily disconnected and removed. However, adding this innovation probably increased cost. This Dictator carries a neat crew cab while undergoing a road test for Modern Transport. *Ian Allan Library*

A strange reversal of the usual pattern was the subsequent production of some bus chassis, such as the Dictator, as heavy trucks. A later bonneted single-decker was the Director (or 'RP'-type), a truck deriv-ative, but with a drop frame and four-cylinder engine; both Aldershot & District and East Kent bought the model.

Of all the buses, the Dictator and Imperial were the most interesting. They were designed by chief engi-neer Charles K. Edwards, who had previously worked for AEC as chief designer. At a time when mechan-ical reliability was improving, the engine and gearbox plus radiator could be disconnected and wheeled out on the front axle. The cylinder head could be removed without disturbing the valve timing or camshaft drive and just three nuts secured the water pump.

Subsequently, heavy duty passenger chassis faded from the scene, although a new single-decker, based on the Equi-load truck, appeared in 1938.

Morton

General engineering company Robert Morton & Sons, of Wishaw, had built a few steam vehicles under licence from Lifu in the first years of this century. From 1907 construction was undertaken by a new company, Belhaven Engineering & Motors. One Morton is said to have received an open-top bus body seating 40, and to have been operated by the Caledonian Railway during 1906.

Napier

Napier is better remembered for its cars, racing cars and aero engines, but from time to time it offered commercial vehicles and passenger chassis. In 1901, the first year of the company's existence, a few chara-bancs were built on modified car chassis and a bus chassis was offered, briefly, five years later.

Commercial vehicle models were produced in a more serious manner from 1912, when a separate department was formed, but dropped altogether some 10 years later. Gearboxes on later models were mounted in unit with the engines.

Northern General

The few larger bus companies that saw a need to design and build chassis to meet their own special requirements generally began in the early part of this century. Northern General Transport, however, found itself in this position in the early 1930s. Traffic was growing, but parts of its territory were littered with low bridges which precluded the use of double-deckers on many routes. It needed modern, high capacity single-deckers.

This led to the production between 1933 and 1939 of some 67 side-engined single-deckers, of a chassis layout not unlike that of the AEC 'Q'-type. On all but the prototype the front axle was set back. All the petrol-engined buses, and some luxury coaches that were also built, had Hercules six-cylinder engines imported from America. These engines were particularly compact and led to less intrusion in the interior than on the 'Q'-type, which had to have a longitudinal offside seat above the engine. NGT managed to get all seats facing forward. The vehicles were 30ft (9.14m) long six-wheelers.

The chassis for the largest batch built, 31 in 1935, were assembled by AEC at Southall, and it has been suggested that this was some kind of deal to assuage AEC's complaint of patent infringement. Only one axle of the twin rear axle assembly was driven. The final 25 built, plus a prototype, were only 27ft 6in (8.38m) long with a single rear axle and seated 40.

Above:
This is a close-up of NGT's side-engined six-wheeler. Note how squat the US-built Hercules engine is, thereby creating minimal intrusion into the saloon of the bus. *Author's Collection*

Below:
A production version of NGT's SE6 which illustrates the type's set-back front axle. Unlike the AEC 'Q', the SE6 had a front-mounted radiator. Seating capacity was 44. *Author's Collection*

During World War 2 one of the 30ft-long buses was converted to two-axle, thus becoming the first of this configuration in the UK. The two-axle buses were built with diesel engines, a modified version of the new AEC 6.6 litre design, installed at an angle of 30°. Most of the petrol-engined buses were converted to diesel in later life, using AEC engines specially designed for the by then outdated Matilda tank. They were bought in pairs (as fitted to the tanks), and those with auxiliaries mounted on the offside of the engine went into the SE6s, while those with nearside ones were used to convert Midland Red-built SOS chassis that also featured in the NGT fleet.

Opel

Well known German maker Opel added trucks to its car and van range at a very early stage. Best known Opels of all were the Blitz range, introduced in 1931. The make sold in the UK in small numbers in the 1930s as an alternative to the Bedford and some remained in service into the postwar period, despite the obvious problem of spares.

Orion

Although built in Zurich, Switzerland, for only 11 years Orions were surprisingly successful in export markets. Five of these horizontal-engined buses were running in London during 1905, two with the LGOC and three with the Victoria Motor Omnibus Co. The first two buses of the Cambrian Railways were of this make and lasted from 1906 until 1912.

Overland

Willys Overland Crossley was an offshoot of Crossley Motors of Gorton, Manchester, and was set up in 1920 to assemble Willys-Overland vehicles for the UK. It later added models of its own designs,

albeit using US-sourced major components, and from 1928 these chassis were sold as Overland Manchesters. The 1.75 tonne truck of 1929 fitted with 3.6 litre five-bearing engine was also offered as a 14-seat coach. By 1933 the company had gone into liquidation.

Pagefield

Best remembered for its refuse collection system and vehicles, Pagefields were made by Walker Bros of Wigan, who were mining engineers. Cars, vans and lorries were also made plus a few buses around 1919/20 on lorry chassis. Then in 1927 a low-frame PSV chassis was introduced. Remarkably advanced for its time, it had a six-cylinder Dorman engine, four-wheel internally-expanding drum brakes, and sub-assemblies that were isolated from chassis flexing. The whole engine assembly could be easily detached and wheeled out, an idea followed a few years later by Morris-Commercial. However, the cone clutch was rather dated. Total PSV production was less than 10. Users included Grant's Saloon Services in Scotland and — more locally — Wigan Corporation.

Palladium

Originally a car maker, Palladium started building commercial vehicles in 1913, achieving some success with a Dorman-engined 3-4 ton chassis, a number of which were bodied as buses. An unusual feature of a

Below:
These two Swiss Orions, with bodies by Christopher Dodson of London, were the first two motorbuses owned by Cambrian Railways. They began running between Pwllheli and Nevin in 1906. *Author's Collection*

purpose-built coach chassis introduced at the 1920 Olympia Show was the option of double cantilever rear suspension. Road Motors of Luton, later taken over by National Omnibus & Transport, had a few of the type. One or two Palladiums were bodied as double-deckers. The maker was based in west London and closed down in 1924.

Peugeot

French maker Automobiles Peugeot had offered commercial vehicles from when it began production in 1894. In 1905 a 1½ ton truck with two-cylinder 1.8 litre engine was available in the UK at a price of £450. It was probably one of these that formed the basis of a 14-seat bus that ran between Fraserburgh, Rosehearty and New Aberdour in 1906.

Pickering

Tweedmouth, near Berwick-on-Tweed, was the unlikely location of this maker of commercial chassis. Established in 1905, it was claiming in 1906 that despite an annual output of 300 'it was kept more than fully engaged'. That too was unlikely; the company folded the same year.

One Pickering single-decker ran in Penrith, while another, a double-decker, was — just — an exhibit at the 1906 Agricultural Hall Show in Islington, London. All that was on the Pickering stand when the exhibition opened was the body for the bus, but the chassis did arrive in time for the two to be married before the show closed. This bus had a four-cylinder Pickering engine of 35-40hp 'which develops its power at 750rpm'. Unusual features included a dual ignition system, Pickering patented wheels with a fixed centre flange, and steering-mounted controls for throttle, air and both ignition systems. The engine drove through a metal to leather clutch and then 'via a telescopic link' to a three-speed gearbox.

Pierce-Arrow

Quality American car maker Pierce-Arrow added trucks to its range in 1910 and later PSVs as well. British ideas, such as worm drive, were incorporated in some of its early commercials as a result of employing engineers from Dennis and Hallford. From 1924 there was a normal-control bus chassis, the model Z. It had a six-cylinder engine as used in the cars and was available in the UK for a time. With a list price of £1,000 it was the most expensive chassis on the market.

Prunel

Another French maker, based near Paris, Prunel built cars and commercial vehicles for just four or five years. A double-decker on a three-ton chassis with 30-33hp four-cylinder engine had a body built by T. H. Lewis of Chalk Farm, London. The body was shipped to France and fitted in the factory. The complete vehicle with invited observers was then driven the 180 miles from Paris to Boulogne in 15hr running time. It then crossed the Channel by ship and covered the 72 miles from Folkestone to London in six hours, all without mishap. The bus was then shown at the 1906 Agricultural Hall Show in Islington.

Ransomes

Better known as a pioneer trolleybus maker, Ransomes, Sims & Jefferies built one battery-electric bus in 1921. It was constructed around a lorry chassis and sold to a colliery in Accrington, Lancashire, to provide works transport.

Regent

Very little appears to be known about the 24hp Regent chassis built in 1905 for omnibus or lorry work and which was demonstrated to the press that year. One noteworthy feature was the use of a single lever 'to operate all the gears, the speeds being placed in consecutive order, with the high speed at the rear of the box'. There were four forward speeds, and the gearbox was mounted immediately ahead of the rear wheels. Applying the handbrake 'put the motor out of gear,' it was said.

Renault

For many years a distinctive feature of numerous Renault models was their unusual bonnet shape, like an upturned coal scuttle. Austin of England used a similar bonnet for some years. By the 1920s the French maker had developed a huge range, from cars to heavy trucks, specialised vehicles to cross the Sahara desert, PSVs and railcars. From the late 1920s there was a range of normal and forward-control coaches, capable of considerable speed. Sir Henry Seagrave demonstrated them in Britain, where a number were sold. Earlier, there had been UK customers for smaller vehicles. For example, Blue Bird Motors of Cwm bought a 26-seat bus in 1925 for its service to Ebbw Vale. The vehicles had a coal-scuttle bonnet, pneumatic tyres at the front and servo-assisted four-wheel brakes — the latter a rarity at that time. Even more impressive were two 1928 45hp six-cylinder normal-control Renaults supplied to John Lee & Son (Rothbury) and Geo Longstaff & Sons (Morpeth). Both were fitted with Strachan & Brown bodies and both worked services into Newcastle. The chassis had extremely long wheelbases, long coal-scuttle bonnets and servo-operated brakes on all wheels; the latter were no doubt essential given the top speed of over 60mph.

Above:
The first — and perhaps only — Regent chassis is demonstrated to the press on a steep hill in Hampstead. Note the early trade plate displayed. *Author's Collection*

Below:
The so-called coal-scuttle bonnet style was a distinctive feature of Renaults for many years. This one dates from 1922. *Author's Collection*

Reo

One of America's better-known makes is Reo, which in the 1920s became the most successful US chassis sold in the UK; the Reo Speed Wagon was particularly popular. Reo had been started by one R. E. Olds in 1904 after what would now be called a boardroom split or coup, in which he was ousted from his very successful Olds Motor Works. That company became Oldsmobile and a major part of General Motors. Olds himself went on to make a success of his second company, Reo, which makes him unique among motoring pioneers.

Reo, like Olds Motor Works, also built cars, having first added commercial vehicles in 1908. Speed Wagons were introduced in 1915, with a new range in the mid-1920s. A few World War 1 Reos had come on to the British market, with Harris & Hasell of Bristol handling the first direct imports here in 1922. However, in 1929 there appears to have been a parting of the ways, with the setting up of Reo Motors (Britain) to assemble and sell the chassis whilst Harris & Hasell produced a new marque (the BAT). The latter lasted less than three years, whereas Reos went on being sold in the UK — albeit in smaller numbers — until 1939.

The first direct imports of Reos into the UK were of small models of little over 1 ton capacity and 27hp four-cylinder engine. Larger models, Sprinters and Pullmans, soon followed with six-cylinder engines and four-wheel brakes. These were officially 'sedan coaches', but four and six-cylinder bus models were also listed. Later, chassis denomination was by letter. Both 20 and 26-seaters were fitted with six-cylinder Gold Crown engines; Reo was unusual among US

Above:
Reos were light and fast, and arguably among the best of the imports; not all US-designed engines withstood fast driving or high mileage. This one, named *Pride of the West*, has a folding canvas roof, but fixed side frames with full-drop windows. Its low build and neat lines give it an imposing appearance. *Arthur Ingram Collection*

makes in building its own engines. The company made much play of this in its sales pitch, particularly with the Silver Crown and Gold Crown engines. The chrome nickel cylinder block of the Gold Crown was said to be seven times harder than the conventional iron blocks used by most makers. With a claimed output of 67bhp at 2,800rpm, aluminium pistons and a seven-bearing crankshaft, the engines contributed to the reputation of high performance, aided by their installation in lightweight chassis.

Several companies that became successful in the coaching field in the late 1920s and early 1930s built themselves up on Reos. Black & White Motorways of Cheltenham began in 1926 with a 14-seat Reo charabanc, acquired as a temporary measure until two 20-seat Reos with London Lorries charabanc bodies could be completed for a new pioneer, Cheltenham-London express service. Seven more Reos were added in the following two years, before the company moved on to Gilfords and Leylands. Yelloway Motor Services bought 12 Reo Major 20-seaters in 1926 and 1927, before acquiring the same number of Reo Pullman 26-seaters in 1928. However, it too moved on to Gilfords and Tilling-Stevens in later years.

Republic

Another American manufacturer to have a degree of success in the UK in the 1920s was Republic, once the largest truck builder in the US. Chassis were conventional, with four-cylinder engines, though drop-frame passenger models were introduced quite early.

Rochet-Schneider

French car maker Rochet-Schneider of Lyon was established well before 1900 and was soon producing trucks and buses fitted with the same engine design. New models from the early 1920s included 1½ and 2½ chassis, the larger having an 18bhp four-cylinder engine. The chassis earned a reputation for durability,

and also for riding quality, enabling the company to build up useful PSV business.

A few chassis were sold in the UK in the 1920s, and the fleet of six charabancs of the Dean Motor Transport Co (taken over by Scottish Motor Traction in 1925) included four of this make.

Below:
The best of both worlds was offered by this Republic exhibited at the 1922 Scottish Motor Show. Called a bus-chara, it could be used as an open charabanc in summer (with cape hood raised if it rained) but the addition of the two-piece detachable top made it an enclosed saloon bus. Two people were said to be able to raise the winter roof, which was in sections, so that a half open, half closed format was also possible.
Author's Collection

Left:
Republic was early in adopting a low-frame chassis. This one with underslung rear springs and Lycoming engine dates from 1924. Clutch and gearbox are mounted in unit with the engine. *Arthur Ingram Collection*

Romar

A rare make of vehicles indeed, even in its native land, was the Romar, seven of which were bought in late 1915 and early 1916 by the Wellingborough Motor Omnibus Co. All were fitted with new or secondhand open-top double-deck bodies, the latter coming from Leylands in the fleet that had been requisitioned by the military authorities. All the Romars had left the fleet by the end of 1918. Another operator to buy the make was Southdown, which was also seeking replacements for requisitioned buses.

Ryknield Motor Co

This foreign-sounding make was actually built in Burton-upon-Trent, a place better known for its breweries. There was, in fact, brewery interest or backing in Ryknield, with some of its lorries bought by breweries. The first PSV chassis was announced in 1905, and 20 were running in Brussels by 1910. Home operators included Leeds, the LGOC and Todmorden, while Manchester saw both single and double-deckers. The chassis were probably better designed and more solidly built than some other makes. By 1907 an unusual feature was the emergency brake for the conductor. It was operated by a hand wheel at the back of the bus and worked through the driver's handbrake. It applied a pull on a compensating beam and finally transmitted the application to single brake blocks on the exterior of the toothed driving rings which transmitted drive to the rear wheels. These toothed driving rings were no doubt noisy. One imagines this brake system was a result of the Handcross Hill accident to a Milnes-Daimler in 1906. After Ryknield went bankrupt Tom Barton (of what became Barton Transport) was offered some 30 chassis; he bought and resold many, whilst a few entered his own fleet.

St Vincent

This Glasgow maker built small numbers of cars and commercial vehicles up to 1910. They included a charabanc with Aster two-cylinder 14/16hp engine exhibited at the 1908 Edinburgh show; it was described as a 12-seat 'passenger lorry', presumably because the bodywork was detachable.

Saurer

To many people Swiss maker Saurer is best known for its postbuses serving many an Alpine pass. This old-established company sold chassis to the UK over many years, although not in great numbers. The Mersey Railway bought 10 in 1905, some of 24/28hp and others of 28/32hp, fitting all with double-deck bodies. However, a House of Lords decision in 1907 ruled that the railway had no right to run buses and all were sold, six to Kingston upon Hull Corporation.

Another early buyer was another railway, the North Eastern, with six in 1906. They carried single-deck bus or charabanc bodies — bodies were often interchangeable in those days — and ran in many parts of the company's area for many years, one lasting almost 20 years.

But the association with those Alpine passes is appropriate, as Saurer sold successfully in South Wales for two routes over roads previously regarded as too arduous for buses. Following a successful demonstration of a 3AD chassis, South Wales Transport bought seven Brush-bodied 26-seaters to inaugurate its Townhill, Swansea, route in 1926. It was not so much the steepness of the hill, but the length — 1½ miles at an average of 1 in 9.6 with a steepest section of 1 in 5.6 — that caused the problem. The engine had a variable camshaft so it could provide braking downhill, there was a second speed-lock on the gearbox, and a sprag to prevent running backwards. So successful were buses and route that the fleet ultimately totalled 17. However, almost permanent second-gear running gave a ruinous petrol consumption of 3.1mpg, which resulted in AECs and Daimlers (by then improved, though not without engine problems on this work) ousting the last Saurer by 1935.

Independent operator Lewis & James of Newbridge (later to become part of Western Welsh) had either heard about the South Wales' Saurers or J. H. Lewis saw one when he was on holiday in Switzerland, depending on which story you believe. Either way, one was ordered for a new route from Bargoed via Aberbargoed to Markham. This had a half-mile of hill with gradients between 1 in 8 and 1 in 5, with a short length worse at 1 in 4.5. The bus, with a Dodson body, was delivered in September 1926 in the operator's Western & Sirhowy Valley fleetname. However, a bill setting up the West Monmouthshire Omnibus Board, with takeover powers for several routes in its area, had just received the Royal Assent, and the route did not start until June 1927. The so-far unused bus was sold to the board for £1,500 — £250 less than it had cost. So successful was this route (its pence per car mile figure was very high) that soon a second and later a third Saurer were bought by the board. Later, starting in 1930, Leylands replaced the Saurers, and the last of the trio retired in 1939.

Other Saurers used in the UK during the 1920s and 1930s were less colourful.

Scheibler

German maker Scheibler had been building vans and light buses before 1900. From 1903 heavier chassis were offered, and a total of 20 appear to have operated in London during 1907. Their success was, however, shortlived.

The Market Place, Devizes

Scout

Scout Motors of Salisbury was a small company building cars and commercial vehicles between 1909 and 1921, with a gap from part way through World War 1 until 1920. A number of chassis with chain drive (and later worm drive) were bodied as chara-bancs, while the newly-formed Wilts & Dorset bought five with bus bodies in 1914/15.

Selden

American truck maker Selden was based in Rochester, New York State. In World War 1 it built considerable numbers of 'Liberty' trucks for the US army. Afterwards, the company went on to export in considerable quantities to Europe and Japan. Its range in the early 1920s was relatively simple and standardised, fitted with Continental engines. Continental was a US engine builder which supplied numerous chassis makers. One of the British trade journals at the time said: 'The Selden, like many American truck chassis, lends itself very well to passenger work'.

Sentinel

The most innovative of the makers of steam road vehicles was Sentinel of Shrewsbury, which built saleable models long after other makers had ceased. However, its one entry into the passenger field, in 1924, was of dated design.

Sentinel-HSG

Sentinel was a maker of steam lorries which, by 1933, had produced relatively advanced designs with shaft drive. However, within a few years, it was anxious, if not desperate, to reduce its dependence on steam and in 1938 bought High Speed Gas (GB). At the motor show that year, in Glasgow's Kelvin Hall, it exhibited a bus chassis with producer gas plant at the rear. The chassis, like the earlier Gilfords (HSG) example, again used a Gilford chassis, but this time with an American Hercules engine. It subsequently gained a Cowieson body and underwent trials at Merthyr Tydfil and in London. At some point during World War 2 the original engine was converted back to petrol.

Shefflex

Shefflex is one of the stranger stories in vehicle building. Sheffield-Simplex of Tinsley (Sheffield) was a luxury car maker which, during World War 1, assembled Commer commercial vehicles under contract. After the contract ended, the company found itself left with quantities of components which were assembled and sold as Shefflex trucks. More problems occurred and, as a result, R. A. Johnstone bought those remaining and apparently had little problem selling them. Encouraged, he restarted production at Tinsley. The company subsequently became Shefflex Motor Co. It began with two goods models, but soon added a 24-seat passenger chassis. By the mid-1930s, if not earlier, refuse vehicles had become the main output.

Shelvoke & Drewry

Harry Shelvoke and James Drewry produced the first S&D Freighter in 1923. They designed it as a low-frame vehicle, easy to drive and able to be driven slowly for use as a dust cart or refuse collection vehicle. It had very small wheels, an engine mounted transversely just ahead of a set-back front axle, and tiller controls for steering and for working the change-speed mechanism of the epicyclic gearbox. Much later, passenger models changed to conventional steering wheels.

In 1924 Bill Gates of Worthing saw the bus potential for a vehicle that was easy for the elderly to board and alight from. His Tramocars fleet led a minor fashion which resulted in some 50 S&Ds being built for PSV use, mainly at seaside resorts such as Blackpool, Bournemouth, Douglas and Exmouth. The final two buses for the Tramocars fleet, delivered in 1938 after it sold out to Southdown, were even more unusual in having the engine mounted transversely behind the back axle.

Sheppee

A retired Indian Army officer, Col H. F. Sheppee had set up the Sheppee Motor Co in York to pursue his enthusiasm for steam-powered road vehicles. As it took him some 10 years to build a total of 14 vehicles, mainly goods chassis, his interest was obviously in design rather than production! It is thought the chassis

Above:
The Sheppee was built in York and its minuscule total production included this steam charabanc. Like the more successful Thomas Clarkson, interest in design improvements was uppermost. *Author's Collection*

may have been from existing vehicles rather than purpose-built. The boilers were liquid fuelled and produced steam at a pressure of 900psi, though no two vehicles were alike. There was a steam charabanc built either before or during 1909.

Simms-Welbeck

The Simms Manufacturing Co of London made mainly electrical components for motor vehicles, continuing with this business up to the time of the Routemaster bus. However, it also produced a few complete motor vehicles which were fitted with its own make of engine. Both van and heavier chassis were built between about 1904 and 1907. A few engines were also supplied to others; the Alexandra (Newport & South Wales) Docks & Railway Co bought two 20/25hp engines for fitting to two 1903 Milnes-Daimler buses it was running. Pioneer London motorbus operator Vanguard (the London Motor Omnibus Co) ran a Simms double-decker which was said to be the only double-decker of this make. A bodied single-decker for the Durham & District Motor Omnibus Co was delivered by road from London in June 1906. The 270-mile journey over two days was covered in a running time of 16hr 52min. Vehicles were known as Simms and Simms-Welbeck.

Singer

Better-remembered as a car maker, Singer occasionally offered van models. However, at the 1929 Commercial Motor Show the company launched a complete range of commercial vehicles under the title Singer Industrial Motors. These had nothing in common with the cars. A 3.1 litre four-cylinder engine developing 60hp, with five-bearing crankshaft, servo-assisted four-wheel brakes and twin rear wheels were standard. In 1930/31 the chassis was described as low-loading, and was available as a normal-control 20-seat PSV.

Spa

An apparently short name represented the initials of a long one; Spa chassis were built in Italy by Societa Ligure Piemontese Automobili of Turin. Established in 1908, the company soon developed a whole range of commercial vehicles. By 1923 there were also two passenger-carrying models, the smaller — a 20-seater — boasting such refinements as pneumatic tyres and an electric starter motor. A bank failure two years later took the company into the hands of Fiat, with Fiat (England) offering both makes for goods and passenger-carrying for some years. It was not until 1947 that Spa was finally absorbed by Fiat.

In Britain, the Royal Agricultural Show was an unlikely but popular venue for both truck and bus exhibits, and the 1928 Show saw Fiat (England) showing three Fiat trucks, one Spa truck and one Spa bus. The bus had a 52bhp four-cylinder engine and a 24-seat bus body.

Star

Star had been making bicycles for some years prior to 1900, later moved on to cars, and before World War 1 had commercial vehicles and a charabanc chassis in its range. After the war it produced medium-capacity goods and passenger chassis that were relatively light yet well made — and fast. Probably they were too well made, and thus expensive, for the highly competitive markets of the late 1920s. Guy bought the company in 1928 and moved production to a new factory, still in Wolverhampton, but by 1932 it was all over.

Relatively late in its life Star produced a low-frame 20-seat passenger chassis, and from it developed its Star Flyer. This was fitted with a 3.2 litre, six-cylinder, overhead-valve engine fitted with seven bearings. There was a spiral bevel rear axle, excellent suspension — and a laden top speed of well over 50mph. A neat touch, and one which exemplified the hand-building of the marque, was the casting of stars on components such as petrol filler-cap, front axle and differential cover. It is a myth that Guy handed (or sold) the design of the Star Flyer to AJS, which built it as the AJS Pilot. Guy itself bodied at least one Flyer.

Scottish Motor Traction was an enthusiastic user, buying 38 in 1928 and fitting them with 20-seat bus or 14-seat coach bodies. The last was withdrawn in 1936.

Below:
A strange purchase, one might have thought, was this Star charabanc acquired new by the Royal Naval Air Service in 1916. Note the high fleet number. *Author's Collection*

Bottom:
A much later Star is this 1928 model, one of a large batch for SMT which received either 14-seat coach bodies or 20-seat bus bodies. *Ian Allan Library*

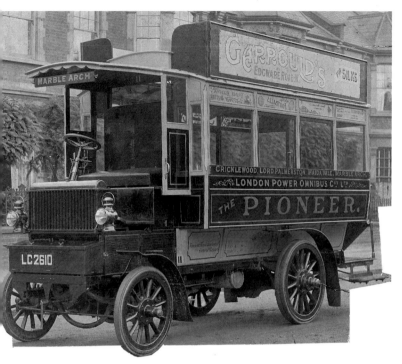

Stewart

US truck and bus maker Stewart had a Canadian assembly plant in the 1930s and exported chassis to Europe. However, it ceased to offer its US-built 20-seater in the UK after about 1931. Two Stewarts were exhibited at the 1929 Commercial Motor Show, both with six-cylinder engines. One had a body by Newns.

Stirling and Scott-Stirling

With advertisements in the technical press in 1906 claiming an annual production of 500 buses, Scott-Stirling could have been thought to be the country's biggest bus builder. But it was not true and by 1908 the company had gone.

Stirling had been an early maker, based in Hamilton, and ran its own-assembled wagonettes with Daimler engines as buses in Stirling. It also built three 14-seaters for the North Eastern Railway in 1903. Later, buses — now known as Scott-Stirlings — were assembled at Twickenham, Middlesex. After a few single-deckers, production turned to double-deckers, in which the driver sat high with the engine beneath and ahead of his feet. By March 1907 the London Power Omnibus (fleetname Pioneer) was running 62 of the type, but making losses of 7d (3p) a mile. By July Pioneer went bankrupt and vanished. The availability of all these secondhand buses also unsettled the whole new bus market.

Straker-Squire

Sidney Straker was an engineer of considerable talent. In 1900, as consulting engineer to Daimler of Coventry, he designed the first Daimler multi-passenger vehicle, a small charabanc. He lived in London, but had interests in Bristol with the engineering company Owen, Brazil & Holborow. His association with the firm began in 1899, and two years later the Straker Steam Vehicle Co was formed. It built steam vehicles, including two double-deckers for the British Electric Traction Group in 1901, a single-decker in 1903 for a service to Stratford-upon-Avon, and also petrol-engined vehicles.

At about the time the firm arranged to sell German-built Bussings in Britain it was renamed Sidney Straker & Squire, and soon had to move to a larger factory in Bristol to cope with demand. By the time the three major London motorbus operators combined in 1908 (into the LGOC), they were operating 261 Straker-Squires. The maker gradually introduced UK-sourced components into its product and at the same time introduced its own designs.

After World War 1 ended the company moved to the London area, announcing a new design with its 'A'-type. This had a four-cylinder monobloc engine of 55bhp, four-speed gearbox and worm drive, and — unusually — was of semi-forward-control layout. It was a fast vehicle and in the early days of pirate (or independent) bus operation in London proved popular since it could easily outpace the slow and lumbering

Above:
Many tram operators were quick to spot the potential of the motorbus. The quaintly-named Gateshead Tramways Motor Service took delivery of these two Straker-Squires with unusual front entrances. Note the single offside headlights and the headgear of the drivers and their assistants. *Author's Collection*

Below:
By the time this Dodson-bodied Straker-Squire was delivered in 1911, the chassis maker was claiming that it was built 'mainly of British components'. The Brighton, Hove & Preston United Omnibus Co had been formed in 1884 and had begun trials with motorbuses as early as 1902. In 1915 the BHPU sold its Brighton-Worthing service, for which this bus is lettered, to the new Southdown Motor Services. *Author's Collection*

AECs of the LGOC. At this stage Straker-Squire also offered its own bodywork and the availability of this complete 'package' built to the stringent requirements of the Metropolitan Police was a further attraction to newcomers.

The quick acceleration and speed were never matched by reliability, unfortunately, and the company went into receivership first in 1925 and again in 1926.

Studebaker

Studebaker is probably best remembered for its large cars in the UK, but this old-established business built horse-drawn vehicles for many years followed by electric ones. Cars and petrol-engined commercial chassis followed later, and by the mid-1920s there was a range of normal-control chassis powered by a 5.9 litre six-cylinder engine used in the cars. Later the range of PSVs went from 14-seaters to large single-

deckers with eight-cylinder petrol engines. A few found their way to the UK, and the early fleet of Black & White Motorways included four, built between 1927 and 1929; all were 20-seaters. Clan Motorways had eight, with 14, 20 or 24-seat bodies running on its express services from Glasgow in 1928.

Sunbeam (SMC)

Sunbeam was a car maker and, like many others, desperately looking for diversification in the hard times of the late 1920s. Buses and coaches seemed to offer hope and in 1929 the company produced the Pathan four-wheeler and Sikh six-wheeler. Both were beautifully engineered (and expensive) and most had an engine of nearly eight litres with a seven-bearing crankshaft, dry sump lubrication and other innovations perhaps inspired by previous experience building aero engines.

Right:
Sunbeams were beautifully engineered, and their double-decker six-wheelers were impressive looking vehicles. But only two were sold. This was the second, which entered service with London independent Westminster Omnibus in 1933. It was fitted with a 64-seat Dodson body. By this time the Metropolitan Police allowed windscreens, but Westminster's managing director did not approve of them. *Ian Allan Library*

Just two of the six-wheelers were sold, though ultimate conversion of a third, unsold, chassis to a trolleybus opened up a new and much more successful field.

Pathans sold rather better as single-deck coaches. Rootes bought the struggling company in 1935 and subsequently two AEC directors joined its board for a time. There followed a single AEC Regent double-decker with Gardner engine and Sunbeam radiator grille; but no other motorbuses or coaches were offered.

Talbot

Better-known for its cars, Clement Talbot built vans, trucks, ambulances and coaches at various times between 1914 and 1938. A 20-seat coach chassis was first introduced soon after World War 1. This was of conventional normal-control layout. Highland Motorways ran a Glasgow-Inverness service in 1928 with Talbots claimed to seat 26. The Rootes Group took over the company in 1935, the same year it bought Sunbeam.

Thames Ironworks

Thames Ironworks was an old-established shipbuilder in southeast London, which diversified into road vehicles. Its first bus chassis was built in 1905 and a year later offered what was claimed to be the first PSV with six-cylinder engine. Charabancs were apparently made in reasonable numbers, but the company is best remembered for its final vehicle, which could have been mistaken for its first. It looked like a horse-drawn stagecoach without the horses, and was a semi-forward-control double-decker. Amazingly, one of these vehicles survives in the National Motor Museum. It was built in 1913, the last year of the company's existence. An earlier user was pioneer operator J. W. Cann's London & South Coast Motor Services of Folkestone, which bought eight, the first few in 1906. However, some of the earliest vehicles lasted barely a year in the fleet.

Thornycroft

John I. Thornycroft & Co was a builder of steam launches, based by the River Thames at Chiswick. It added vehicle building to its products after one of its lightweight vertical steam engines was fitted to a van in 1896. Within two years a move to larger premises at Basingstoke was necessary to meet demand.

The rather bizarre roofed double-decker steam bus that operated briefly in London during 1902 has attracted a disproportionate amount of attention; in the same year the Belfast & Northern Counties Railway put into service in Belfast two similar buses, but fitted with 14-seat single-deck bodies. They ran for at least six years — before being replaced by horsebuses, but the chassis were converted to lorries, one of which worked until 1925. The railway, which by now had become the Midland Railway (Northern Counties Committee), bought two more Thornycrofts in 1905, this time petrol-engined charabancs for summer excursions.

From 1902 the company had been building paraffin and petrol-engined lorries and by 1905 it had a considerable range of petrol vehicles available in the UK. Two-cylinder 16hp or four-cylinder 30hp engines were later offered for passenger chassis seating up to 34. The famous 'J'-type was first built in 1913; during World War 1 some 5,000 were built, with more following after the war. Not all wartime ones went for military service; the Great North of

Below left:
Like some other makers, Sunbeam sometimes supplied demonstrators to larger operators and issued a press release implying that they had been bought by the operator. This 52/120hp six-cylinder-engined Pathan with coachwork by H. E. Taylor of Norwich was indeed 'supplied' to SMT in 1930, but its stay there was less than a year. *Ian Allan Library*

Right:
One of the earliest vehicles built by Thames Ironworks Shipbuilding & Engineering was this partly open, partly closed coach for London & South Coast Motor Service. A motor show exhibit of 1906, it had a body constructed of fire-resistant timber. *Author's Collection*

Left:
This early Thornycroft 'motor chara-banc' was operated by the Lake District Road Traffic Co and, when photographed, had been in the fleet for eight years. No doubt it was running on gas because of World War 1 fuel shortages. *Author's Collection*

Centre left:
Phoenix Motor & Omnibus Co was a one-bus London independent operator, which began with this Thornycroft 'J' early in 1924. The business and bus were sold in 1927. The bus had a standard London-style Dodson body, and the chassis too had to meet the stringent requirements of Scotland Yard on turning circle and other details. *Author's Collection*

Below:
Thornycroft had considerable success with sales to the Isle of Man in the late 1920s, supplying 46 buses in three years. Among the last was this 1929 BC Forward with Hall Lewis 28-seat body. However, there were no more bus sales to the island. *Author's Collection*

Scotland Railway bought three from Basingstoke and fitted its own bus bodies in 1915/16. The 'J' became a popular choice for PSVs after the war. Scottish Motor Traction bought some 50 ex-WD chassis between 1920 and 1924, overhauled them and lengthened the chassis by 12in (300mm) before fitting new 27-seat charabanc or 28-seat bus bodies. Portsmouth Corporation Tramways bought 10 'Js' in 1919, fitting open-top double-deck bodies to them; one still survives.

A particularly successful model was the 1¹/₂ ton A1 introduced in 1924. Over 1,000 were said to have gone into service by the end of 1925. They had the gearbox in unit with the engine, and were also offered as 20-seat bus chassis. Later there was the larger A2 as well. A much bigger chassis was the Lightning coach of 1927, 'a surprise to all our competitors,' said Thornycroft. Its 70bhp side-valve six-cylinder engine had 'wet liners for the cylinder block, two detachable heads, a camshaft driven from the rear end of the crankshaft, seven main bearings and full pressure lubrication'. It was said to be capable of 50mph fully laden, so it was as well it had servo-brakes on all four

wheels. It was of normal-control layout, with seats for up to 26.

Unit construction for the engine, clutch and gearbox was soon extended to larger vehicles, and chassis frames were lowered between the axles.

Railway business was good in the late 1920s. The Great North of Scotland Railway had bought more 'J'-types in 1919 and again in 1921; its successor, the London & North Eastern Railway, bought a batch of 38 32-seat Thornycroft 'BCs' in 1928/29. The Isle of Man Railway was another success, with 22 buses, nearly all 'BCs', supplied in 1928; these followed 19 'A2s' in 1927 which went mainly to companies in which the railway had an interest. Subsequently the vehicles operated with the railway-owned Isle of Man Road Services. But jewel in the crown was the Great Western Railway, which also bought numerous Thornycroft goods vehicles. It bought 40 'A1s' with 19-seat bodies in 1925 and returned to the make in 1928 for 15 'A1s' and six others. In 1929 five 'A1s', 12 'A2s' and 11 'BCs' were acquired. The 'BCs' seated 26 or 32. Virtually all the GWR and LNER-owned vehicles passed to the bus companies in which the railways had bought a financial stake and so there were no more railway orders, and precious few from the bus companies.

During the 1930s it was probably the export side that kept the bus business afloat. The years 1930 and 1931 must have been poor for sales, but at the 1931 Olympia Show the company launched two new models and had two or three of each bodied as demonstrators. These were the Daring double-decker and the Cygnet single-decker. Older, fairly dated designs had sold at the rate of four or five a year, so seven Darings for 1932 was a slight improvement, but just 14 Cygnets sold was a poor result. Petrol-engined Cygnets were said to be very thirsty.

By 1934 Thornycroft was offering its own diesel

engine, a 7.88 litre six-cylinder direct injection unit. Two buses so fitted went to the Stalybridge, Hyde, Mossley & Dukinfield Joint Board and two more to Southampton Corporation. However, the SHMD examples soon gained Gardner engines. SHMD was the company's biggest supporter, with more than 80 Thornycrofts in its fleet at one stage. Its manager, incidentally, was a former employee! SHMD bought its last Darings in 1936, while Southampton took a total of four in 1936/37 with Gardner 5LW engines. These were the last double-deckers built. Some of the Southampton ones were sold to Nottingham for further service in 1946 and lasted until 1948, so they cannot have been that bad. Certainly they were far better than the four-cylinder 'LC-DD', four of which were bought by Cardiff Corporation in 1930 — their brakes were said to need adjusting three times a day, though their mechanical performance was improved by 1934 when Gardner 6LW engines were fitted.

The problem in the mid-1930s was, of course, that the opposition had improved its product by leaps and bounds and was selling in sufficient numbers to support research and development — unlike Thornycroft.

There were also some smaller models offered in the 1930s. There was a lightweight Ardent 20-seater and subsequently a Dainty. Later, the Sturdy, a low-weight, high capacity truck, was also offered as a 26-seater called the Beautyride. By 1939, this was the only PSV still listed.

Tilling-Stevens and TSM

Early motorbuses were heavy, primitive machines, difficult to drive. Those who did drive them could often unwittingly cause considerable damage to frail gearboxes and other components. This led London operator Thomas Tilling to experiment with a petrol-electric. Three men designed it: the engineer and manager of Tilling's motor department, Percy Frost Smith; Frank Brown, chairman of David Brown & Sons of Huddersfield, which manufactured the final drive; and W. A. Stevens, managing director of W. A. Stevens of Maidstone, which designed the electric transmission and assembled. The bus was generally known as the SB&S. Surprisingly, J. & E. Hall of Dartford, builders of the Hallford, whose chassis was used as the base got no mention.

The petrol engine drove a dynamo, which in turn fed current to two electric motors, each placed outside the main frame and each driving one rear wheel via a carden shaft. This bus entered service in London in 1908; it was known to the Tilling crews as 'Queenie' because it behaved so well. It ran some 60,000 miles, during which various improvements were made. An improved version was sold in small numbers as Hallford-Stevens but Tilling did not buy any.

Instead it developed the Tilling-Stevens petrol-electric, which it built in its own workshops in Bull Yard, Peckham, London using electrical equipment from W. A. Stevens. The first model was the TTA1, production of which started in 1911. The following year Tilling bought control of W. A. Stevens and by the time production of this model ended in 1914, it was running 174 of them. A few had also been sold to other operators. A distinctive feature of the TTA1 was the Renault-style bonnet; the radiator was mounted behind the engine because it would not be so exposed to road dirt. The 30hp four-cylinder engine drove a 20kW dynamo and, unlike the SB&S, there was just one motor, which powered a worm and wheel live back axle via a short propshaft. The chassis frame was of pressed steel, and varied in depth.

One unforeseen advantage of the Tilling-Stevens was that it was of no interest to the military, whereas the authorities commandeered huge numbers of 'B'-types and Daimlers among others.

The postwar AEC 'K'-type with 46-seat body was

Left:
This example of the first production petrol-electric (model TTA1) was one of two hired by Thomas Tilling to the Great Eastern Railway in the summer of 1914 for use on a new Dovercourt-Harwich service. Other TTA1s were, of course, sold to outside operators. *Author's Collection*

Right:
Later petrol-electric models were of more conventional appearance. This demonstrator dates from 1921 and was one of the postwar improved TS3A type, with seats for 48. *Author's Collection*

Centre right:
Photographed on Brighton's seafront in postwar years, this conventional Tilling-Stevens B9B had been new to Southdown in 1927, and gained a new Harrington body in 1934, at which time the chassis may have been updated. Sold in 1938, it was later bought by Unique Coaches (Brighton) and lasted until 1954. *Author's Collection*

Below:
Despite the introduction of a new double-deck model in 1931 with six-cylinder engine, few double-deckers were sold in the 1930s. However, in 1933 the newly-formed Benfleet & District Motor Services of Benfleet, near Southend, bought three D60A6 chassis with Park Royal bodies. At least one later acquired an AEC 8.8 litre diesel engine. Benfleet & District was later taken over by Westcliff-on-Sea Motor Services, which subsequently became part of Eastern National. *Ian Allan Library*

on London's streets in numbers before the first TS3As, with their 48-seat bodies, entered service there in 1921. The TS3As had the driver alongside the engine. The TS3 had been put into production earlier, and the TS7 followed in 1923. However, these and later designs were mechanically and electrically little changed, although radiators were now at the front.

The chassis sold to many operators, apart from Tilling's own business; Wolverhampton Corporation was one sizeable user. The company began to make conventional petrol chassis too in 1919, and in 1926 introduced the B9 low-frame Express single-deckers. They were offered in normal and forward-control forms and sold well, as did the succeeding B10. However, the company also persevered with petrol-electrics, producing two new models (a four-wheeler and a six-wheeler) in 1929 which attracted little interest.

Thomas Tilling tried one of the new petrol-electrics (a TS17A with special light alloy frame (to reduce weight) and its own body, and then a couple more, plus an early AEC Regent in London and Brighton, and a Leyland Titan and a Daimler CF6 in Brighton only. It then returned the TS17A chassis to Tilling-Stevens and went out and ordered almost 300 Regents, and followed this by disposing of its share-holding in Tilling-Stevens. It was all very odd. Why had Tilling's subsidiary been allowed to persist with an outdated double-deck design, with a relatively high chassis, for so long? Was, perhaps, Tilling manage-ment more interested in buying and running bus busi-nesses?

The new company badged its chassis TSM and developed further conventional models, later offering Gardner diesel engines as an option. But sales fell drastically, particularly after the Bristol bus building business came into the Tilling fold.

Two surprises in 1937 were the purchase of the ailing Vulcan of Southport (mainly for its truck models) and the appearance at the Motor Show of two three-axle chassis with underfloor engines and seven-speed pre-selector gearboxes. Known as the Successor, the model had horizontally-opposed diesel engines of 7.45 litre; one was shown in chassis form, the other with an elegant Duple coach body. Probably neither ran for an operator.

The company also changed name back to Tilling-Stevens and its fortunes were subsequently helped by a revival in interest in petrol-electric chassis for use as mobile searchlights in World War 2.

Traffic

The American-built Traffic was a fairly conventional normal-control chassis, of which a few were used in the UK as buses a year or so after the end of World War 1.

Turgan

This French maker changed from cars to commer-cials, and from steam power to petrol. A steam double-decker was built in 1900 and in 1906 just one petrol-engined double-decker began running in London between Oxford Circus and Streatham Common. Turgan ceased trading in 1907.

Unic

French maker Unic is best remembered in the British market for its taxis, some of which could still be found working in London during the 1950s, though of venerable age. Vans and light goods vehicles were also sold here for many years, but the 1920s saw passenger chassis of smaller size also on offer. For example, the Scottish Motor Show of 1922 saw goods

vehicles from about ³/4 ton to 1¹/2 ton, with a
passenger version based on the 1 ton goods model. It
had pneumatic tyres all round and a coach body with
seats for 14. There was a four-speed gearbox and a
leather cone clutch. Tobin of Margate, an operator
acquired by East Kent Road Car, had bought mainly
Unic 14 or 17-seat charabancs between 1922 and
1927, having a total of 12; he traded under the fleetname of 'Unique'! PSVs were last listed in the UK in
1932, when 14, 20 and 28-seaters were offered.

Vulcan

Any long-serving employee of Vulcan would have
felt no stranger to financial crises and management
reorganisations, for these were numerous over the life
of the company, which, nevertheless, survived a long
time. Vulcan began, like so many, making cars.
Thomas and Joseph Hampson were brothers who
outgrew their Southport premises twice within a few
years, then moving to nearby Crossens, reforming the
business at the same time to the Vulcan Motor &
Engineering Co. Wartime saw production of just
commercial vehicles, but problems in 1919 resulted in
both brothers leaving. Not long after, Vulcan joined
the unsuccessful Harper-Bean consortium, which was
also shortlived. There was another reorganisation in
1928, but by 1931 the company was in the hands of
the receiver. Production continued and in 1938 the
factory was sold to a trailer maker whilst Tilling-
Stevens took over the assets and goodwill, transfer-
ring production to its Maidstone factory under the
new name of Vulcan Motors.

The first acknowledged passenger version of
Vulcan chassis came in 1926 as 20- and 26-seat
models of conventional layout. After that there were
almost bewildering annual changes with larger
chassis being added: a 30-seater in 1928, 32 and 36-
seaters in 1929, and even a 53-seat double-decker (the
Emperor) in 1930. By this date the models were
named; Countess, Duke, Duchess, Prince and Princess
were all single-deckers. Forward-control layout was
standard on some models, six-cylinder petrol engines

came in — initially on the 20-seater in 1928 — but it
all became somewhat chaotic, at least to the outsider,
with no passenger models being listed in one or two
years, and then several the next.

The truth was, no doubt, that things were pretty
desperate, and probably almost anything would have
been built at the right price for a purchaser with cash
in hand. One remarkable success, or dramatic failure
depending on how you look at it, was the order from
Glasgow Corporation for 25 Emperors, delivered in
1931/32. They joined a fleet that was already running
numbers of (very satisfactory) Leyland Titans and
AEC Regents, alongside which the Vulcans were a
considerable disappointment. One can only assume
that the transport committee selected Emperors
because of their low price. Within three or four years
Glasgow had fitted Leyland radiators and engines to
most, but by 1940 they had all been scrapped. Even
before that date their public appearances in service
seem to have been rare.

In a year when Vulcan (in theory) offered no
passenger models, it built a couple for Douglas
Corporation. They were small-wheel forward-control
models on which Vulcan-built bodywork was
mounted. They were designed to meet the requirements of the Douglas general manager for a pair of
summer runabouts, with an open-sided toastrack
layout on the nearside. A long folding and windowed
door design stayed, concertina-like, at the rear in fine
weather but, if it rained, it could be slid forward to
keep the passengers dry. Three similar bodies were
also produced by Vulcan for use on Douglas horse-
trams.

W & G

The full name of this company was W. & G. du Cros.
It was based at Acton in London and its diverse
production included ambulances, PSVs and refuse
collection vehicles. The last-named were usually
badged du Cros, presumably to avoid associating
anything so mundane with passenger-carrying vehicles. The mid-1920s saw the company offer

goods and charabanc chassis, with a fast, low-frame six-cylinder bus introduced in 1926, and later forward-control models were added. Passenger chassis sold well for a time, but faded rapidly and production ceased in the early 1930s, although chassis were still listed in buyers' guides up to 1936. Most vehicles went to smaller operators, but there was a 'Corporation' model bus, as W & G called it. This was a long, normal-control vehicle. Bournemouth Corporation, then running mainly trams, bought 15 of the type with front entrances for one-man operation.

Walker

Walkers were probably the most successful battery-electric trucks built in the USA. A number were exported to the UK. Just one appears to have been bodied as a bus, in 1921. It was bought by Liverpool Corporation, which also built the 25-seat body. It was used to carry children between their homes and a special school.

Wallace

One of the more imaginative entrants to the market after World War 1 was the Wallace, produced by Richmond Motor Lorries of Shepherd's Bush, London. S. A. Wallace had been chief engineer of AEC and began importing a selection of components from US makers for assembly in the UK (rather than a complete model in component form). The main components were the Continental Red Seal four-cylinder engine, a three-speed gearbox and a bevel-drive rear axle.

Trucks and charabancs were offered, but assembly ended in 1922. At least one Wallace was bodied as a single-deck bus, while White Motors Service on the Isle of Man had an 18-seat charabanc on pneumatic tyres.

Ward La France

American maker Ward La France is best-known for its fire appliances, though it also built truck chassis. Production was on a surprisingly small scale, using bought-in parts throughout. Pneumatic tyres were offered from an early stage.

One Ward La France operated in South Wales for some years. It was owned by E. E. (Ernie) Snow, an enterprising and inventive operator who built up a fleet of luxurious charabancs after World War 1. This Ward La France had hood and door mechanisms of Snow's own design, and a 10-note organ that was used to wake sleeping residents when the charabanc returned from excursions.

Watson

Henry Watson & Sons of Newcastle-upon-Tyne was an engineering concern producing castings. It had also assembled the British Berna. Then, after World War 1, the company announced its own product, a $3^{1}/_{2}$-$4^{1}/_{2}$ ton bonneted truck with four-cylinder engine. Engine and gearbox were mounted in a subframe which ran inside the longitudinal chassis frame. A passenger-carrying derivative was subsequently offered, with a bigger engine. Production petered out some time in the late 1920s.

THIS ILLUSTRATION SHOWS OUR " CORPORATION" MODEL BUS, AS SUPPLIED TO THE BOURNEMOUTH CORPORATION TRAMWAYS DEPT., AND IS BUT ONE OF NUMEROUS TYPES WE HAVE SUPPLIED TO PROMINENT UNDERTAKINGS IN ALL PARTS OF THE COUNTRY. LET US QUOTE YOU FOR YOUR REQUIREMENTS.

WRITE FOR CATALOGUE NOW.

OUR RANGE OF MODELS INCLUDE :—
30 CWTS., 2-TON AND 2½-3 TON—COMMERCIAL—20, 26, 30, 32 AND 36 SEATERS— PASSENGER.

W. & G. DU CROS,
LTD.

177, THE VALE, ACTON, LONDON, W.3.

Phone :
CHISWICK 0800.

Left:
Advertising by W & G in the late 1920s made much of its order for Bournemouth Corporation. Bournemouth used them on feeder services to its trams, but its next order went to Karrier.
Author's Collection

White

One of the best known, longest-lived and most successful makers in the USA was White. It originated as the White Sewing Machine Co, of Cleveland, but retitled itself without the sewing machine part of its name in 1906, by which time it was already building steam trucks and vans as well as cars. Petrol-engined cars followed a few years later, then trucks and by 1918 buses too. Few of its products found their way to the UK, but United Automobile Services bought a number from the United States Army in France after World War 1. They had pneumatic tyres, seated about 20 and were left-hand drive. They were fast, and used as 'chasers' on routes where there was competition.

Willys-Overland and Willys-Knight

Willys-Overland was a long-established American truck maker. It had links with other makers and with car manufacturers. At one time there was a UK branch of Willys-Overland in Stockport, which in the 1920s sold a one-ton chassis based on the Overland Four Car. In the late 1920s Willys-Overland built an export PSV chassis known as the Willys-Knight, with a six-cylinder sleeve-valve engine of this make. Willys Overland Crossley, a company jointly owned with Crossley, later assembled Willys-Overland chassis in the UK.

A few Willys-Overlands and Willys-Knights oper-ated in the UK, usually with smaller operators. In the mid-1930s Western National Omnibus Co and Southern National took over a number from local operators selling out. Some of them had locally-built Mumford bodies seating 14 or 18. There were various others, loosely described as Willys, that seated between 14 and 20.

Wolseley and Wolseley-Siddeley

If Frank Searle had not persuaded the LGOC to build his design of bus chassis, the company would have placed a large order for Wolseley-Siddeley chassis, of which there were already 90 in the fleet. From 1901 to 1905 Wolseley's remarkable range of products, which included cars, vans, trucks, buses and fire appliances, was masterminded by general manager Herbert Austin, who then went off to start his own company.

Following Austin's departure, the vehicles became known as Wolseley-Siddeleys as J. D. Siddeley took over Austin's position. A single petrol-electric bus was built in 1907, the engine driving a BTH electric

Below:
The original Wolseleys had two-cylinder horizontal engines but later models were more substantially built, with a four-cylinder vertical engine. The biggest fleet running them was that of the LGOC. Note the short-working board displayed at the bottom of the side windows: it reads 'Oxford Circus Only this journey'.
Author's Collection

motor on each rear wheel. The Great Western Railway was an early user of Wolseleys, but in 1906 returned one to the maker as unsatisfactory, taking in part exchange two new ones similar to those running in London. Three more similar vehicles were subsequently acquired; all five were double-deckers. Wolseley's one-ton chassis was often sold as a charabanc. True bus building appears to have ceased before World War 1, though truck production continued. Ultimately all commercial vehicle production ceased. Later Morris acquired Wolseley and built Morris Commercials in the factory.

Yellow Coach

Chicago-based Yellow Coach Manufacturing was formed in 1923 as a subsidiary of a bus company. It was the idea of John D. Hertz, a car salesman who earlier developed a special design of car for sale as a taxi. Thousands of his Yellow Cabs were built and sold. Subsequently he bought control of Chicago Motor Bus and its bus building subsidiary, American Motor Bus Co, and joined them with Fifth Avenue Coach Co of New York. In addition, a new factory was provided.

Key personnel included George Alan Green, who became vice-president of Yellow Coach. He had worked for Vanguard in London, left, but subsequently became chief assistant engineer of the LGOC under Frank Searle. Green then went to America, becoming general manager of Fifth Avenue, and was responsible for the design of its open-top double-deckers. Green had a flair for what today would be called marketing, and saw a need for three reliable and durable types of vehicle: a 29-passenger city bus (Yellow Coach Type Z), a more comfortable 25-29 seater for longer distances (Type Y), and a 17-21 seater for feeder services and for premium-fare express work (Type X). Yellow Coach was later to pioneer the transverse rear engine with angle drive. General Motors bought control of the company in

1925, subsequently merging it with its own operation.

The LGOC had always kept an eye on US developments, even sending teams on study tours from time to time, and bought two Yellow Coaches. It put a 'Z'-type, complete with a Chiswick-built 25-seat coach body, into service in 1925 and the following year added an 'X'-type with its own 11-seat body. Both coaches went into the private hire department. The 'Z'-type had a four-cylinder Silent Knight sleeve-valve engine made by an Illinois company (which was later acquired by Hertz) under licence from Daimler in Coventry.

Another key member of Yellow Coach not so far mentioned was George J. Rackham, its chief engineer for three years. He had worked with Vanguard, was later the LGOC's chief draughtsman and had followed Green to the States. He later came back to the UK to design Leyland's legendary Titan, before moving to AEC to design Regals, Regents and Renowns.

Yorkshire

One of the better known builders of steam lorries was the Yorkshire company. It had a patented boiler mounted transversely over the front axle. In 1917 the Yorkshire Patent Steam Wagon Co built one steam bus in its Hunslet, Leeds, works for Provincial Tramways Co of Grimsby. After being used as a single-deck bus for two years it became a lorry for the operator.

British
Buses
since
1900

Part Two
1946-2000

British Buses since 1900

Part Two 1946-2000

Stephen Morris

Half title:
The one-off SMT lightweight intergral bus, based on Albion running units, seen at St Andrew Square, Edinburgh.
John Aldridge

Title page:
Foden's last sortie into the bus market, in conjunction with Northern Counties, proved short-lived. Only seven were completed, two for Greater Manchester Transport. The Foden-NC had a rear transverse Gardner 6LXB engine and Albion transmission.
Ferodo Ltd

British Buses since 1900

Part Two 1946-2000

Stephen Morris

Contents — Part Two

Acknowlegements

Thanks are due particularly to John Aldridge, author of the prewar section of this book, who was particularly helpful and supportive in supplying information, took the trouble to read through the manuscript and has even added one or two bits himself; Kevin Lane, who undertook some of the picture research; Mike Sutcliffe, who gave Kevin Lane access to his photo collection, and Mike Fenton, whose work on Quest 80 was very useful. Thanks are also due to Heather, my wife, and David, my son, who had to put up with a house full of reference material and a husband/father respectively who was even more irritable than usual during the original production of this book, and then had to put up with it all again for the revised edition.

Also acknowledged gratefully is reference to a number of publications, especially some of the PSV Circle chassis lists, a number of Venture Publishing and TPC titles such as *The British Bus Story* volumes for the 1950s, 1960s and 1970s, the *Best of British Buses* series, especially the postwar Daimler volume, and Doug Jack's *Beyond Reality*, plus Ian Allan publications down the years on various chassis manufacturers, such as Geoffrey Hilditch's *Looking at Buses*, Robin Hannay's *Dennis Buses in Camera*, Jasper Pettie's *Guy Buses in Camera*, and Stewart Brown's Albion and Crossley book in the same series. R. C. Anderson's *History of Midland Red*, published by David & Charles, was helpful for the BMMO section, while much information was gleaned from *Buses Illustrated*, *Buses*, *Classic Bus* and *Passenger Transport* plus Ian Allan's *British Bus Fleets* series of the 1950s and 1960s.

Foreword

Given that in 2000 there is but one British-owned bus manufacturer active in the UK market, it is remarkable that one can list no fewer than 48 British manufacturers which have been active in the UK market over the last 55 years. And that is to overlook ERF, a British manufacturer, now in German ownership, which still builds buses, though not for use in this country. Some of the manufacturers listed may only have built buses in penny numbers — one or two indeed built only one each — but others were sizeable in their day. Together they represent a kaleidoscope, and an apt reminder of why those of us over, shall we say, a 'certain age', find buses so fascinating.

The following chapters look at bus manufacturers which have actively built buses in Britain since the war, not ones which have simply imported them into this country. Thus the likes of Scania and DAF, both active in the UK market, do not appear, though Volvo does with its UK-built products. It is a shame though that the list of contents reads largely as an historical catalogue, and many once familiar names are no longer with us.

STEPHEN C. MORRIS B Mus, FCIT, FILT
Shepperton, Middlesex, February 2000

Introduction

The postwar period has turned out to be a traumatic one for the British motor industry as a whole, and this is especially true of the bus and coach industry. Immediately after the war, and indeed for the ensuing 20 years or more, imported vehicles were the exception rather than the rule, and were unheard of in the bus and coach sector. Who would have thought that by the turn of the century Dennis would top the British bus market and indeed be the only British-owned bus manufacturer left?

Contrast that with the situation immediately after the war when Britain could boast nine what may be called 'mainstream' bus chassis builders (AEC, Albion, Bedford, Bristol, Crossley, Daimler, Dennis, Guy and Leyland), plus other commercial vehicle builders like Atkinson, Austin, Commer, Foden, Ford and Seddon which were to come into the market subsequently, those like Maudslay and Tilling-Stevens which had been more significant before the war and would play some part, albeit minor, after the war, and the Birmingham & Midland Motor Omnibus Co, Britain's biggest company bus operator which ploughed its own furrow, building its own buses whose plain styling disguised cutting-edge technology under the skin.

The British postwar bus was a solid, no-nonsense affair. Before the war the British bus had reached a peak of refinement, and there were various interesting technical developments going on. AEC had built its first RT-class buses for London in 1939, bringing together numerous new features such as air brakes and air-operated preselective transmission packaged together in a body style which set new standards for grace and elegance and featured a very low bonnet line for improved visibility for the driver.

The RT was of largely conventional layout, but tentative experiments had gone on to get the engine out of the way on single-deckers; Leyland had explored both rear engines and mid-underfloor engines before the war, and other manufacturers, notably AEC, were going the same way.

The war put paid to such fripperies; basic, solid, low-cost engineering was the order of the day, and only Bedford, Guy, Daimler and Bristol had been permitted to build new buses. Everyone else was concentrating on the war machine. They came back into the field from 1945/46 but generally models such as Leyland's Titan PD1 and AEC's Regent (and their single-deck equivalents, in this case Tiger and Regal respectively) cut little new ground. Nor could they be expected to; after the war it was just a matter of concentrating on getting new buses into production — simple, reliable ones at that — and never mind the frills.

It is perhaps surprising then that by the end of the 1940s most manufacturers had new ranges on the market. To the passenger most may have looked or seemed little different from what went before, but there were new levels of refinement and particularly performance, while innovations continued under the surface, such as synchromesh gearboxes to make life easier for the driver. Development that had been interrupted by the war was back in full swing.

Moreover new buses were needed. Operators had had a tough time in the war and prewar buses, which under other circumstances would have been maturing nicely, had been run into the ground and needed replacing. There was no shortage of passengers, and fleet replacement schemes got under way.

The standard British 1940s postwar bus had a front-mounted diesel engine, with half-width cab alongside. Double-deckers would almost without exception have the entrance at the rear, either with an open platform or maybe enclosed by platform doors. They would be 7ft 6in wide and 26ft long, typically with 56 seats, although by the end of the 1940s dimensions had been relaxed to 8ft wide by 27ft long, giving around 60 seats. Longer vehicles could be built on three axles for higher capacity, though in practice only trolleybuses were available for UK consumption in this format after the war. AEC, Guy and Leyland in particular had offered three-axle

motorbuses before the war, with limited success, but none
was offered on the home market in postwar years.
Trolleybuses were a different proposition, as the need to
maximise the use of expensive infrastructure meant that
there was a requirement to maximise passenger capacity.
Single-deckers could already be 27ft 6in on two axles.

Generally, only manufacturers of lighter vehicles, such
as Bedford, continued to offer petrol engines after the
war, and its OB chassis, a more refined version of its
wartime OWB, with a small petrol engine in a
conventional bonnet at the front, formed the basis of
many a 29-seat coach in this period.

However, passengers on single-deck routes may well
have noted a major change from the end of the 1940s;
from 1949 underfloor-engined single-deckers began to
appear and these represented a major change in the
appearance of buses, with a full front and entrance in an
overhang ahead of the front axle. BMMO was one of the
first with its own vehicles, while AEC brought out its
Regal IV in 1949, with refinements such as brakes and
preselective gearbox both operated by air pressure.
Meanwhile Leyland had collaborated with body-builder
Metro Cammell Weymann to go one stage further by
eliminating the traditional separate chassis at the same
time. However, Sentinel is credited with the first
underfloor-engined bus after the war. Sentinel was one of
the last builders of steam lorries, having produced
particularly effective horizontal-engined vehicles during
the 1930s and similar technology (though using diesel
power!) was logically adapted to buses. Indeed it offered
only horizontal engines in its postwar range, goods
vehicles included.

The underfloor engine allowed a useful increase in
seating, to 40, and later relaxation of the rules to allow

30ft single-deckers on two axles increased this to 44.
There was also the potential for one-person operation,
with passengers boarding alongside the driver, though
this aspect was only to make an impact several years
later; buses with more than 20 seats could only be one-
man-operated under special dispensation from the Traffic
Commissioners.

Leyland soon found resistance to chassisless, or
integral, vehicles, and offered a separate chassis, the
Royal Tiger, some of which, confusingly, were built with
a style of MCW body identical to the Olympic. What
these early underfloor-engined chassis did share was a
very high unladen weight, and in the 1950s cost-saving
became more significant as passenger numbers peaked
and began their long, steady decline. Thus lighter-weight
versions were produced; in the case of Leyland and AEC
these were the Tiger Cub and Reliance respectively,
which were both introduced in 1953. Ironically the
Reliance later developed into a premium, heavyweight
coach chassis. There was also a chassisless version of the
Tiger Cub, or lightweight Olympic if you prefer, called
the Olympian, which sold in very small quantities on the
home market.

Meanwhile, lighter-weight double-deckers were also built on new versions of existing chassis, and during the 1950s the traditional exposed radiator on double-deckers was often disguised by styled sheet metalwork, only Leyland continuing to offer exposed-radiator models well into the 1960s.

In 1954 Walsall Corporation had a batch of 30ft double-deck trolleybuses built on two axles and this paved the way for longer vehicles on two axles. Trolleybuses were subject to different rules and regulations from those applying to motorbuses (they were officially considered to be some sort of railway!) and thus it was sometimes possible to introduce new approaches on trolleybuses while they still could not be applied to motorbuses because of legal restrictions. Walsall's trolleybuses thus proved that a 30ft double-decker on two axles worked perfectly well, and two years later 30ft two-axle motorbuses were legalised. The demand thus created was met in the main by lengthened versions of existing chassis. Single-deckers of 36ft were to be proven in the same way later in the decade; Glasgow introduced 10 36ft 50-seat single-deck trolleybuses and by 1961 36ft single-deck motorbuses were authorised.

Going back to 1954, however, London Transport had commissioned a new generation of bus principally for the replacement of trolleybuses. Built by AEC and Park Royal (though prototypes involved other builders too) the legendary Routemaster had to be capable of carrying 64 passengers within the same laden weight as the 56-seat RT, with no loss of comfort and with extra facilities for the driver.

The Routemaster achieved its aim despite a high level of comfort and power steering plus automatic transmission. Again, chassisless construction was adopted, using an aluminium structure which proved not only very light but also immensely strong and durable. It retained traditional layout and was thus the ultimate development of the front-engined, halfcab bus; no further major developments were made to this type, although new versions of existing models and one complete new model — the AEC Renown — had yet to emerge.

The Renown, resurrecting the name of the prewar three-axle double-decker, was largely conventional, but had a low frame and dropped-centre rear axle to enable low-height double-deck bodywork to be built on it (though in fact some operators, such as Leicester and Nottingham, used the low floor to create extra internal headroom instead). This was not a new concept; it had been developed as far back as 1949 by Bristol, which had been nationalised under the 1947 Transport Act and was thus permitted only to supply vehicles to the state sector, once orders in hand at the time the Act came into force

Below:
In some ways a typical independent operator's fleet of the mid-1950s, though with rather superior depot accommodation compared with many. This 1955 shows the Worksop depot of Major's Coaches, just before it was taken over by East Midland. Visible are a late-Utility Guy Arab II and a pair of contrasting Dennis Lancet coaches.

had been fulfilled. Bristol sold its new bus as the Lodekka, and also allowed Dennis to build an open-market version of it under licence as the Loline. Leyland had produced its own, none too satisfactory low-height bus, the Lowlander, which was built by Albion — since 1951 part of the growing Leyland group.

Leyland, however, was pursuing a different avenue. Just as engines had gone elsewhere on single-deckers, Leyland developed a double-decker with a transverse rear engine. The first two prototypes were largely conventional in appearance, with the engine under the stairs on the rear platform. However, before production began an integral version had been developed with MCW, with the engine in isolation behind the lower saloon, and the entrance ahead of the front axle. It went into production in 1958 as the Atlantean, by which time it could be built to 30ft length, and the decision had been taken to abandon the integral version and simply build a separate chassis, though MCW still built the bodywork for the first versions. Its main advantages were high seating capacity — up to 78 seats could be fitted in — while the driver could supervise boarding and unloading, even if he wasn't allowed at this stage to take the fares.

Daimler quickly followed with its Fleetline, which offered two advantages over the Atlantean. Firstly, it could be fitted with low-height bodywork — on the Atlantean this could be achieved only by fitting a sunken side gangway upstairs towards the rear, reverting to the awkward pre-Lodekka arrangement, albeit not for the whole length of the bus, until it turned to Daimler and used the Fleetline gearbox in a low-height version. Its second advantage was that, while Leyland insisted on fitting engines of its own make, Daimler could offer Gardner engines, which had been a favourite for bus

work since diesel engines were first fitted to buses. This proprietary unit was very economical — despite little major design change since the early 1930s it was not until the mid-1980s that another manufacturer managed to match its fuel consumption — and was also very reliable and produced plenty of torque at low speeds, which was ideal for bus work.

At this stage no other manufacturer was pursuing such developments in the bus world, although Guy tried a different approach from Leyland and Daimler. Its Wulfrunian used a Gardner 6LX engine mounted ahead of the front axle, with the entrance alongside and a staircase over the nearside front wheel. This was combined with other complexities, and its problems proved insurmountable. The weight imbalance was too great, especially given the sophistication of the front suspension and brakes, and as one of the classic flops of the bus world it brought Guy down with it.

The die was now cast, even if bus operators were expected to cope with a drop in reliability. Tried and tested components which worked well in a conventional location, with plentiful natural airflow around them and mounted alongside the driver, where he could hear or feel if something was amiss, suddenly proved much less reliable when tucked away in a powerpack at the back of the bus. Although many operators stuck doggedly with the front-engined layout as long as possible, the industry was gradually persuaded that higher fuel consumption and much-reduced reliability was a small price to pay for fashion and a few extra seats!

However, one-person operation of double-deckers was legalised in 1966, which rather changed the equation. The first operator to take advantage of the new legislation was Brighton Corporation, which used conventional forward-

Right:
New look for the 1970s. South Yorkshire PTE tried a variety of modern types on its 51 service; from left to right they are a Leyland Titan, an MCW Metrobus (both demonstrators), an East Lancs-bodied Leyland Atlantean, an East Lancs-bodied Dennis Dominator and a Van Hool-McArdle-bodied Ailsa.

entrance Leyland Titans, requiring the driver to turn round in his seat to serve passengers and giving him no ease in the physical job of driving to make up for his extra workload. Eastern National and Eastern Scottish tried a similar approach with Bristol Lodekkas. Most operators, however, recognised the importance of having the entrance placed opposite the driver if he was expected to relieve passengers of their fares as they boarded.

Bristol had now joined the move to rear engines with its VR, this appearing in prototype form in 1966 with in-line engine on the offside. However, it changed horses, abandoning what could have been a very versatile design for the now-conventional arrangement of a transverse engine. By now Bristol had been liberated from the constraints to sell only to the state sector, as Leyland had taken a 25% shareholding in 1965, and this had enabled it to sell new products to all comers. Its RE rear-engined single-decker was undoubtedly the most successful of a troublesome crop of new rear-engined single-deckers from the likes of Leyland, AEC and Daimler. These designs had the advantage of a low entrance and high capacity, now that single-deckers could be built up to 36ft. This gave seating capacity on a par with double-deckers, at 53, and allowed for one-person operation before it could be applied to double-deckers.

AEC's foray into rear-engined double-deckers was shortlived; an intention to build five rear-engined Routemaster prototypes was commuted by Leyland and only one was built. It shared the basic structure of the Routemaster and used about 60% of standard Routemaster components. London Transport FRM1, the sole example built, still exists as a museum piece, and many have a sneaking suspicion that the design could have been a great success. Not all the lessons learned in

building it were consigned to the dustbin, however, and it had at least some bearing on the later Leyland Titan. Internally it seemed rather better-designed than other rear-engined types at the time, with a particularly neat interior, and if it had proved to be as well-designed structurally as the Routemaster there seems little doubt that it could have been a winner. In all lines of British engineering there seem to be 'might-have-beens' which look so promising. London instead went for the Fleetline for one-person operation and, while there was nothing particularly wrong with the Fleetline as a bus, by the time it had been hacked about to suit London's 'unique' requirements it was something of a disaster. One also suspects there was a certain death wish on it from the start in London — but we're getting a bit ahead of ourselves.

The 1968 Transport Act had a profound effect on the bus world. Its main effect was the formation of the state-owned National Bus Company, encompassing almost all the major company operators; those which had been part of the BET Federation had sold out to their state-owned THC counterparts a little earlier. In addition, the municipal operators in four major conurbations were amalgamated into Passenger Transport Executives, and to speed one-person operation the Government introduced a 25% capital grant, later increased to 50%, for new buses which met certain parameters, notably that they could be operated without a conductor. This spelt the end of the conventional double-decker, and by 1968 production of the Leyland Titan, AEC Regent and Routemaster, Daimler CVG6, Guy Arab (Guy had been taken over by Daimler and continued as a separate entity after its Wulfrunian disaster) and Bristol Lodekka had ended.

As a result these well-built and reliable vehicles had a much shorter lifespan, in most cases, than they were

Left:
One of two London Transport standard double-deck types for the late 1970s/early 1980s was the Metrobus, one of which stands in Hounslow bus station. The 222 is now run by Dennis Lance low-floor buses.

Right:
Deregulation strikes! A 20-year-old North Western Leyland Atlantean leads a convoy of buses in Liverpool in October 1994. Although bus mileage has increased with deregulation — especially in the Metropolitan areas — there has not been a corresponding increase in passengers. Indeed the reverse is the case.
Michael H. C. Baker

Leyland had gradually been expanding its dominance of the bus world. It had merged with ACV, an amalgamation of AEC, Crossley, Maudslay, Thornycroft and bus bodybuilders Park Royal and Roe in 1962, and its shareholding in Bristol was increased to 50% in 1969, by which time the rest of its shares were owned by the National Bus Company. One of the most momentous events in the British automotive industry was the merger of what had become Leyland Motor Corporation since the ACV merger and what was then British Motor Holdings. Up to 1966 BMH had been BMC, but the takeover of Jaguar had brought about the change of title. Jaguar owned Daimler and Guy, so by now Leyland was becoming something of a monolith in the bus building industry.

Certain operators were dismayed at this situation, and other manufacturers were not slow to exploit it. Firstly came Scania, in conjunction with bodybuilder Metro-Cammell Weymann, which was concerned that Leyland's move to integral construction would rob it of any business. Its Metro-Scania was a direct rival to the Leyland National and, while it sold in fairly small numbers, a double-deck counterpart proved rather more of a serious rival. However, it was significant in that it was a toe-hold for overseas manufacturers, which would ultimately lead to the virtual demise of UK manufacturers.

Dennis, which had pulled out of bus building in 1968 — and indeed had shown little enthusiasm for bus building for some years before that — was also encouraged to introduce a new rear-engined double-decker, the Dominator, which was intended as an alternative to the Daimler Fleetline which Leyland was in the process of phasing out, and this was later to lead to a whole range of products and set up Dennis as the last remaining British manufacturer. The Dominator sold reasonably well, largely to municipal and PTE operators — South Yorkshire PTE took to it, unusually with Rolls-Royce engines — and was later to spawn other models, notably the Falcon single-decker, which, with a rear horizontal Gardner engine, was a sort of latter-day Bristol RE.

Meanwhile, the coach business was largely in the hands of Leyland companies for the heavyweight market — notably the mid-engined Leyland Leopard and AEC Reliance — and Bedford and Ford for the lightweight, the former with a mid, vertical engine, the latter with a front

designed for, and were replaced by vehicles suitable for one-person operation. This need also brought about an increase in the popularity of lightweight single-deckers, built by the likes of Bedford and Ford. In 36ft form they could carry nearly as many passengers as a double-decker, yet were much cheaper to buy and, with their dependence on high-volume, medium-weight trucks for parts, were cheap to run and maintain. They entered fleets of small, independent operators which had traditionally used secondhand double-deck stock.

Of more significance was the second-generation rear-engined single-decker, of which the principal example was the Leyland National. This was designed by Leyland in conjunction with the National Bus Company and embodied very strong, integral construction, which avoided the problem encountered with the earlier generation where conventional bodywork had tended to sag with the weight of the engine in the rear overhang. The Leyland National also had air suspension, paving the way to near-universal adoption of this feature, giving not only a better ride but making for easier maintenance than conventional leaf springs. Other features were power steering and ergonomic design to the benefit of both driver and passenger. It was a highly-standardised bus, with a very limited range of options — indeed at first they were offered with a choice of only three plain colours: red, green or white. This was in stark contrast to the traditional way of building buses, which were more often than not bespoke products for individual operators, and such an approach enabled it to be mass-produced, car-like, by semi-skilled labour in a brand-new, purpose-built factory in Workington, Cumbria. Around 7,700 Leyland Nationals were built from 1971 to 1985.

engine though inclined to fit under the floor. They were soon joined by another importer, Volvo, with a similar but rather more sophisticated and powerful mid-engined heavyweight, the Swedish-built B58.

Volvo's Scottish importer, Ailsa Trucks, also saw potential for a simple, rugged front-engined double-decker, though with the entrance alongside the driver, Guy Wulfrunian-style. It had several advantages over the ill-fated Wulfrunian: it retained conventional suspension and brakes, used a semi-integral body from Alexander to overcome structural difficulties, and had a small, turbocharged Volvo engine. Such a power unit was at first regarded with disdain as not being 'man' enough for the job, but Volvo engineers knew their stuff and, for the most part, the engine confounded its critics. However, despite the dislike of rear engines, the Ailsa did not sell in huge numbers outside Scotland. Perhaps it had come too late; by now engineers had got used to rear engines, and the problems of early vehicles had been sorted out to a large extent.

Leyland intended to continue the rationalisation of its range. The Leyland National had been seen as the way forward, with a perceived move to single-deckers. However, Leyland had misread the market and, with one-person operation of double-deckers now perfectly feasible, large operators moved back to double-deckers. Leyland's Project B15, which came to be known as the Titan, was a sort of double-deck Leyland National; the concept was largely similar — a fully-integral bus with air suspension, though independent at the front, and lots of sophistication. It was hit by major production problems and became essentially a London vehicle, large early orders for provincial centres going mostly

unfulfilled and never being repeated.

Just as the Titan entered production, MCW had ended its relationship with Scania and began building a rival to the Titan — the Metrobus — using a Gardner engine and German Voith transmission. It was not so sophisticated as the Titan, but MCW was rather more successful at getting production underway and it sold more widely than the Titan. Moreover, it could be produced as a separate underframe and as such was bodied, albeit in fairly small numbers, by Alexander and (later) Northern Counties. Plans for Titans to be built by Northern Counties for its parent Greater Manchester PTE came to nought.

Leyland also soldiered on with an ageing range of double-deck and coach chassis, the latter being outclassed now by foreign competition. The coach business was deregulated in 1980, and Leyland was able only to offer chassis which had evolved since the 1950s. Operators turned overseas for such features as air suspension and powerful turbocharged engines, often mounted at the rear to give better luggage accommodation and minimise noise intrusion into the saloon. UK bodybuilders had also fallen behind with styling, and it was overseas manufacturers which were the main beneficiaries of deregulation. Rather belatedly Leyland introduced the Tiger, with air suspension and a more powerful, turbocharged engine, and followed it with a stylish rear-engined integral, the Royal Tiger Doyen. This was the equal of anything the Continental manufacturers could offer in terms of styling and comfort, but by now coach operators had lost faith in Leyland. It could not offer the same level of back-up on Continental work and there were doubts over build quality.

Meanwhile, the major British express operator, National Express, called for a new high-floor rear-engined coach. Dennis and Duple responded with a coach version of the Falcon with Duple's high-floor Goldliner body, powered by a turbocharged Perkins V8. Most of Dennis's models at this time could be equated with vehicles of earlier generations — in this case the coach version of the Falcon was a sort of latter-day Daimler Roadliner; the Roadliner had not been one of Daimler's high points . . . Sadly National Express's timescale had been too tight to allow proper development and, while the Falcons went like the wind and were superbly comfortable, smooth and quiet, there had been no time to get the bugs out of them. Failures which should have occurred on the test track and been ironed out thus occurred very publicly, in service, and almost cost Dennis its hard-won reputation.

On the double-deck front there was also a rethink at Leyland in the face of opposition to the Titan, and the same mechanical units were put into a chassis, though with a brand-new front axle and suspension arrangement. The resulting Olympian was able to take low-height bodywork, which the Titan wasn't, and could be bodied by a range of manufacturers. After a slowish start it replaced the Atlantean, Fleetline and Bristol VRT and proved highly successful.

Meanwhile, single-deck sales had fallen drastically and the Leyland National was reaching the end of the road. Bus deregulation was announced in a Transport Bill in 1984 (enacted as the 1985 Transport Act), bringing with it privatisation of the National Bus Company and provision for other public sector operators to go private too.

This stifled all investment in large vehicles, for a number of reasons. Bus Grant had been steadily phased out during the early 1980s, at a time when increasing European legislation on safety, accessibility and emissions was making buses ever more complex and therefore expensive. Subsidies for bus operations, which in many cases were substantial by present-day terms, if not by Continental European terms, were cut back to the bare minimum, and operators were also left in a state of uncertainty, with any profits likely to be creamed off by newcomers. The newcomers were coming in at the lowest possible cost using rolling stock cast off by larger operators reducing their fleet sizes, so they offered little hope to the bus manufacturers. And any money that was available was being spent not on new buses but on raising capital to buy bus companies, either from public-sector owners or from private-sector owners.

There was, however, a major move to van-based minibuses which were cheaper to buy and to run and could be used to open up areas inaccessible to large buses. The main bus builders found themselves unable to offer suitable products, though MCW was soon to come up with the integral 25-seat Metrorider. Deregulation killed the demand for large single-deckers and Leyland therefore took its time over introducing the replacement for the Leyland National, the Lynx, though it did sell reasonably well once introduced, boosted by large orders

from West Midlands Travel and the Badgerline and West Riding groups.

As part of its privatising zeal the Government also wished to rid itself of British Leyland, which it had picked up during difficult phases in the 1970s. The car, truck and bus businesses were sold separately. General Motors, which owned Bedford, was interested, but it was unacceptable to have such a strategic interest as Land Rover owned overseas — ironic in view of the subsequent outcome, which saw it owned by BMW and later, controversially, sold on to Ford. GM wanted the truck business plus Land Rover, and its failure to gain these meant that it decided Bedford was unable to carry on alone — much investment in new models was needed which volumes looked unlikely to sustain — and closed it down.

There was a similar situation at MCW. In 1986 the Laird Group, which owned MCW, looked at the possibility of buying Leyland Bus, which could have made a strong, combined bus-building group. Ultimately Leyland Bus was sold to its management in 1987, which sold it on to Volvo the following year. Then, at the end of 1992, having given many undertakings of a bright future, Volvo closed Leyland as volumes were still down. It reopened its Irvine truck plant, where the Ailsa had been built, to bus production, revamped the Olympian as a pure Volvo product and built that and a new small single-decker, the B6, there. Meanwhile, the Laird Group decided not to continue sustaining losses at MCW, which it closed at the end of 1988, its model range passing to Optare, a relatively new bodybuilder which had been formed at the former Roe factory, shut by Leyland in 1984.

Dennis, however, prospered. Its Javelin medium-weight coach was an innovative design and came in just at the right time to pick up sales from Bedford. It is not unreasonable to surmise that, had GM invested in a new coach range, this would have turned out very much the same as the Javelin. Dennis repeated its success with a small rear-engined single-decker, the Dart, which was introduced at the 1988 Motor Show, and production began in 1990. This was a spectacular success, as it was just the right size to take over from minibuses where they had developed traffic to the point where they were now too small; at the same time it was big enough to take over from full-sized single-deckers on routes where traffic was declining. By 1994, 2,000 had been built. It used simple technology in an imaginative way to create a reasonably sophisticated bus, a formula used again for the full-sized rear-engined Lance. The Lance was hardly an outstanding success for Dennis, but formed the basis of the first British sortie into a new European technology, the ultra-low-floor bus.

Itself not a huge success — around 100 were built — the low-floor version of the Lance sowed the seed of a whole new genre of British bus, and again Dennis was in the vanguard. It developed its Dart into a low-floor bus, the first of which went into service in early 1996. Dennis had proved that accessible low-floor bus technology

could be cheap and simple. Nowadays very few buses
that are not low-floor and accessible enter service; the
first low-floor double-deckers had made a tentative
showing on DAF by the end of 1998 and in 1999
hundreds flowed into service. Yet again, Dennis took the
lead with its Trident, which scored over the DAF with a
low-floor gangway throughout the lower saloon. Volvo
had tried to adapt its new, pan-European B7L to suit the
double-deck market, realised its mistake and lost
valuable time to Dennis while it redesigned the side-
engined B7L into a transverse-engined double-decker.
The first began to appear in early 2000. All three
mainstream double-deck body builders — Alexander,
Plaxton (which had taken over Northern Counties) and
East Lancs — developed new bodies for them, all built to
the newly-legalised width limit of 2.55m.

Optare, meanwhile, having introduced its low-floor
Excel as a rival to the Dart as well as to larger Continental
offerings, developed a rear-engined low-floor minibus,
the Mercedes-powered Solo, which gave conventional
van-based minibuses a tough time of it.

Volvo, Scania and DAF all brought in large single-
deck products to compete in the low-floor market, and
Volvo also tried again with its British-built B6, creating
the low-entry B6LE and, later, B6BLE, which still did
little to dent Dennis's supremacy. DAF also had a pot-
shot at Dennis, with its new SB120, a Dart SLF clone
developed in conjunction with Arriva — both DAF's UK
importer and a likely operator of the type.

By the turn of the century the process of consolidation
in the operating industry was all but complete; there were
now several big groups listed on the Stock Exchange,
giving them ready access to capital. Meanwhile, driven in
part by the requirement for accessible buses on local

authority tendered services, smaller operators were
investing in new rolling stock in a big way, though often
by taking advantage of leasing deals available through
specialists in the field, like Dawsonrentals, Mistral and
Arriva Bus & Coach. Investment in new buses was back
up to decent levels, and some 5,000 new full-size buses
were registered in Britain in 1999. Dennis capitalised on
its strength and finished the century as runaway leader in
the British bus market.

Meanwhile, traditional leader Volvo suffered not only
from a lack of the right models but from the fact that
some of its big group customers had gone elsewhere;
Travel West Midlands, in the National Express Group,
was buying Mercedes-Benz, and Stagecoach had turned
to MAN, while another slow starter in the British psv
industry, Iveco, was mopping up some coach sales from
Volvo. By the end of 1999, however, the B7L had come
on stream, and things were beginning to look brighter for
Volvo; it had regained the custom of Travel West
Midlands, which took 102 of the first B7Ls, and early
indications suggest this new model could be a winner for
Volvo.

The first century of the British motorbus had certainly
been turbulent. Dennis apart, the British-owned bus
manufacturer is a thing of the past, but at least the market
has matured again.

ACE/Ward

One of the delightful things about the British automotive industry is the way from time to time a small company will have a go at producing something which isn't otherwise available on the market. This is particularly so in the bus industry; numerous small companies have come and gone, leaving a legacy of an oddball vehicle here and there. Sadly they seldom have the staying power to survive, even if their ideas are good. They tend to be undercapitalised and have great difficulty in assuring potential users of their credibility.

ACE is the most recent example. It had some good designs, and like many such companies began life when an operator wanted a vehicle which nobody built. ACE, based in Huddersfield, began life as Ward Brothers. Wards had (indeed still has) a medium-sized coach business in Lepton, to the south of Huddersfield, and was particularly keen on Seddon Pennines with Perkins V8 engines. After Seddon stopped building such vehicles it started work in 1980 to build its own 36ft coach chassis with a mid-mounted Perkins V8, called the Dalesman. It was fitted in 1981 with a well-appointed Plaxton Supreme IV coach body. Engineer Keith Ward disliked power steering, not least for its effect on tyre wear, so the vehicle was built without that feature. It had a ZF six-speed synchromesh gearbox, which can be a tricky box in many well-established manufacturers' products, yet Wards managed a superb installation which worked extremely well.

Above:
The start of a new manufacturer. What was to become ACE began life as Ward, with this Perkins V8-powered mid-engined Dalesman C11-640 chassis. It had a Plaxton Supreme body and is seen on a cold day in the Pennines on a *Buses* road test.

Left:
A Perkins-engined ACE Puma of Huddersfield operator Abbeyways at a show in Renfrew. Bodywork is by Plaxton, the low-driver version of the Paramount 3200 body. Abbeyways had connections with ACE through managing director Steven Ives.
Sandy Macdonald

Above:
Another ACE Puma at Renfrew, this time with Van
Hool bodywork.
Sandy Macdonald

It bowed to pressure to fit power steering on production vehicles.

Its next project was another 'Seddon clone' the GRXI, a rear-engined service bus with a horizontal Gardner engine and SCG semi-automatic gearbox, very similar in many respects to the Seddon Pennine RU. Six were built in 1983 for Darlington Transport, and no further orders were received. Wards closed down in 1984 having built 18 chassis in total.

However, from the ashes arose a company called AEC (Albion Equipment Co), started by another Huddersfield coach operator, Steven Ives plus two of the Ward Brothers. It announced a range of three chassis, the Puma, Cheetah and Cougar, all using Perkins engines. Not surprisingly Leyland which had rights not only to the original AEC name but also to Albion, objected and it was quickly renamed ACE (Advanced Chassis Engineering). The Cheetah was the successor to the Ward Dalesman, but with a dropped driver position as was then fashionable, while the Puma was a short-wheelbase midicoach chassis, of which 12 were sold, one with a DAF DHT 8.25litre engine. The Cougar took longer to come on stream, and was a rear-engined 10m bus chassis with a ramped floor. Only two were built and the company closed down in 1992.

AEC

AEC, based in postwar years at Southall, Middlesex, was very much one of the 'giants' of bus manufacturing, having been established originally as the 'builder of London's buses' as it used to advertise itself.

After the war it essentially had two ranges, one for London and one for the provinces. Just before the war London's RT version of AEC's double-decker, the Regent, had seen the light of day and postwar production began quickly. The RT was ahead of the field with a powerful 9.6litre engine, air-operated preselector gearbox, air brakes and a low bonnet line to give excellent visibility. Some 4,650 London RTs were built after the war until production ended in 1954.

The RT was also offered to provincial operators, but more conventional Regents were also offered, starting immediately after the war with a stop-gap Regent II, largely following on from prewar practice and built to a rather basic specification. The Regent III was available in various forms with a range of engines from 7.7 to 9.6 litres capacity, preselector, synchromesh or constant-mesh gearboxes and air or vacuum brakes. The bonnet line was higher than the RT, and a few operators specified concealed radiators in the 1950s. There was a parallel Regal single-deck version, which was successful as both a bus and a coach, spawning some very attractive coach versions especially once 30ft versions were legalised.

Before the war AEC had been experimenting with engine positions, and had built an underfloor-engined bus for Canada as well as underfloor-engined railcars for the Great Western Railway. Similar technology was embodied in the Regal IV introduced in 1949, with a standard preselector gearbox and air brakes. This formed the basis of either a bus or a coach and offered not only style but a higher seating capacity, albeit for a very substantial weight penalty over the front-engined Regals. A London version the RF, was built in 1951-53.

The commercial vehicle industry as a whole, and the bus industry in particular, became obsessed with weight saving in the 1950s as economies had to be introduced following the beginnings of a tail-off in passengers as car ownership grew. In AEC's case, following lightweight versions of the Regent III, a new lightweight range was introduced to supersede the earlier models. In 1953 came the Reliance, a lightweight underfloor-engined single-decker, following the realisation that underfloor-engined buses would not fall apart without a structure like the Forth Bridge under the floor. The same components could be had in a Park Royal-built integral, the Monocoach. An unsuccessful foray into an underfloor-engined double-decker, the Regent IV, showed there was no advantage to be gained from increasing the complexity of a double-decker at this stage, so the lightweight double-decker was the Regent V, which offered a stylish concealed radiator as standard.

Although conceived as lightweights both Regent V and Reliance grew into heavyweights in later life, the Reliance in particular turning out to be AEC's last chassis, metamorphosed into a sophisticated premium motorway coach by the time of its demise in 1979.

Meanwhile London Transport too was looking at increasing seating capacity within the same laden weight as an RT for trolleybus replacement, resulting in the classic Routemaster, of which prototypes appeared in 1954 and production began in 1958. This embodied many advanced features such as coil suspension, independent at the front, automatic transmission and power steering, arranged in two subframes built into an aluminium integral body structure by Park Royal. AEC built 2,873 of them, though some had Leyland engines, and in 1966 developed a rear-engined version, of which only one prototype was built.

Similar, though simplified, technology was adopted for a new provincial double-decker, the Bridgemaster, of which Crossley-bodied prototypes appeared in 1956. Production buses were bodied by Park Royal from 1958, using steel rather than the Routemaster's aluminium. It had a dropped-centre rear axle to enable low-height bodywork to be built without recourse to a sunken gangway upstairs. It was not one of AEC's more auspicious products and sold only 179.

In 1962 AEC sold out to archrival Leyland. It had taken over Crossley and Maudslay in 1948 to form Associated Commercial Vehicles, merged with Park Royal, which also owned Charles H. Roe, in 1949 and had taken over Thornycroft in 1961, and thus represented a substantial sector of the bus and commercial vehicle business. However, it was able to continue as a separate entity and still built its products at its Southall, Middlesex factory. Its last new double-decker was launched at this time, the Renown, which used AEC Regent V components in a low-height form, and provided a more conventional replacement for the Bridgemaster. About 250 Renowns were built.

Meanwhile a rear-engined single-decker was in development, the Swift. Although using AEC components the Swift was a product of the merger with Leyland, for the same chassis was also built with Leyland components as the Panther. It used the 8.25litre AH505 engine, though some had the bigger 11.3litre AH691 engine, also fitted to London's heavyweight version, the Merlin. Semi-automatic transmission was standard, though the Swift was available for rural use with a five-speed constant-mesh unit.

There was to be one further AEC; at the 1970 Commercial Motor Show an impressive rear-engined coach with a V8 engine appeared, the Sabre. It had a new ECW body, and although the chassis never got beyond prototype stage the body was reworked for the Bristol RE. By this time AEC was building only single-deckers; the Regent V and Routemaster had ended in 1968, and AEC had no new rear-engined bus to replace them. The Swift continued in production until 1975 and the Reliance, by now a premium heavyweight coach, far removed from the original concept, alone kept the AEC name going until this very popular marque was closed down in 1979. The final Reliances had 691 or even bigger 760 12.5litre engines with ZF six-speed gearboxes or semi-automatic transmission and were fine, high-speed motorway performers. They were superseded in the Leyland range by the less powerful and less refined Leopard, of which a special version with ZF gearbox was built to cater for the AEC market, though many AEC customers preferred to turn to Volvo or DAF.

Above:
A splendid scene in Leeds in about 1950 shows West Riding 74 (BHL 190), a Regent III with Roe centre-entrance bodywork passing a Leeds tramcar.

Below:
The single-deck version of the Regent III was the Regal III. Seen when new in 1949 is a Weymann-bodied example for East Midland.

Right:
The Regal III was also popular as a coach. This one has bodywork by Longford to a classic late-1940s style, and is seen in 1964 in service with West Riding. It was new in 1949 to Bullock & Sons, which was taken over by West Riding the next year.
J. Fozard

Centre right:
London Transport's own version of the Regal IV was the RF type, which was often to be found on the extremities of LT's operations. Seen in May 1962, still requiring a conductor and open front door, to keep the Metropolitan Police happy, this picture of RF421 in Shepperton High Street was taken from outside what, 32 years later, was to become the *Buses* editorial office, where much of this book was written!
Michael Dryhurst

Below:
The provincial version of the Regal IV made a superb, if very heavy, coach, with a quality of ride and noise levels, and ease of driving, which would rival many coaches built 30 years or more later. This one, for Scottish operator Northern Roadways, had Burlingham Seagull bodywork.

Above:
After AEC's heavyweight period came some lightweight designs, not least the Regent V. This Devon General bus had lightweight MCW Orion bodywork — and would also have featured a straight-through exhaust, giving a splendid sporty, rasping crackle. Behind is the old order, a rather heavier Weymann-bodied Regent III.
Kevin Lane

Centre left:
AEC's lightweight single-decker was the Reliance, though this was to grow in size and weight over the years. Many a BET company had Reliances with this style of body-work in the late 1950s/early 1960s, built by a variety of builders. This Yorkshire Woollen District one had Park Royal bodywork and was new in 1960.

Bottom left:
This Reliance was a late survivor with Chiltern Queens and is seen at Reading in 1975. Unusually it carried the body from the one-off Dennis Pelican.
Kevin Lane

Top:
Though Burlingham's Seagull body of the 1950s was a classic, the Seagull 60 was less universally acclaimed. This new one on an AEC Reliance for Scottish Omnibuses in 1961 looks handsome enough, though.

Above:
Also with Scottish Omnibuses is a pair of AEC/Park Royal Monocoaches seen at St Andrew Square in Edinburgh in December 1954.

Above:
The AEC/Park Royal integral Bridgemaster was not an outstanding success. This one began life with South Wales but is photographed with Yorkshire Woollen District in Dewsbury in 1969.
Michael Fowler

Left:
The Routemaster proved remarkably enduring; it was introduced in 1954 and was still in service in 1994 when photographed at Victoria. This London Central bus is the 30ft long version, RML2345, as refurbished a year or two earlier.

Right:
Much lamented was the fact that the rear-engined Routemaster project never got off the ground — though had thousands of them been built they may have been despised as the bus that ousted the Routemaster! Who knows? FRM1 was originally built with no opening windows, though after it caught fire the opportunity was taken to fit some opening windows when it was repaired and returned to service. It is seen on the 76.
K. Pratt

Below:
After the Bridgemaster failed to catch on AEC introduced the Renown on a separate chassis. North Western was a major customer, with this Park Royal body which was rather better proportioned than that for the Bridgemaster. 1964-built 119 is seen on North Western's parking ground behind Mersey Square in Stockport in the company of a Marshall-bodied Bristol RESL.

Above:
Though it began life as a light-weight the Reliance developed into a premium heavyweight motorway coach. This Plaxton Supreme-bodied coach of Premier Travel makes an imposing sight as it leaves Drummer Street bus station in Cambridge in 1982. Next to it is a slightly older Reliance with Plaxton Panorama Elite bodywork.
Kevin Lane

Centre left:
Though not considered one of AEC's finest, the London heavy-weight version of the Swift, the Merlin, put in useful service on the intensive Red Arrow network.
A. Fox collection

Below left:
AEC's last new model was the Sabre with a rear-mounted V8-800 engine and a new body by ECW. The body was adapted for the Bristol RE, though the Sabre never entered production. The one-off vehicle, seen at the 1970 Commercial Motor Show at Earls Court, nevertheless saw a full service life.

Ailsa

Throughout this book you will find references to the 1948 Commercial Motor Show, which was highly significant in that several postwar models made their debut there. Another significant show in postwar years was the 1973 Scottish Motor Show, at which three psvs were seen for the first time. One was the Seddon Pennine VII, a thoroughly British, very solid chassis, but the other two were something different in that they introduced some foreign content and represented different ways forward for the double-decker. One was the Metro-Scania Metropolitan; the other was the Scottish-built Ailsa.

Ailsa was based at a former munitions factory near the Ayrshire coast at Irvine — almost in sight of the island of Ailsa Craig whence came its name. It had been set up to import Volvo trucks into Britain in 1967, and in 1971 started the Ailsa Bus Company initially to import B58 coach chassis into Britain.

However, in 1973 it announced an unusual Volvo-engined psv. At this stage rear-engined chassis had become universal in terms of production, although not in the affections of engineers. The bugs had not yet been ironed out of them, and problems were exacerbated by shortages of spare parts and long delivery times. The engineers hankered after something simpler, and thus the Ailsa was born.

Guy had previously shown how not to build a front entrance bus with a front engine and never recovered from its Wulfrunian fiasco. Mechanically the Ailsa was much simpler, with no independent air suspension or disc brakes to cloud the issue. The other problem was the space taken up by the Gardner

'lump', which Ailsa overcame by using a compact, high-revving turbocharged Volvo TD70 6.7litre engine which pushed out a highly creditable 190bhp, even if the torque levels were rather lower than most people liked for bus work. This unit was immediately viewed with suspicion by engineers; as Midlander, himself an engineer, reported in *Buses* when the Ailsa was announced, ' . . . 6.7litre swept capacity is likely to be too small for a double-deck design with an unladen weight of just over 9 tons'. This was the accepted logic of the time, though in fact that engine was used in heavier lorry applications and proved very much more capable, reliable and economical than anyone first thought. And being so small, it didn't take up as much room on the platform and in the cab as the Gardner had done on the Guy.

The Ailsa had an unusual design of perimeter underframe — a bit like that on a Bristol Lodekka, only more so, and was designed to be integrated into an Alexander body structure. The rest of the design was well-proven in the main, with a mid-mounted SCG gearbox and Kirkstall front axle with ZF power steering, though the rear axle was a drop-centre hub-reduction unit made by Hamworthy, which was perhaps a little more exotic than most. Despite the ability this created for low-height variants all bar one was built to full height. Indeed the Hamworthy axle was to be something of a weak point on it, and when a Mark III version was introduced in 1980 a conventional Volvo rear axle was substituted.

Being built in Scotland and being mechanically straightforward it was not surprising that the Scottish Bus Group should be a major customer, and the first big order was for 40 for Alexander Fife. Thereafter it

Right:
An Alexander-bodied Ailsa in service with West Midlands PTE at Oldbury in 1982.
Kevin Lane

remained primarily a Scottish vehicle, as Strathclyde PTE and Tayside also took in large numbers. However, there were significant customers in England too; West Midlands PTE took 50 in 1975, after three pre-production vehicles, and South Yorkshire PTE took 62 with Irish-built Van Hool-McArdle bodywork of particularly striking appearance in 1976.

The Mark II version came out in 1977, with detail modifications and the choice of Voith or Allison transmission as options to the standard SCG, and in 1980 the Mark III was introduced. Originally the Mark III was to have been marketed as a Volvo B55, though it was decided to revert to the name Ailsa. However, there is much confusion around this period as to whether one should refer to Volvos or Ailsas! An air suspension option came with the Mark III. New body options came in in about 1980 too, with Greater Manchester taking some late Mark IIs with Northern Counties bodies, Tayside had both Northern Counties and East Lancs while Derby City Transport and Strathclyde PTE each had two with Marshall bodywork.

The last new model to emerge from Ailsa was the Citybus. This used an Ailsa-style perimeter frame but with Volvo B10M mechanical parts, ie a mid-mounted 9.6litre horizontal engine, SCG gearbox and full air suspension. The prototype was bodied by Marshall for Strathclyde PTE. However, when production began in 1983 the Citybus was sold as a Volvo, and as volumes were small at first it was soon decided to offer a special version of the standard B10M, built in Sweden, as the Citybus instead of the Ailsa-built version. The Ailsa plant was used by Volvo for lorry manufacture and bus production was taking up valuable space where much larger numbers of lorries could be built. Ailsa production ended in 1985 with 40 B55s for Indonesia; the last British ones were built the previous year for Strathclyde PTE. Just

over 1,000 had been built, nearly half of them for Scottish consumption, and no fewer than 321 went to Indonesia. Although thought-of as almost as an 'SBG special' in fact Scottish Bus Group had only 192 of that total, a figure which both Strathclyde and Tayside came close to matching. The Irvine factory then concentrated on lorries, but by hook or by crook is both nearly first and last in this book!

Albion

Albion was based in Scotstoun, near Glasgow, and was not exactly a mainstream bus builder, though it enjoyed some popularity in Scotland — notably with Glasgow Corporation — while in England Red & White also favoured the marque.

Its Venturer CX19 double-decker had entered production just before the war and recommenced production in 1946, with the options of Albion's own diesel or, surprisingly, petrol engines or the Gardner 6LW. It was the only postwar double-decker to offer a petrol engine, though in practice the only ones built were a 1948 export order to South African Railways; Albion sold strongly in territories such as South Africa and Australia. An updated CX37 with a more powerful Albion diesel engine superseded it in 1947. Glasgow Corporation was the main customer for the postwar Venturer, with 138 delivered between 1947 and 1953.

The single-deck equivalent was the Valiant, which

was built largely as a coach. However, Albion also
had quite a reputation for its lighter-weight products,
and offered a four-cylinder half-cab single-decker, the
Valkyrie CX9, although the CX13 version offered
either Albion's six-cylinder engine as fitted to the
Valiant or the Gardner 5LW.

The lightest Albion single-decker was the Victor,
intended largely for rural work and lightweight
coaching. The first postwar version, the FT3AB, had
a four-cylinder Albion petrol engine but the more
popular FT39, introduced in 1948, had a four-cylinder
diesel.

Albion ceased heavyweight production for the
home market in 1951, and later that year was taken
over by Leyland. On the home market it then concentrated on lightweights, after a very heavy underfloor-
engined single-decker with a horizontally-opposed
eight-cylinder engine, the KP71NW, got nowhere. In
1955 it launched a much smaller underfloor-engined
chassis, the Nimbus, which was a midibus before its
time. A larger model in 1957 was the Aberdonian,
which again followed the lightweight theme; by this
stage Leyland had launched its lightweight Tiger
Cub and the Aberdonian used similar mechanical

components, though with a typically tuneful five-speed Albion constant-mesh gearbox which also came to be offered in the Tiger Cub, and this weighed in at 17cwt less even than the Tiger Cub. Again it sold reasonably well in Scotland, though one unusual English customer was Manchester Corporation, which added to this unusual move by having them bodied by Seddon. Other customers included Venture of Consett and the Ulster Transport Authority, which took 57. Like other Albions it was also something of a success on the export market.

A bigger Victor was announced in 1959; this was aimed at the market dominated by the Bedford SB, for a 41-seat front-engined forward control lightweight coach.

While Albion's range was kept separate from that of Leyland — although several Leyland Titans and

Above:
The Nimbus was a small lightweight bus chassis; Halifax Joint Omnibus Committee had a batch of 10 in 1963 with attractive Weymann 31-seat bodywork. 258 squeezes through Heptonstall, where its diminutive dimensions were probably more appreciated than its diminutive four-cylinder engine, in 1964.
Philip Torcliff

Centre right:
The Nimbus was known as a bus, but also appeared with coach bodywork; this 29-seat Plaxton body makes for an attractive small coach. It operated for Maurice Watson Tours of Huntington, Yorkshire.
A. Hustwitt

Bottom right:
The Lowlander was a low-height version of the Leyland PD3. No attempt was made to lower the cab, resulting in a bizarre appearance more often than not. Alexander made no attempt to disguise this odd arrangement on its bodywork, which adorns this East Midland example.
Michael Fowler

Atlanteans for Glasgow carried Albion badging — Leyland used the Albion factory to produce a low-height version of the PD3, which was marketed as the Albion Lowlander. It was rather a late entrant to this market, in 1961, and appears to have been something of a knee-jerk reaction to the AEC Bridgemaster and Dennis Loline. Whilst it had a low chassis frame and dropped-centre rear axle the front end was pure PD3, leading to a rather bodged arrangement involving raised seats at the front upstairs to give the driver adequate headroom. Most were sold in Scotland, where 197 went to the Scottish Bus Group, but others sold to Ribble, East Midland, Yorkshire Woollen and Southend Corporation.

Albion's last home-market effort was the Viking, introduced in 1963 with a Leyland O.370 engine at the front opposite the entrance, and two years later the VK55 version had the same driveline but mounted in-line at the rear, principally for the Scottish Bus Group and for export. The Viking and similar Clydesdale continued for export until the 1980s, though latterly badged as Leylands.

Alexander

Walter Alexander was — and still is — well-known as a bus bodybuilder. However, it did have one dabble into a fully-integral vehicle in the 1970s. This was its S-series midibus, a 27-seater which entered production conveniently around the time Seddon stopped building the 4.236, often credited as being the first true midibus. The A-series was a more conventional large minibus design, however, rather than a scaled-down 'big bus'.

Alexander's main factory is at Falkirk, although it serves mainly the Irish market (both sides of the border) from its Alexander (Belfast) factory at Mallusk to the north of Belfast. This factory al tends to produce mini and midibuses, and was chos to build the integral S-series. It was based on the Fo A-series, which offered some potential for a 27-se bus but had rather a high frame, hence Alexande decision to build it in integral form with a lower flo level than Ford could offer. The prototype emerged November 1974 and did a demonstration round various operators. The 7m long body had de windows and a roof line not dissimilar to the Sedd though with a very utilitarian front end which did no favours. A more stylish front and rear we designed by Ogle for production models. They we based on the A0609 version of the A-series, with t Ford six-cylinder 3.6litre 87bhp diesel engine a offered a choice of Turner manual gearbox or Allis automatic.

Had it arrived 10 years later it would have sold li hot cakes, but the industry had only limited use small vehicles at this stage. Nevertheless it so tolerably well. The first were a batch of eight 2 seaters for West Midlands PTE at the end of 19 and one was shown at the Scottish Motor Show t year. Other early customers were Grampian a National Bus Company, which had small numbers Eastern Counties, Southdown and Hants & Dors Central SMT bought two in 1980 and took an earl demonstrator.

Below:
National Bus Company took a number of the Alexan S-type integral minibus, based on Ford A-series part Western National 3 began life with Southdown.
Martin Curtis

Atkinson

Ever since man first learned the noble art of putting diesel engines into buses there has been a great desire for those diesels to be manufactured by Gardner. The problem was that to develop a diesel engine was an expensive business so most manufacturers which built their own engines insisted on fitting those engines to their chassis to keep the volumes up. When it came to the new rash of underfloor-engined single-deckers after the war the clear leaders in the field were AEC and Leyland — who would fit only their own engines, though there were a few Gardner-engined AEC Regent V double-deckers. Bristol fitted Gardners in its underfloor-engined buses, but these were not available on the general market.

North Western Road Car Co had been a keen Bristol user until sales became limited to the state sector, and would have liked a Gardner-engined single-decker with conventional transmission. Thus nearby lorry manufacturer Atkinson, of Walton-le-Dale, Preston, introduced such a chassis, the Alpha PM745H with an underfloor Gardner 5HLW horizontal five-cylinder engine and five-speed constant-mesh gearbox. This was followed by a PM746H, which was similar but with the more powerful Gardner six-cylinder 6HLW and a lightweight PL744 with the four-cylinder 4HLW engine. North Western and Lancashire United were major customers, taking 19 and 40 respectively, but smaller operators also took small numbers while Venture of Consett amassed a fleet of 24.

In 1954 Atkinson branched out into double-deckers, offering two PD746 models, largely conventional half-cab, front-engined vehicles, available with either manual or semi-automatic transmission. In the event only one of the latter was built, for the Stalybridge, Hyde, Mossley & Dukinfield board (it is preserved in the Manchester Museum of Transport), which had bought two PL745 single-deckers the previous year and had another two in 1955 and three in 1959. Production largely fizzled out around 1955, though penny numbers were built in the following years culminating with three single-deckers with modern Marshalls bodywork for Sunderland in 1963, the first for more than four years.

There was also a lorry-derived 30ft front-engined single-deck chassis with the Gardner 4LW engine, the L644LW EXL, which was intended primarily for export, though Sunderland had two with Roe bodywork and Carruthers, Dumfries, had a 27ft 6in version with Plaxton bus bodywork.

Altogether Atkinson built 117 psv chassis for the UK between 1950 and 1963, 100 of them by the end of 1955.

Austin

Although Austin was a very large builder of light-weight commercial vehicles it was never a major force in the bus industry. Its main passenger model, built from 1947 to 1950 was the CX, which was very similar to Bedford's rather better-known OB, with a six-cylinder, 3.5litre (later increased to four-litre) petrol engine in a conventional bonnet ahead of the driver, styled in a similar fashion to the Bedford. Indeed the type was sometimes referred to as the 'Birmingham Bedford'. It was essentially a small coach model, suitable for vehicles of around 29 seats and found some popularity amongst coach operators.

There was also a forward-control version, the CXB, which Mann Egerton fitted with an attractive coach body, immediately identifying the vehicle as an Austin with a front grille similar to contemporary goods vehicles and even having some resemblance to that on the A30 car.

Later generations of Austin light vans, such as the J2, also appeared as the basis of minibuses, notably with bodywork by Martin Walter. The last Austin-badged psvs, also badged Morris, were the 440EA which was sold notably with 19-seat Ascough Clubman bodywork, built in Ireland, and the 550FG which formed the basis of a small, 24-seat coach from 1969, though by 1971 both were being sold a Leyland Redlines.

Above:
Coach versions of the Atkinson Alpha were rather more rare. This PM746H, new in 1955, had Plaxton bodywork for Bracewells (Feather Group) of Colne, an enthusiastic Atkinson user which bought nine in four years.

Left:
Austin often built coaches in association with Kenex, which built the body on this 1948 CXB. The grille was of a style fitted to a number of Austin vehicles, cars included, at this time.

Above:
The 1¹/2 ton Austin van was very common in the 1950s as the basis of Royal Mail vans, ice cream vans, laundry vans etc etc. This one, for Micro Coaches, Bristol, had an attractive Reading coach body and was built in 1956.

Below:
The 152 was also a very common type of vehicle in various guises. This version was the Omnicoach, with a 1,489cc, 42bhp petrol engine. 'Winking indicators and tubeless tyres are included in the standard specification; heater and radio are optional extras' says the Austin press release, dated 31 August 1960, which accompanied the photograph. The Omnicoach was available in 10-seat and 13-seat versions and formed the basis of the first postbuses.

BMMO

The Birmingham & Midland Motor Omnibus Co Ltd, better known as Midland Red, was remarkable amongst British bus operators in that it built most of its own buses. Prewar they were known as SOS, but after the war they were known as BMMO.

Its prewar designs had also been sold to other operators such as Northern General and Trent, but after the war it built buses in its Carlyle Road Works at Edgbaston in Birmingham solely for its own use. Though Midland Red at the time was the biggest company operator, running just short of 2,000 buses in the 1950s and 1960s, one might still have thought that the scope for development of buses on such a small scale was limited. In actual fact BMMO's products were quite remarkable for their innovation, successfully using techniques which would even today be considered avant-garde. Nor did the company take the easy option by using proprietary components; it even built its own diesel engines.

Its first postwar double-decker to enter production was largely conventional. This was the D5, which followed on from a prototype built during the war, the REDD (rear-entrance double-decker, as opposed to the FEDD forward-entrance double-deckers which had been built before the war), which was later redesignated D1. Both used BMMO's K-type eight-litre six-cylinder engine and constant-mesh gearbox. The first 100 D5s were built in 1949 and another 100, designated D5B, came the next year. They were bodied by Brush to a distinctive style, using four-bay

construction, and an innovation was the use of a full-width bonnet and concealed radiator.

The next BMMO double-decker was the D7, of which 350 were built between 1953 and 1957. The D7 was bodied by Metro-Cammell and had an altogether tidier, smoother appearance than the D5. In keeping with the spirit of the age they were rather lighter than the D5s, though mechanically similar, and had seven more seats.

However, the greatest innovation in the early postwar years was in single-deckers. Rather surprisingly Midland Red had been able to continue

development work during the war and converted four buses which had been built as rear-engined single-deckers to underfloor engine, using a horizontal version of the K-type engine. As a result it was able to get ahead of the field and introduce its mid-underfloor-engined S6 as early as 1946.

Of even greater interest was the S5 prototype, which used similar components but in an integral, chassisless form, certainly an innovation at that time. However, the development was put on the back burner for a time and production was concentrated on vehicles with separate chassis, the S8, an 8ft wide version of the S6, coming in 1948, and an updated S9 in 1949-50. One hundred of each were built, followed by 156 S10s, again broadly similar, and 44 S12s which were built to the new 30ft length, allowing

seating capacity to be increased to 44, in 1950-51. The S10s were later extended to the same size. Meanwhile parallel coach models were built, the main mechanical difference being the use of a five-speed overdrive gearbox, though with more stylish bodywork. Finally 99 S13s came in 1952, most of them dual-purpose.

The next major development was the S14. The prototype for this highly-innovative design was effectively the 100th S13, built in 1953. Mechanically it followed on from previous designs, with that horizontal K-series 8-litre engine, although a Hobbs automatic gearbox was fitted whereas production buses retained the four-speed constant-mesh unit. It was of integral construction with rubber suspension all round, independent at the front, and hydraulically-actuated disc brakes. It weighed in at under five tons unladen, remarkable for a bus of such technical innovation with a heavyweight driveline. As a result only single rear tyres were necessary.

The die was now cast for future BMMO production; integral construction, lightweight materials, independent front suspension and disc brakes were all to become hallmarks of the marque. The S14 was built from 1956 to 1958, during which time 219 entered service, along with 97 of the similar but more luxurious S15s, the last of which were built in 1962. But the most glamorous S14 spin-off was undoubtedly the C5 family of coaches, which included the impressive CM5 and CM5T motorway coaches. These legendary vehicles with possibly the most handsome styling of any BMMO product really captured the imagination by being ready for motorway work from the first day of the M1, and using a turbocharged version of the K-type engine and overdrive gearbox to reach reported speeds of 100mph. BMMO apparently had wanted something even more spectacular, and had tried to persuade the Ministry of Transport to relax the regulations to allow 45ft-long vehicles with 60 seats, and even converted an S8 to that length to press home the point. It was unsuccessful in this particular endeavour.

Subsequent BMMO models developed the same theme. Once regulations were relaxed to allow 36ft long vehicles the larger S16 was introduced in 1962, but shared the same mechanical components as the smaller S14 and S15, with which it compared unfavourably, so only 50 were built.

Meanwhile BMMO had introduced a new double-decker, the D9, in 1958. This employed similar techniques to the S14 and in many ways can be likened to the Routemaster, with its integral construction and independent suspension, though initially had disc brakes until these proved troublesome on a double-decker. A new 10.5litre version of the K-type engine had been developed for it, coupled to semi-automatic transmission. The other unusual feature was the set back front axle, though a traditional half-cab layout was retained, giving the D9 a unique appearance. In 1960 BMMO went one stage further with its D10 which, like single-deckers, put the engine on the side under the floor and had the entrance ahead of the front axle. However, to keep the floorline low the crankcase was at the nearside of the vehicle, with the cylinders inboard, under the gangway. Two were built, one with a second door and staircase at the rear. However, the underfloor-engined double-deck concept was then to lie fallow for more than 20 years. However, BMMO went on to build 344 D9s before production ended in 1965.

Later single-decker designs also used the 10.5litre engine and semi-automatic transmission, resulting in a new breed of 36ft motorway coach, the CM6, and various single-deck designs, the S17, which was essentially the S16 with a bigger engine and semi-automatic transmission, S21, S22 and S23 which used a similar body structure to the CM6, though with bus styling, and brought BMMO production to an end in 1970 when National Bus Company had taken over Midland Red. By now larger numbers of standard Daimler Fleetlines and Leyland Leopards were entering service and these were considered a more practical way forward, especially as it was becoming more difficult to find suitable craftsmen to build the vehicles. The S21-23 classes together numbered 14 vehicles.

Left:
Midland Red 3694, built in 1950, was the prototype BMMO S13. It was bodied by Brush and was one of the first 30ft vehicles in the fleet. The conductor stands back deferentially to allow his rural passengers to board in a rather idyllic 1950 scene.

Top:
The S14 and S15 were the first production integral BMMOs, which also featured rubber suspension and disc brakes. This is an S15, the more luxurious, dual purpose version.

Above:
The first 36ft BMMOs were the S16 type, which had the same mechanical units as the 30ft S14 and S15 and were thus rather underpowered. This one is seen in Bearwood.
Patrick Kingston

Left:
One of the later BMMO designs was the S22, of which one is seen in Coventry on the X94 to Wellington in January 1968.
T. W. Moore

Centre left:
One hundred D5s were built with Brush bodywork in 1949/50.

Below:
Stuck in rush-hour traffic in Coventry, with plenty of Coventry Transport Daimlers in the background, is a BMMO D7. Midland Red had 200 D7s, with Metro Cammell bodywork, in 1954-57.
T. W. Moore

Above:
BMMO's last double-decker to go into full production was the integrally-built D9; a 1966 example is seen in Leamington on a local service.
T. W. Moore

Right:
Possibly the most revolutionary BMMO double-deck design was the D10, which resembled the D9 but had an underfloor engine to give a front entrance. Only two were built (the other had an additional door and staircase at the rear, though was later rebuilt as a single-door bus) and they were the first successful underfloor-engined double-deck designs.
K. D. Jubb

Above:
A typical postwar Beadle integral. This one, for Bristol, had Morris Commercial running units, but the same body style appeared on a variety of different bases, including Sentinel.

Beadle

John C. Beadle (Coachbuilders) Ltd of Dartford was in the ascendancy for a fairly short period after the war. Its great stock-in-trade was taking components from prewar buses and building them into its own patented all-alloy integral construction as single-deck buses or coaches. It started with four 33-seat proto-types built between 1945 and 1947, using respectively Commer, Leyland Cub, Bedford and Dennis Ace components, with Gardner 4LK engines in the Leyland and Dennis. Its first order was for 24 Leyland Cubs for Lincolnshire Road Car, while 12 vehicles were built on Morris Commercial parts in 1949/50 for Bristol, Hants & Dorset, Western National, West Yorkshire and United. However, the majority used components from prewar Leyland Titan TD4/TD5 and Tiger TS7/TS8 or AEC Regents and Regals for major operators not very far from its home ground, such as Maidstone & District, East Kent and Southdown, with smaller numbers for operators such as East Yorkshire, Yorkshire Traction and Yorkshire Woollen. Not just secondhand parts were used; 50 new Bedford OBs were built into Beadle structures in 1948/49 for Tilling-group operators. Altogether it built around 400 buses in this way, in addition to conventional bodies on chassis.

Beadle began to adapt its integral structure in other ways as early as 1948, when it could lay claim to having the only underfloor, horizontal-engined vehicle at the 1948 Commercial Motor Show, quite an achievement when big guns such as Leyland and AEC were beavering away at similar designs. In this case its integral structure had been adapted to fit Sentinel (qv) running units, the first of 26 Beadle/Sentinel combinations to be built over the following years.

In 1954 Beadle introduced a new integral model, again with an underfloor engine. Unlike the main-stream manufacturers, which used horizontal versions of existing vertical engines Beadle used an engine which had been designed as a horizontal engine from the start, the Commer TS3 two-stroke. This remark-able unit, which became well-known in Commer lorries, had three cylinders, each with two horizon-tally-opposed cylinders, to produce a highly respectable 105bhp from only 3.26litres. A coach version, the OE Mk II, followed in 1956. Altogether Beadle built 141 such Commer-based vehicles until production ceased in 1957, for which Devon General, Southdown, Yorkshire Woollen, PMT and Smiths of Wigan were significant customers. Beadle also produced smaller models, the Canterbury coach and Thanet bus, which were sold under its own name but were in fact based on modified Karrier Bantam chassis, with the option of either Commer TS3 diesel or Rootes petrol engines.

Beadle is now known as a motor dealer in North Kent.

Bedford

As the British commercial vehicle arm of American automotive manufacturer General Motors, Luton-based Bedford had established itself in the prewar years as a competent manufacturer of small, light-weight, normal-control coaches. It began production in 1931 and was the only manufacturer entitled to build single-deckers during the war. It had launched its petrol-engined OB in 1939, a slightly larger version of the earlier WTB, with a new front end and usually bodied with a Duple body to a design which was to become very familiar after the war, albeit with a few alterations. The war quickly interrupted production, but it resumed as the Utility version, the OWB, in 1942, and more than 3,000 had been built by September 1945.

Postwar OB production began a month later, and the type quickly established itself as the standard lightweight coach, operated by thousands of small coach operators — though bus versions were also built. Typically it had Duple's Vista body, with 29 seats, of which the first appeared in March 1946, though there were plenty of other builders for it. The OB retained the semi-normal-control layout of its prewar predecessor, and also retained the 3.5litre petrol engine, which produced 72bhp but was usually known by its RAC rating as a 28hp unit. It was 24ft long and had a gross vehicle weight of 7tons 3cwt. Some bodybuilders, such as Yeates and Burlingham, converted chassis to forward-control. Production continued until 1950, when it was replaced by the larger and heavier forward-control SB, by which time 7,200 had been built for the home market, and several thousand more were exported.

Bedford also built a comparable range of goods vehicles, and to confuse matters a small number of OBs were built for non-psv use while some of the goods chassis, such as the OLAZ, were bodied as buses which were visually very similar to the OB.

Though production ended in 1950 many survived into the era of preservation and there has been something of a renaissance of the OB for continued service over the last decade or so.

If the OB had been the standard British independent coach during the late 1940s, the SB became the standard British coach for the next decade. It was a front-engined chassis but of larger dimensions than the OB and was forward control. When introduced in 1950 it was intended as a 33-seater, but grew to the typical independent operator's 41-seater by 1956. It was also offered with a petrol engine, a 4.9litre unit of similar design to the OB's 3.5litre engine, though a diesel version with a 5.5litre Perkins R6, the SBO (O for oil engine) was introduced in 1953. The Perkins was later replaced by Bedford's own 330. The SB had a number of rivals, such as the Ford Thames, Commer Avenger and later the Albion Viking, but remained Bedford's sole passenger model for the 1950s and was by far the most popular vehicle of its genre, as a cheap, lightweight, simple and very effective chassis suitable for most small coach operators' use. It was still available, as the NJM, up to the end of Bedford production in 1986, though in latter years it was more likely to be specified for military use than for passenger work. It sold in excess of 50,000 units, including export to very many territories.

Below:
Contrasting Bedfords in the Cedar Coaches fleet, also based in Bedford. Nearer the camera is a Plaxton Paramount-bodied YNT, and next to it a classic OB, a type still able to give sterling service.
Kevin Lane

Bedford was to remain faithful to the front-engine concept with its next generation, introduced from 1962. In that year it returned to the 29-seat concept with its VAS, though now in forward-control form, as a sort of diminutive SB. It too was available with a choice of petrol or diesel engines and remained in Bedford's catalogue to the end. It was never to prove as popular as the SB, being rather more specialist, but found a rôle as a useful vehicle for feeder work for tour operators, welfare work, airline crew work and the like. It too remained in production to the end, as the PJK.

The next year Bedford produced its first vehicle suitable for 36ft coaches, the VAL, and this adopted an imaginative approach. Rather than developing axles specifically for a 36ft coach Bedford, which relied heavily on truck components in its psv range, instead used three lighter-weight axles from its truck range, in a 'Chinese six', or twin steer, set up, with diminutive wheels and, unusually at that time, power steering. The engine was mounted at the front, though ahead of the axles which were set back to allow a front entrance. At first the 6.54litre Leyland 400 was standard, although a new Bedford diesel, the 7.6litre 466, was introduced in the VAL70 in 1966. Duple, which since the days of the OB, had been most readily identified as the 'standard' coachbuilder on Bedford chassis, introduced a stylish new body for it, the Vega Major, which created a very striking-looking coach, though the Plaxton Panorama body was also made available, and one or two continental designs from builders such as Van Hool and Caetano were to appear on it in later years. Its small wheels gave a good ride for coach use, but also made a low

floor available for buses, and a few operators took VAL buses, notably North Western which had a distinctive Strachans body built, specially contoured to fit under a low bridge. It remained in production until 1972.

The third model introduced in the 1960s was the VAM, a 33ft-long two-axle vehicle, suitable for 45-seat coach bodies but also used as a service bus by numerous operators, including major company operators which were not readily associated with light-weights. Among these were some of the nationalised Tilling undertakings, when no suitable Bristol model was available for their requirements, and the likes of Western National even had them with an ECW body similar to that built for the Bristol MW. It was intro-duced as the VAM5, with Bedford's 5.4litre 330 diesel, but later variants, like the VAL, were the VAM14 with the Leyland O.400 and the VAM70 with Bedford's 7.6litre 466.

Bedford was still the standard choice for light-weight vehicles, especially amongst the independent sector, though Ford was emerging as an increasingly strong competitor with its R192, which was very similar in concept and size to the VAM, and bigger R226.

The VAM was superseded in 1970 with the start of a new Bedford range. The YRQ used very similar components to the VAM, but arranged with the engine under the floor amidships. Hitherto the stan-dard arrangement of underfloor engines was to use horizontal units, but Bedford managed to fit its 466 engine in vertically. Two years later the VAL was superseded by a 36ft version of the YRQ, the YRT, which had heavier components all round, shared with the 16-ton KM lorry range. Specification upgrades led to the largely similar YMQ and YMT, and a short-ened version of the YMQ, the YMQS, was also made available.

There was something of a diversion from Bedford's mainstream production at the end of the 1970s. At the

1978 Motor Show it unveiled a highly-promising small bus, the JJL. This had a vertical 330 engine mounted transversely at the rear, driving though an Allison automatic gearbox and had a very stylish 27-seat body built by Marshall though developed in Bedford's own design studio. Unfortunately it never reached production; only four were built which saw service with a number of municipal operators, notably Maidstone and Brighton before being scattered amongst various independent operators. Unusually for such a rare type they achieved pretty well a full service life. Bedford's parent company foresaw little market for it and decided not to go into production. Given the runaway success of the Dennis Dart, a very similar design in many respects, it is possible that GM made the wrong decision, though perhaps the JJL was developed before its time had come. Another great British might-have-been . . .

During the 1980s the demands of coach operators were increasing; vehicles were required to work harder and run at high speeds over very high mileage, and the traditional lightweight began to be eclipsed by more sophisticated models, many from overseas. Bedford introduced turbocharging across the range in 1982, both to increase power outputs and to reduce emissions, and even the lowly NJM, as the SB had become, was available with turbocharging towards the end of its life — though in the same year as turbocharging was introduced Blue Coach Tours of St Helier, Jersey, was still buying 7ft 6in wide SBs with petrol engines. The YMT gave way to the

turbocharged YNT, which also boasted the six-speed ZF gearbox beloved of the heavyweights, rather than the five-speed Turner with which Bedford had latterly been associated. However, Bedford was still lacking a 12m chassis (though specialist conversions of the YNT were available), and this came in 1984 with the full 16-tonne, air-sprung YNV, the first Bedford psv to gain a name — Venturer. This had a 205bhp 8.2litre Blue Series turbocharged engine — still mounted vertically amidships, under the floor — and a ZF gearbox. It was a competent coach, with many heavyweight virtues yet still with a light weight and low cost, but fashion had dictated that Bedford was now a spent force, at least in the UK. The thousands of sales the company could record in a good year were down to a couple of hundred or so by the mid-1980s. Then General Motors tried to buy the struggling Leyland group from the Government during 1986 and was turned down on strategic grounds. The American giant decided that Bedford was too small to survive in its own right, and closed it down; production of buses and coaches ceased in 1986. The Bedford range passed to AWD, which never reintroduced psv chassis, and then to Marshall of Cambridge, along with the rights to use the Bedford name.

Bristol

The postwar history of Bristol Commercial Vehicles is an unusual one, in that of all manufacturers it was affected the most by the politics of the times. Like some other manufacturers, such as BMMO and AEC, its origins were in supplying vehicles to the operator which owned it, though its products quickly became

much more widespread than simply the Bristol Tramways Co, more often then not in conjunction with the bodybuilding subsidiary of another fellow Tilling group company, Eastern Counties, which later became a separate entity as Eastern Coach Works (ECW).

In 1937 it had launched a new range, the K double-decker and L single-decker, entirely conventional front-engined half-cab chassis with a Gardner 5LW engine and crash gearbox. Production of Ks restarted during the war, though with AEC engines, and postwar versions of both were offered in 1946, with a lowered radiator and bonnet line. Gardner 5LW, 6LW, AEC or Bristol's own AVW six-cylinder engines were available with four-speed or five-speed overdrive gearboxes. However, under the 1947 Transport Act various bus operators, including Bristol with its Motor Constructional Works, passed into state ownership, and Bristol was restricted to selling only within the state sector, though outstanding orders to other sectors could be completed. In some ways having a single, tied customer, tended to stifle development, and compared with the likes of Leyland and AEC Bristols tended to lack refinement and, in certain respects, engineering innovation. On the other hand their rugged simplicity, unstoppable reliability and excellent fuel consumption were denied to operators in other sectors who had learned to appreciate their charms.

The lack of technical innovation tended to be in the driveline department; Bristol drivers had to wrestle with crash gearboxes long after other manufacturers had made life easier. However, in other respects they were ahead of the field. The company operators of the nationalised Transport Holding Company tended to operate more in rural areas and as a such had a wide-

Above left:
A very promising Bedford design, which never got into full production, was the JJL, with a stylish Marshall-built body. They worked for a time at Brighton on the town centre shuttle service using an unusual livery in shades of orange.

Above:
A classic Bristol line-up at Eastern National's Braintree garage in 1971. Dual-purpose and bus versions of the MW flank an FLF-type Lodekka.
J. Rickard

Right:
A North Western Bristol L5G braves the snow in Buxton in February 1963.
A. Moyes

spread requirement for lowbridge double-deckers, with the awkward sunken gangway arrangement upstairs. Bristol was the first to address this problem, with its lowheight Lodekka. As introduced in 1949 twin prop shafts were used to take the drive to separate double-reduction differentials, using gears to bring the drive up from the low propshaft level to hub level and allowing thereby a dropped-centre axle. Production buses, which went into service from 1954, had a simpler arrangement with just one prop shaft. This new model, the LD, replaced the K-series, which had grown into the larger KS and wider KSW. Meanwhile the replacement for the L, which had like-

Top:
An early LD-type Bristol Lodekka of United at Bishop Auckland in 1959. Later LDs had a shorter radiator grille.
M. A. Sutcliffe

Above:
For rural use Bristol developed the diminutive SC4LK front-engined chassis. It was ideal for Crosville's operations in the more rural parts of North Wales, typified by this view of SSG606 near Henfryn in the Clwyd Valley in 1966.
A. Moyes

wise developed into the larger LL and LWL, was the LS, an underfloor-engined model offering a choice of Gardner 5HLW or 6HLW engines and a horizontal version of the Bristol unit, with integral bodywork by ECW, though some for the Scottish Bus Group were bodied by Alexander.

The LS was later replaced by the MW, with a separate chassis, though this dropped the Bristol engine option, while the very successful Lodekka was developed with a longer LDL version, and then from 1959 a new range with flat floors was introduced, the FS, with longer FL and forward-entrance FSF and FLF models. The Lodekka remained in production until

1968, by which time over 5,000 had been built. From 1956 onwards Dennis had been licensed to produce the Lodekka for outside customers as the Loline.

Bristol also built small numbers of smaller buses; the SC4LK was a small front-engined single-decker, in the mould of the Bedford SB and indeed using axles supplied by Bedford, though with a Gardner 4LK engine. This was replaced with a small underfloor-engined bus, the SU, which used a four-cylinder horizontal Albion engine.

Another innovation from Bristol in 1962 was the introduction of a single-deck chassis with the engine horizontally at the rear, the RE. This was available in two lengths and two frame heights, the high version giving space side luggage lockers for coach work. It was the first of a new wave of rear-engined single-deckers, and was also the most successful. The use of a front radiator helped improve weight distribution as well as cooling (indeed with several feet of piping and a cool-running Gardner engine cooling could be too good), while the engine was mounted closer to the rear axle than on other designs, with the Lodekka dropped-centre axle allowing a prop shaft to run over

Left:
The MW was the standard underfloor engined Bristol single-decker for the late 1950s/early 1960s. Scottish Omnibuses used this fleet of MW coaches to transport 1,000 wedding guests for Lord Bruce's wedding in Edinburgh; each carried a shield in Bruce tartan.

Above:
Seen leaving Basildon on the famous 151 Southend-London (Wood Green) service is a semi-automatic Bristol FLF6G of Eastern National.
W. T. Cansick

Left:
Bristol produced the most successful of the new-generation rear-engined single-deckers in the 1960s with its RE model. Seen in Wells in 1972 is a Bristol Omnibus one with the usual ECW bodywork in the reversed livery then used by Bristol for one-man operated services.
P. W. Robinson

Below left:
In 1965 Bristol products were once again available on the open-market. The first model sold to customers outside the THC was the RE, which was particularly popular with municipalities such as Colchester.
Kevin Lane

Above right:
Bristol introduced the lightweight underfloor-engined Bristol LH in 1968. It was available in various different lengths; the shortest was the LHS, which continued to be available primarily as a small coach chassis after the rest of the range was deleted. London Country had a few ECW-bodied LHSs.
Kevin Lane

Right:
National Bus Company standardised on the Bristol VRT for double-deck use. These two were in the PMT fleet; the one nearer the camera came from National Welsh.
Kevin Lane

the top of the axle to a gearbox mounted within the wheelbase. This arrangement put less strain on the vehicle's structure than other designs with all mechanical components in the rear overhang, and the remote mounting of the major components made for better heat dissipation. In true Bristol fashion a rather awkward manual gearbox was standard, though later the company was to bow to the inevitable and fit a semi-automatic unit, which improved the driver's lot no end.

Under THC ownership Bristol was set up as a separate manufacturing company, Bristol Commercial

Vehicles, in 1955. Then in 1965 Leyland took a 25% share in Bristol, allowing it to be opened up to other customers again, and the RE was made available with Leyland engines. It quickly sold to operators outside the nationalised sector.

Bristol was very late developing rear-engined double-deckers compared with Leyland and Daimler. Its first efforts appeared in 1966, unlike the other two using an in-line vertical engine in the rear offside corner. It was intended as a whole family of double- and single-deck vehicles, though after a couple of prototypes it was hurriedly re-engineered as the VRT, with the engine mounted transversely at the rear. The longitudinally-engined VRL remained on the stocks, but was specified only by one British operator, Ribble, with Leyland O.680 engines as a rather splendid 36ft motorway coach. Others were sold as buses to South Africa.

The National Bus Company was formed in 1969, and took over 50% of Bristol. Leyland increased its shareholding to become an equal partner with NBC, which adopted the VRT as its standard double-decker. Early versions were not up to Bristol's usual standard for reliability, but later Series 2 and Series 3 models improved things somewhat. It clocked up sales of 4,474 before being superseded by the Leyland Olympian in 1982, though its success was largely due to National Bus Company. Again Gardner engines were standard, though later buses had the option of Leyland's 500-series fixed-head unit, and a few were built with Leyland O.680s when Gardners were difficult to come by.

At about the same time as the VRT was introduced Bristol announced a new single-decker, the light-weight LH. This was available in three lengths, the 9m LHS, 10m LH and 11m LHL, with mid-mounted Leyland 400 or Perkins engines. Now that the ban on outside sales was lifted it sold reasonably well as a coach to private-sector operators which might otherwise have bought Bedfords, though as a bus it received support from the National Bus Company and London Transport in particular.

Leyland and National Bus Company set up a joint Bus Manufacturers Holdings company in 1975, which controlled Bristol, ECW and Leyland National, until NBC decided it was losing too much money and passed its shareholding to Leyland in 1982. Leyland had begun production of its Olympian at Bristol in 1981, ending VRT production at the same time. Meanwhile production of the RE continued for Northern Ireland and New Zealand, the last for Ulsterbus being built in 1982 despite the fact that home market customers had been refused REs since 1975, in favour of the Leyland National. Bristol built 4,629 REs.

Various factors conspired to depress the bus market during the 1980s; privatisation, deregulation and the phasing-out of bus grant all came about in the early years of the 1980s, and Leyland, anxious to cut surplus capacity, quickly decided to close Bristol, of which it had just gained control. Just over 1,000 Olympians were built there before the factory closed in September 1983.

Cannon

Cannon is a small, family-owned engineering company based in Sion Mills, near Strabane in Co Tyrone, just inside the Northern Ireland border. It had made itself a useful business refurbishing trucks, and branched into psvs in 1998, spotting some little niches in the market for small, no-nonsense buses.

It was at about the time when the whole market was going for low-floor vehicles, but Cannon knew that not everyone would find the modern technology appropriate. It introduced two models to offer operators an alternative, including the Softline, which took advantage of some of the problems the Mercedes-Benz Vario was having in the minibus market. Unlike the Vario, which is derived from a van and comes as a chassis cowl for bus use, the Softline is a purpose-built, front-engined, bonneted midi chassis, powered by a 133bhp Cummins four-cylinder B-series engine driving through a ZF five-speed manual gearbox or Allison automatic. It has air-over-hydraulic disc brakes and Albion axles. Cannon's other high-floor chassis is the Hiline, which is almost identical to the short-lived Leyland Swift, with a six-cylinder Cummins B-series mounted vertically under the floor.

Neither model has sold in huge numbers, but the Hiline has found a niche in the Channel Islands, one place where the Swift also found a home. The Hiline offers 160 or 180bhp and a ZF five- or six-speed manual gearbox or Allison automatic. The first two went to Pioneer on Jersey. Both chassis are offered in conjunction with bodywork by Leicester Carriage Builders, which builds the Islander dual-purpose body on the Hiline and the Nemesis on the Softline, and are finding a niche in the welfare market.

A new chassis was unveiled at Coach & Bus '99, the Low Line. It is a 9.5m low-floor chassis powered by a rear-mounted four-cylinder Cummins B-series engine, in 170bhp Euro 3 form, though a version with a longer overhang and a six-cylinder engine is promised.

By the end of 1999 Cannon had built or received orders for 26 chassis in total.

Commer

Luton-based Commer was part of the Rootes Group, which took it over along with Humber in 1928. Its first postwar chassis was the Commando, which was in similar vein to the Bedford OB, though slightly bigger. It was in production from 1946 to 1949, during which time some 1,300 were built, with Commer's own four-litre petrol engine or the Perkins P6 diesel. It was popular for military use, especially with the Royal Air Force, though psvs were also built.

Left:
Also at Expocoach '98 was this Cannon Softline, with Leicester Carriage Builders Nemesis bodywork.

Above:
An early Commer Avenger coach with the same style of front as fitted to contemporary Commer lorries. Built in 1949 it was one of a batch of four with Harrington 21-seat bodywork for Motorways (Overseas) of London SW1.

Right:
From 1954 Commer offered its new TS3 two-stroke diesel in the Avenger III. This early example has a Duple butterfly-fronted body of the type more readily associated with Bedford SB.

Below:
The Commer Avenger chassis, with the low-mounted TS3 diesel engine which avoided engine intrusion into the saloon.

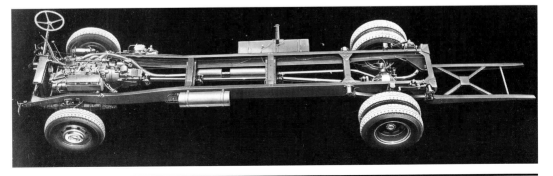

Quite a number had unusual one-and-a-half-deck observation-style bodywork, often for use by airlines for transfer work.

Commer was another manufacturer in the vanguard of underfloor-engined buses, though in a rather different vein from other manufacturers. Whereas the likes of AEC and Leyland were developing high-capacity single-deckers with the engine mounted amidships under the floor Commer was more interested in the coach market with the underfloor engine at the front, with a conventionally-positioned front axle. Here the aim was to rid the coach of engine intrusion. Like many manufacturers its new model was ready for the 1948 Commercial Motor Show; the Avenger was ahead of the pack of lightweight coach models in being forward control, thanks to the under-floor engine. The engine was Commer's own six-cylinder, 109bhp overhead valve unit. It was not a true horizontal unit, but the cylinders were set at 66° from vertical, a solution favoured much later by Ford and Scania as a way of minimising engine intrusion without going to the expense of developing a true horizontal unit. Many of the early Avenger Is featured the same frontal styling as Commer's contemporary truck range, which also used the underfloor engine.

The Avenger is not often considered a mainstream chassis, yet almost 1,000 Avenger Is were built before the larger Avenger II was introduced in response to the Bedford SB, which now took the lion's share of the market; thereafter Commer sales fell. Most of the sales were to small independents, though BOAC took sizeable numbers and many were exported.

In 1954 Commer offered its new TS3 diesel engine in the Avenger III. The TS3 is probably Commer's best-known achievement, though the engine had been developed by Tilling-Stevens which became part of the Rootes Group, of which Commer was a part, in 1953. The TS3 was a remarkable unit, a tiny, 3.26litre three-cylinder two stroke with supercharging and horizontally-opposed pistons, which despite its size was capable of producing 90bhp, and was later uprated to 105bhp. The sound effects were perhaps its most memorable feature! With its small dimensions and horizontal cylinders it was a natural for the Avenger, and was also supplied to Beadle and Harrington for their own integral designs (qv). However, the bus industry was never too adventurous with technology, and preferred more conventional engines with higher torque ratings, and the Avenger became an also-ran to the Bedford SB. Production of what had become the Avenger IV finished in 1964, by which time volumes had become very small indeed. Nonetheless sizeable batches were delivered to Southdown in particular, including 15 with Burlingham Seagull and 15 with Harrington body-work.

There were to be other Commer psvs, though; the 1500-series van was reasonably popular as a minibus in the 1960s — Crosville even took a pair in 1964 — and gained immortality as the archetypal postbus. It was rebadged Dodge (qv) in 1976 following the takeover of the Rootes Group by Chrysler three years earlier.

Crossley

It is perhaps a shame that Crossley Motors had a certain amount of difficulty translating its engineering innovation into production excellence. Crossley was well-known for its innovation, both in its bus and its car designs before the war. Unfortunately it was let down by a reputation for poor reliability and engine design.

The company had been based in Gorton in Manchester, though its factory was damaged during the war and postwar production began in a new factory at Errwood Park, just in Stockport. During the war it had developed a new double-decker, the DD42, and this was to be its mainstay model in the postwar years, along with a single-deck equivalent, the SD42. Crossley had been a major supplier to Manchester Corporation, which had evaluated the prototype DD42 in service. It was a largely conventional half-cab design, of which the most notable visual feature was a very low bonnet line, giving excellent visibility for the driver. Beneath the surface though was a new Crossley oil engine, the HOE7, which was to be the standard power unit for its postwar buses, whereas units such as the Gardner 5LW had also been available in prewar models, and it was coupled to a Brockhouse Turbo Transmitter torque-convertor transmission rather than a conventional gearbox.

Production buses turned out rather differently; constant mesh and later synchromesh gearboxes were considered in most cases a better bet than the unusual

Left:
Reading was quite a keen operator of Crossley DD42s; this one had lowbridge bodywork.

Below:
Disguising its Crossley origins well is this 1950 DD42 for Birmingham, with 'new look' front.

Right:
A CVE Omni owned by Kent County Council and operated by East Surrey around Edenbridge. Note the kneeling rear suspension to enable wheelchairs to be loaded at the rear.

Brockhouse unit, and whilst the prototype engine had acquitted itself very well last-minute redesign of the cylinder head was to strangulate the engine's air flow, leading to poor performance and a tendency to smoke. Crossley historian Mike Eyre attributes the head redesign to an reluctance to pay licence fees to Swiss manufacturer Saurer on whose patents the original head was designed. That reluctance may have led to the demise of the company. In 1948 it sold out to AEC, which bought Maudslay at the same time, to create ACV (Associated Commercial Vehicles).

Crossley DD42s tended to be a municipal bus; there were exceptions, but most turned up with municipal operators, more often than not with Crossley's own bodywork. The two biggest customers were Manchester, which had 301 postwar (plus the 1944 prototype) and Birmingham, which had 270, with its own style of bodywork. Birmingham's had the later downdraught version of the engine, with a revised cylinder head with more straightforward air intake arrangements, which overcame most of the earlier shortcomings of the engine. The last 100 delivered to Birmingham unusually had Birmingham's 'new look' front, with concealed radiator and wide bonnet.

However, Crossley's biggest triumph was a huge export order for Holland, to help re-equip the country's bus fleet after the war. Most of the 1,175 for Holland were SD42s with a supercharged, 150bhp version of the Crossley's engine, though 250 were tractor units to haul passenger semi-trailers.

When production ended of genuine Crossleys AEC built a small number of buses under the Crossley name, largely to gain extra stand space at Commercial Motor Shows but also to suit local pride; Darwen

Corporation for instance had a batch of Regent Vs with Crossley rather than AEC badges, showing Lancastrian solidarity (even if Crossley had ended its days just in Cheshire). The original Bridgemaster model was also developed at Crossley, which continued building bodywork until 1958, though it used AEC components and was later built at Park Royal on AEC subframes.

CVE/Omnicoach

City Vehicle Engineering set up production of an unusual minibus design at former railway engineering premises at Shildon, Darlington, in 1988. This was at the height of the 'minibus revolution', though when some of the shortcomings of van-based designs were becoming apparent. Its Omni was a licence-built version of an Austrian Steyr-Puch design, which used front-wheel drive in order to give a step-free entrance and low floor. Steyr's design was a halfcab, though CVE decided not to go back to that style once beloved of British builders, so its Omni had a slightly more conventional appearance than the Steyr — even if it was still a striking design. It was re-engineered for the British market with a Land Rover diesel engine, though other units became available, such as the Perkins Phaser.

The Omni's low-floor credentials meant it sold rather better to the welfare sector than it did to psv operators, though a few entered service in the psv sector for specialist applications. CVE went out of business in 1990, but the Omni design passed to a new builder, Omnicoach, set up the following year. It now used a Mazda turbocharged diesel engine, and a longer, three-axle version was also developed.

Daimler

Daimler boasted a fine reputation for the refinement and quality of its cars, and this extended to its buses. Early on it had taken to using fluid transmission, with a preselector gearbox, which not only made life easier for the driver, it gave rise to one of the most characteristic features of Daimler's vehicles, a delightfully melodious transmission. Daimler also used very effective flexible engine mounts to give its buses a smoothness which few could match.

Based in Coventry, Daimler restarted bus production in Wolverhampton during the war and afterwards introduced its Coventry-built Victory series, better known by its type designation which changed according to the engine specified. Daimler offered a choice of engines; its own CD6 in the CVD6, AEC in the CVA6 and Gardner 5LW or 6LW in the CVG5 and CVG6. Another Daimler characteristic on all its vehicles, buses included, was the fluted radiator top. The CV was available as a single-decker or double-decker, and in single-deck form was popular for coach use. Many major municipalities took Daimlers, the most common variant being the CVG6, and Birmingham specified its 'new look' concealed radiator from 1950, later adopted as standard by Daimler. The last traditional exposed radiator chassis was built in 1953, and the fluted radiator top disappeared, though a stylised version adorned the grille of some of the 'new look' examples. Manchester then specified a narrower bonnet with the headlights separate in 1957, and this too was adopted as standard.

At around the same time 30ft models became available, with semi-automatic transmission as an option to preselective, and a David Brown synchromesh gearbox was also offered, the designation, with Gardner 6LW engine, becoming CSG6.

Daimler was sold by its BSA parent to Jaguar in 1960, and the following year Jaguar also took over Guy, whose constant-mesh gearbox replaced the David Brown unit in manual gearbox versions, as CCG5 or CCG6. Home production ended in 1968, although 34ft long versions were built for Hong Kong until 1971. Some 11,000 had been built.

An interesting diversion was the CD650 introduced in 1948. This was a rather more sophisticated beast altogether, with power-hydraulic systems for the brakes, preselector gearbox and to give power steering. Power was provided in abundance by a new 10.5-litre (650cu in) Daimler engine, for which a wider version of Daimler's standard radiator was supplied, giving an impressive appearance for an impressive bus. The notoriously conservative British bus industry did not take to it; only a few were built, mainly for Derbyshire independent Blue Bus and Halifax Corporation. However, it did sell slightly better as an export single-decker.

The same engine was used in horizontal form in Daimler's next single-deck design, the Freeline, which began life in 1951. It used a five-speed preselective gearbox, and there was an option of Gardner 6HLW engine. Again it was much more successful as an export chassis than a home-market one, though around 70 were built as coaches for UK use, with another 20

Left:
Salford City Transport took a large batch of MCW-bodied Daimler CVG6s in 1951, and needed no more new buses for about 10 years. They had an unusual short version of the standard Daimler exposed radiator. Also unusual is 437's reversed livery.
M. A. Sutcliffe

Above:
Manchester was also a keen Daimler user; for most of the 1950s and 1960s it dual-sourced between Leyland and Daimler. In 1954/55 it took 70 rather elegant MCW-bodied CVG6s, of which two are seen in Piccadilly when new.

Left:
With the later style of front is Huddersfield 431, a 1964 Roe-bodied CVG6LX-30, a type bought by Huddersfield for trolleybus replacement. It is seen in Bradford soon after the formation of West Yorkshire PTE; although the Daimler shows no evidence of PTE ownership the Bradford AEC Regent and Daimler Fleetline behind carry the PTE's new livery.
Kevin Lane

Below left:
Sunderland used a distinctive style of Roe bodywork on a batch of nine Daimler Fleetlines in 1963.
M. A. Sutcliffe

185

Top left:
Alexander brought a new style to rear-engined double-deckers in the early-1960s, as shown on this 1965 Fleetline of North Western, seen at Lower Mosley Street bus station, Manchester.

Top right:
The Fleetline was intended for double-deck use, but a single-deck version was also made available. This rather neat Roe-bodied bus was new to Halifax in 1967. *L. J. Wright*

Above:
West Midlands PTE standardised on Daimler Fleetlines, a type chosen by most of its constituent operators. An MCW-bodied Fleetline picks up in central Birmingham. *Kevin Lane*

Right:
Daimler's purpose-built rear-engined single-deck chassis was the Roadliner, which looked highly impressive when bodied by Marshall for PMT, the biggest UK user of the type. Reliability was sadly less impressive.

or so buses. However, well over 500 were exported.

Daimler turned its attentions to rear-engined chassis in the 1960s. The first was the Fleetline, a transverse rear-engined double-decker introduced in 1960. This broadly resembled Leyland's Atlantean, which went into production two years earlier, though with the important difference that a dropped-centre rear axle was used to give an overall low height. An ingenious semi-automatic gearbox was developed for it, in which the drive passed back through the gearbox through a hollow shaft running through the centre of the gearbox, to give a compact driveline. Daimler engines were to be offered, but the more popular Gardner 6LX became the standard unit, with the 6LXB offered from 1969.

Rather less successful was the single-deck Roadliner. This 36ft rear-engined chassis began with a horizontal Daimler CD6 unit, unusually mounted transversely, using otherwise the same driveline as the Fleetline. However, production buses used a simpler, in-line driveline and straight rear axle, with a Cummins V6 engine chosen for its compact dimensions. However, this proved a highly unsuccessful unit in this application, and a later move to a Perkins V8 did little to improve the model's fortunes, neither did a last-ditch attempt to fit the AEC-built Leyland 800-series 13.1litre V8. It had air or rubber suspension, and made an impressive coach chassis, with a

power output of 192bhp from its fast-revving Cummins, and had the virtue of a low, step-free entrance for bus use. Fewer than 200 were built for the UK market, and a single-deck version of the Fleetline proved rather more popular.

The Fleetline was altogether a very popular chassis, and unlike previous Daimler models sold strongly to company operators as well as municipalities, helped by the lack of a rear-engined double-decker from AEC. London Transport also standardised on the Fleetline for rear-engined deliveries, and its inability to adapt to rear-engined types brought something of a smear to the Fleetline's reputation.

Jaguar had merged with the British Motor Corporation (BMC) in December 1966, to form British Motor Holdings (BMH), which merged again with Leyland in May 1968 to form British Leyland, thereby bringing Daimler and Guy into common ownership with Leyland, AEC and Bristol. As a result Leyland O.680 engines became available in the Fleetline from 1970. However, in 1973 Leyland decided to move Fleetline production from Coventry to its own factory, after 7,224 Daimler Fleetlines had been built. Another 1,500 Daimler Fleetlines were built by Leyland, before the name was changed to the Leyland Fleetline at the end of 1974. Production continued until 1980, by which time almost 11,750 Fleetlines had been built.

Dennis

For the first 90 or so years of its 105-year history, Dennis, based in Guildford, Surrey, was really one of the 'also-rans' of the bus industry. It was never an insignificant manufacturer — but then it wasn't all that significant either! At one time it produced so many short runs of odd models that it was considered that anything suggesting a production line was frowned upon at Guildford. That may be an overstatement of the case, but Dennis always made a great play of being flexible in its offerings.

For a period the company even came out of bus manufacture altogether; few buses were built after 1965 and bus production ground to a halt for 10 years from 1967. What is remarkable indeed is the fact that Dennis is not only one of the most significant players in the British bus market as we enter the new century — achieving overall leadership of the British market in 1999 by knocking Volvo from its perch — but is also now the only British-owned manufacturer, having outlasted many much more significant bus manufacturers, not least the mighty Leyland and AEC.

A protracted battle over Dennis's ownership came to an end in October 1998. The company had worked very closely on a number of models with Plaxton, and a quiet merger with Plaxton's parent, Henlys, seemed a logical next step in a bus-manufacturing world which was becoming increasingly globalised. However, Mayflower, owners of Alexander, launched a counter-offer and eventually won the day; as a result, future development is likely to involve Alexander rather more closely. Indeed first fruits of this are collaboration with Thomas Built in the

USA, which is to build Alexander-bodied Dennis Darts as complete vehicles under its own name, to give a light-weight, fuel-efficient, low-floor design in North America, to compete with more locally-sourced heavyweights.

Returning to earlier times, Dennis's main postwar models were the Lance double-decker and Lancet single-decker. These were basically conventional half-cab types with front engines and manual gearboxes, though with an ingenious preselective overdrive on the Lancet. There was a choice of Gardner engine or Dennis's own 7.6litre O.6. The Lance K2 had the Gardner engine, while the K3 had Dennis's engine and the K4, built for Dennis's local operator Aldershot & District from 1954, had the Gardner 5LW and 'new-look' front.

While other manufacturers used identical bonnets and radiators on both single- and double-deck models, the Lance and Lancet had quite different styles. Most Lancets were built as coaches for independent operators, but Aldershot & District, Yorkshire Traction, East Kent and Merthyr Tydfil were other major operators of the original postwar J3 type, which was also available in full-front form as the J3A. The later 30ft version was the J10 series.

Unusually for a manufacturer of heavyweight conventional chassis, Dennis also offered a lighter-weight, normal-control bus, the Falcon, with a choice of Dennis petrol or diesel engine or the Gardner 4LK. Again, larger operators included East Kent and Aldershot & District. A full-front forward-control version was also built in small numbers.

Dennis joined the underfloor-engine bandwagon in 1950, with its sophisticated Dominant model, which featured a horizontal version of the O.6 engine, available with a turbocharger and Hobbs automatic transmission. However, Dennis introduced a rather simpler — and lighter — underfloor-engined Lancet in 1952, and this proved rather more successful in both coach and bus forms. Following the trend to yet lighter weight, as demonstrated by the Leyland Tiger Cub and AEC Reliance, Dennis introduced the lightweight Pelican in

Below:
A 30ft long Dennis Lancet III with full-front Gurney Nutting 39-seat bodywork of Major's Coaches, Worksop.

1956, which used some Falcon components, including a horizontal version of the five-litre Dennis engine. Only one was completed, but gave good service.

Rather more successful than other Dennis postwar designs was the Loline double-decker, which was a licence-built version of the Bristol Lodekka. It was first shown at the 1956 Commercial Motor Show, in 30ft form; most Lolines were to this length. It was available with a variety of engines, including Gardner 6LW, 6LX, Leyland O.600 and, primarily to suit City of Oxford Motor Services, a loyal AEC user, the AEC AV470. A forward-entrance Loline II came in 1958, and, as the F-series Lodekka included various improvements such as a flatter floor and improved frontal appearance, similar improvements to the Dennis resulted in the Loline III in 1960 — though the new version had more Dennis content than the earlier models. Most Loline IIIs were 30ft long and forward-entrance, coinciding with the FLF version of the Lodekka, though the first two, for Leigh, had rear-entrance bodywork. The last were built for Halifax in 1967, with semi-automatic transmission, and Dennis then withdrew from the psv market, though a pair of Pax V lorry chassis were bodied by Dennis as buses for Llandudno later that year.

Dennis had come into the ownership of the Hestair Group in 1971. By the mid-1970s some operators were concerned at the monopoly being built up by Leyland, and Dennis was persuaded to re-enter the market. It

Above:
Aldershot & District was again a major customer for the normal-control Dennis Falcon; indeed it was the only customer for this P5 model, of which it had 23 with Strachans 30-seat bodywork. 248 (LOU 76) was built in 1954 and had a Gardner 4LK engine.

Left:
The Loline was a licence-built version of the Bristol Lodekka made available for operators outside the state sector. This Loline I was operated by Middlesbrough Corporation and had Northern Counties rear-entrance bodywork.
M. A. Sutcliffe

Right:
The last customer for the Loline was Halifax, which took a batch of Loline IIIs with Gardner 6LX engines, semi-automatic transmission and Northern Counties bodywork in 1967.

Above:
The first Dennis model when it restarted bus production in 1977 was the Dominator. National Bus Company tried five with Willowbrook bodywork with Maidstone & District, whose Medway Towns routes had some formidable hills and sizeable loadings and were thus ideal for testing new bus types. 5302 is seen at Walderslade in 1980.

Right:
The Dominator was also available as a single-decker, often with the distinctively-styled Marshall Camair 80 body. Looking very smart having just been acquired from Merthyr Tydfil in 1985 was Chester 113 (CKG 215V).
Roy Marshall

developed a new, rear-engined double-deck chassis, with a Gardner 6LXB engine mounted transversely, driving through a Voith automatic gearbox. In order to test the driveline, a former Leeds Corporation Daimler CVG6 was fitted with a 6LXB engine and Voith transmission, and ran in service with a number of operators including London Transport and Leicester City Transport, the latter becoming something of a champion of Dennis's new range as it developed.

Once the double-decker, named the Dominator, was launched, a single-deck version followed. The double-decker sold steadily, mainly to the municipal sector, though the breakthrough came when South Yorkshire Transport adopted the Dominator as its standard bus, normally with Alexander bodywork. South Yorkshire had

become a keen user of Voith transmission, which suited its hilly terrain, though it specified the Rolls-Royce Eagle engine in place of the Gardner. As developed, the Dominator had been intended as a low-height double-decker with a Dennis-built drop-centre rear axle. However, South Yorkshire's Dominators used a Kirkstall straight, hub-reduction unit as low height was not an issue, and this later became standard. South Yorkshire initially ordered 144 in 1979, increased to 174 before deliveries began in 1981, and eventually built up a fleet of over 300.

By the 1990s the Dominator was effectively a spent force, unable any longer to offer a serious alternative to the highly-successful Leyland, later Volvo, Olympian. However, it remained in the catalogue and Bournemouth

Top left:
In the days before the purpose-built Dart was available Dennis built a midibus version of the Dominator, the Domino, for Greater Manchester and South Yorkshire PTEs. They had Perkins engines and Maxwell transmission, and the Greater Manchester ones had smart Northern Counties bodywork. They replaced Seddons on the Centreline service in Manchester.

Above left:
The South Yorkshire Dominos were the first vehicles bodied by the fledgling Optare. Though a competent body, Optare had yet to find its feet on the styling front.
Kevin Lane

Top:
As Dennis branched out into underfloor engined designs it came up with a full heavyweight, offering the Gardner 6HLXCT engine and Voith transmission, the Dorchester. Though intended as a coach, Geoff Amos of Daventry had some with rather functional, high-capacity Reeve Burgess bodywork for schools use.
Kevin Lane

Above:
The rear-engined Falcon was a promising design, offering an in-line engine and straight driveline. Most popular was the HC version, with the Gardner 6HLXB engine, though East Lancs contrived to come up with some less than inspired body designs for it. This one is Chesterfield 43 (TWJ 343Y).
Kevin Lane

The Falcon V had a vertical vee-formation engine of either Perkins or Mercedes-Benz manufacture. After coach deregulation Dennis built 10 for National Express with high-floor Duple Goldliner bodywork; National Express wanted a British-built vehicle able to compete on equal terms with the foreign competition. Unfortunately it wanted them in a hurry, and inadequate time for testing showed itself in woeful unreliability; it was a shame, as they performed superbly and could compete with the best for ride quality, comfort and noise levels. They should have been a major boost to Dennis's credibility, but had the reverse effect; Dennis had to make up much ground to attain the position it now enjoys.

took 18 in 1990-2, while its champion in the early days, Geoffrey Hilditch, bought 33 for his Drawlane group and Ensignbus unexpectedly purchased 24 for LT contracts. A new variant with the Gardner LG1200 engine was offered when the 6LXB could no longer meet modern emissions regulations, but only two were built and the Cummins L10, now with either Voith or ZF transmission, was offered instead. By now exactly 1,000 Dominators had been built. Its last chance came in 1992, when Strathclyde Buses' Larkfield depot caught fire; Strathclyde ordered three to try out, with thoughts of buying 150. In the end Strathclyde bought Leyland Olympians and did not even take the three, which accordingly were diverted to Mayne's, the Manchester independent. London & Country became the surprising

Perhaps the greatest white elephant of Dennis's return to the bus market was the Mercedes-powered double-deck version of the Falcon V. However Greater Manchester's pair, with Northern Counties bodywork, were still in service 10 years after they were built. Dennis's East Lancs-bodied demonstrator ended up as a playbus in Stevenage when only two years old; when the author drove it the sound effects reminded him of a Flying Fortress!
John Robinson

last customer for the Dominator, when it bought four as late as 1996, five years after there had been any serious production of the model.

The Dominator spawned three-axle versions, the Condor and Dragon, which sold well in the Far East and continued selling after the Dominator came to an end. Indeed it outsold the Dominator quite considerably before production ended in 1999. In latter years it featured the Cummins L10 engine as standard, supplanted by the Euro 2 M11, whose identical outward dimensions to the L10 disguise the fact it has a larger capacity of 10.8 litres, from 1996.

In 1980 a purpose-built single-deck chassis was developed from the Dominator. This was the Falcon, with a Gardner 6HLXB mounted horizontally behind the rear axle. Other versions were available, notably the Falcon V, with Mercedes-Benz or Perkins V8 engines, the former suitable for double-deck use, the latter developed in conjunction with National Express for high-speed long-distance coach use. Neither helped Dennis's efforts to re-establish itself; the National Express vehicles in particular soon showed up their rapid development through frequent, high-profile failures. If the Dominator was a reborn Daimler Fleetline, the Falcon V was a latter-day Roadliner.

By far the most successful versions of the Falcon were the Gardner-powered H (which, Bristol RE-style, had the gearbox mounted remote from the engine) and broadly-similar HC (with close-coupled engine and gearbox). The HC remained in production until 1992, Drawlane and

Above:
The most popular body for the Dart is Plaxton's Pointer, now the standard for Badgerline group companies amongst others. Two are seen with Badgerline subsidiary South Wales Transport in Swansea.

Left:
Dennis's current full-sized rear-engined single-deck range is rather more successful than the Falcon. London Buses was the first customer for its Lance, which has a vertical in-line Cummins C-series engine at the rear and a delightfully simple construction. London's first ones were for Selkent, replacing Routemasters on the 36B, and have attractive Alexander bodywork.

Below left:
The Lance is proving a versatile design; the first variation on the theme was the SLF low-floor chassis, which East Kent uses on the Canterbury Park-&-Ride service with Berkhof bodywork.

Left:
A Dennis Javelin with UVG S320 bodywork.

Below:
The combination of Dennis Dart chassis and Reeve Burgess (later Plaxton) Pointer body was to become almost the standard British bus of the 1990s. The first was this one for Southampton Citybus.

Leicester again being the final customers, with late batches of 27 and 16 respectively.

While Dennis had been out of the bus market, it had continued to produce lorries, fire engines and refuse vehicles, and the next bus model was built on the same production line as these. This was the Lancet — Dennis was keen on reusing old names. The Lancet was a lightweight, mid-engined chassis, using a Perkins vertical engine, either the straight-six 6.354 or the V8 540. It sold modestly as a bus, and was also offered in short-wheelbase form, in which version it sold reasonably well as a coach with Van Hool bodywork, often called the 'Lancette'.

The Lancet was also developed into a Gardner-engined heavyweight, known as the Dorchester, which sold reasonably well to the Scottish Bus Group, but had few other takers.

The 'Lancette' had shown there was a market for a medium-weight coach and in 1987 Dennis took a new approach with the Javelin. There was much less flexibility of specification than with traditional Dennises; it had a vertical Cummins C-series engine and a ZF gearbox mounted immediately ahead of the rear axle, an arrangement which allowed space for luggage within the wheelbase, like a rear-engined chassis, but with a rear boot too. The Javelin went into full production in 1988 and benefited from Bedford's demise; it quickly became the successor to Bedford in the coach market and gave Dennis its real breakthrough.

The Javelin finally gave Dennis a credible presence in the coach market and, while an obvious Bedford replacement, also showed an ability to perform well in the sector of the market previously dominated by the heavyweight manufacturers. Whilst it wasn't quite up to the rigours of really intensive express work, as Oxford Bus Company was to find on its punishing Oxford-London motorway services, it could do most things as well as a heavyweight, with the advantage of anything up to three more miles per gallon and the ability to take lots of luggage. Not only did it have an underfloor hold in addition to a rear boot, but its light weight also gave it capacity to carry more luggage without exceeding axle weight limits.

Offered originally with just a 245bhp C-series, the Javelin was later made available with a 290bhp version of the same engine (later increased to 300bhp under Euro 2 compliance), giving it the ability to cope on equal terms on the sort of work at which Volvos excelled.

At first only Plaxton and Duple bodies were offered, but in time Caetano, Berkhof, Marcopolo and even Neoplan were added to the list. The Javelin was also available in a bus version, which had a limited appeal amongst smaller operators, again as a Bedford replacement, and also with Eastern Counties and Eastbourne Buses. But its greatest success was as a military vehicle; when Ryder Truck Rental won the contract to provide the British forces with troop transport, it turned to the Javelin in a big way, starting off with an order for 500. Wadham Stringer provided the bodywork, which was later developed as a low-cost coach body, ideally suited to day-trip 'bucket and spade' work or school contracts.

The Javelin peaked during the 1990s, and, as coach operators were persuaded to buy the likes of Iveco and MAN, and discovered that rear engines weren't as frightening as they may have thought, demand for mid-engined designs began to dwindle. The Javelin remains in production, but a depressed coach market, keen pricing from competitors, the end of orders for military use and an ageing product have all conspired to reduce demand to a trickle.

Above left:
A Plaxton Verde-bodied Dennis Lance of Clydeside.

Left:
It was always intended that the Dennis Lance should be made available as a double-decker; this materialised as the Arrow. This is a pre-production bus with Northern Counties Palatine II bodywork, being driven by the author.
Stewart J. Brown

Below:
The Plaxton Pointer body was modified for the low-floor version of the Dart, and then revamped as the Pointer 2. This London United vehicle is a dual-door version with air-conditioning.

In the late 1980s Dennis had become rather good at spotting niches in the market, and the rear-engined Dart was to be its greatest triumph yet. While minibuses had become the norm, nobody had ventured into producing a small, simple bus chassis with a rear engine. The Dart was a narrow-track vehicle, conceived to be 2.3m wide and 9m long, with a Cummins B-series in-line engine at the rear and Allison transmission. It was bodied by Dennis's partner within Trinity Holdings, Duple; both had become part of the Trinity Holdings group in January 1989, following a management buyout from Hestair. Duple designed a stylish stainless steel body for it called the Dartline, with an unusual S-shaped front profile and deep bonded windows. London Transport was a key customer, but to suit the driver-licensing provisions at the time wanted an 8.5m bus which could be driven on a minibus licence. The Dart, like the Javelin, was designed as a front and rear module with a simple chassis frame within the wheelbase, so it was an easy matter to chop half a metre out of it. It flooded into London Transport service.

The Dart came too late to save Duple, ravaged by the 1980s slump in coach sales, but the Dartline body was passed on to Carlyle. Meanwhile other builders were allowed to body the Dart, resulting in new products in 1990 from Wadham Stringer, Wrights — with its quirky, retro-styled Handybus, system-built using the Alusuisse bolted-aluminium system and representing a totally different concept from the Dartline — and Plaxton subsidiary Reeve Burgess, which developed its competent aluminium Pointer body, launched in 1991, of which production was later to pass to Plaxton. A longer, 9.8m model had appeared by the end of 1991.

London Transport, in particular, bought large numbers of Carlyle-, Wright- and Reeve Burgess-bodied Darts, while many other operators were attracted by it, such that 2,000 were built in four years, half of them with Reeve Burgess or Plaxton Pointer bodywork. This was in a bus market that was still depressed by the effects of deregulation and privatisation, and yet more success was to come for the Dart as a variety of factors conspired to accelerate fleet replacement. Part of this was sheer necessity; bus fleets were simply old. Apart from the obvious problems of trying to keep old buses on the road, they were giving the industry a poor reputation, and the Vehicle Inspectorate was toughening up too. One often heard reports of old Leyland Nationals and the like turning up for annual test, and testers saying 'I'll pass it this time, but don't bother to bring it back next year'.

The Dart was conceived as a much better option than minibuses for small-capacity vehicles, but by the time it had grown to 9.8m you could, at a push, get 40 seats into it, making it an ideal low-cost Leyland National replacement. If ever a bus was in the right place at the right time, it was the Dart.

In 1992 a new full-size single-decker, the Lance, was introduced, with an in-line Cummins C-series engine and ZF gearbox at the rear. At first it appeared that this had come at just the right moment, too, as the Leyland Lynx ceased production at the same time. Despite this, it was destined never to be one of Dennis's happier models, but it picked up some sizeable orders, not least from the Badgerline Group, while West Riding and London operators Selkent and Metroline took quantities, and Optare offered it as the Sigma, which sold to Go-Ahead Group and Trent in reasonable numbers.

The Lance was always conceived to be developed into other things. The first of these was the first British ultra-low-floor bus. London Transport was interested in developing this technology, which was taking a hold on the Continent, particularly in Germany. Developed originally as a way to speed up boarding times, London Transport was interested in its ability to give access to buses to the less able and those in wheelchairs, and put out a specification for which bus builders could bid. It seemed a foregone conclusion that the orders would go to overseas manufacturers, but Wrights took up the challenge enthusiastically on the bodywork side while, by fitting ZF independent front suspension and lowering the frame, Dennis was able to adapt the Lance to suit, coining the name Lance SLF; SLF — short for Super Low Floor — was soon to become almost a generic term for low-floor buses. Their efforts were rewarded with orders from LT; 68 were ordered, 38 on the Dennis and 30 on a modified Scania N113, and the Dennises were first into service; 29 January 1994 was the significant first day for British-built low-floor buses into service, on London United's service 120 from Hounslow. Whilst only around 100 Lance SLFs were built, a revolution had begun.

The other Lance development was as a double-decker. Dennis felt strongly that transverse engine layouts were over-complicated and inefficient, and the compact dimensions of the Cummins C-series meant the Lance could be developed into a double-decker, complete with in-line engine. The first appeared, for Nottingham with Northern Counties bodywork, at Coach & Bus '95, and the type was launched formally the following spring, weeks after the last Dominator had been completed, and was rechristened the Arrow. If the Dart had been the right bus at the right time, the Arrow certainly wasn't.

Also at Coach & Bus '95 had been the first low-floor version of the Dart, the Dart SLF. This adapted the existing Dart very effectively; it was widened to 2.4m and even kept the front beam axle. It took on none of the complexity of the Lance SLF, even though it received air suspension for the first time; Dennis had proved that low-floor technology needn't cost the earth or be unduly complex.

As far as the Arrow was concerned, Dennis had shot itself in the foot. Overnight, no-one was interested in a bus that wasn't low-floor. The Lance wasn't enjoying the best reputation and, while the Arrow had a lot to commend it in terms of weight, simplicity and carrying capacity, it failed to catch on. Nottingham took a few more, London & Country bought 10, leaving only Capital Citybus as the Arrow's champion. It took the last to be built just as it was taken over by FirstGroup in 1998; around 70 had been built.

Top:
The Dart SLF is now available with a variety of bodies; this one has Marshall bodywork for Scottish operator Coakley.
Murdoch Currie

Above:
Alexander developed its ALX200 body for the Dart SLF; this one is with Stagecoach Bluebird in Aberdeen.
Paul Chancellor

Left:
East Lancs Spryte bodywork on a Dart SLF for Capital Citybus...
Russell Young

Right:
...and UVG UrbanStar bodywork on an SLF for Marchwood Motorways, on Solent Blue Line service in Southampton.

The first Dart SLFs entered service in early 1996 and demand for the conventional step-entrance Dart, of which no fewer than 4,500 had been built, dried up almost instantly. It was increased in size, to 2.4m wide and lengths of 9.2m, 10m and 10.6m, and fitted with air suspension and a Euro 2 engine. In 1997 an even bigger Dart was announced, the SPD. This was 11.3m long which, when you allowed for the reduced wheelarch intrusion of this small-wheeled design, gave it the internal space of a 12m bus. With increased power output

Above:
Returnee from Kenya; a Dennis Dragon built for Stagecoach Kenya and bodied in Mombasa using a Metsec kit, now in service with Stagecoach Manchester on Magicbus services.

from the Cummins B-series it needed a heavier-weight gearbox, receiving the Allison World Series which in turn necessitated a longer rear overhang. It was launched exclusively with Plaxton bodywork (SPD stood for Super Pointer Dart) but in 2000 it was also made available with East Lancs, Marshall or Alexander bodywork as the Super Dart. Voith transmission was also offered as a new option.

The SPD could have been expected to be a runaway success, but there seemed to be fears that Dennis had stretched the point far enough. However, the following year Dennis came full circle, announcing an 8.5m Mini Pointer Dart, which *has* proved another runaway success, going back to picking up minibus business from operators wanting something purpose-built; more than 200 entered service in the first year of production.

By the beginning of 2000 Dennis was well on the way to its 8,000th Dart (the 3,000th SLF was delivered during 1999), and the model was making its presence felt on the export market — and not just in Hong Kong. In a joint deal with DaimlerChrysler-owned Thomas Built, production of complete Darts with Alexander bodywork was about to begin in the USA, while sales to Canada, Spain, Portugal and Holland were healthy too.

In 1997 Dennis announced its first low-floor double-decker — the three-axle, export-only Trident. This was the replacement for the Dragon, with a Cummins M11

engine in-line at the rear, in Arrow fashion. The first were 12m long for Kowloon Motor Bus, to serve Hong Kong's new airport. More than 500 Tridents were ordered off the drawing board by Hong Kong's three main operators.

With its belief in in-line engines, Dennis started developing a similar two-axle chassis for the UK, and quickly found it could not produce a sensible package for a low-floor double-decker within the right lengths for British operators. It redesigned the chassis with the Cummins C-series mounted transversely at the rear, using Voith or ZF transmission and a ZF drop-centre rear axle. The first chassis was unveiled in January 1998, confusingly also named the Trident despite being on two axles. Bodied examples were to appear a year later, by which time no fewer than 650 had been ordered, well over half of which were in service by the end of 1999. The Trident quickly became the new standard double-decker in London, with more than 200 in service with Stagecoach, 117 with Metroline, 87 with FirstGroup, and further examples with companies such as Blue Triangle and Metrobus; Stagecoach also runs Tridents in Newcastle, Grimsby and Manchester. Other provincial operators include Lothian Region, Oxford, Brighton & Hove, Bournemouth, Preston, Nottingham and Solent Blue Line.

One further new model was launched by Dennis at the end of 1999; this was the new R-Series coach, again launched in conjunction with Plaxton and its new Panther and Paragon range. The R-Series, expected to enter service for the 2000 coach season, is a rear-engined model powered by the Cummins M11 engine, rated at 350bhp (model R350) or 405bhp (R405) with a ZF automated layshaft gearbox or a Mercedes manual one. This puts Dennis into a different sector of the market from that occupied by the Javelin.

Dennis was a remarkable success story in the 1990s and enters the new Millennium as the confident leader of the British market.

Top left:
Dennis is now enjoying considerable success with its Trident low-floor double-decker; this one is with Connex and has Alexander ALX400 bodywork.
Geoff Rixon

Above left:
Another London Trident is this one with Plaxton President bodywork for Metroline.

Left:
Dennis launched its R-Series rear-engined coach in conjunction with Plaxton's new Panther and Paragon bodies at Coach & Bus '99.

Dodge/Renault

Dodge has had a number of incarnations and allegiances down the years. It is a well-known American name, but in Britain has a more chequered history, latterly tied up more with French manufacturers than American. It also became part of the Rootes Group, itself taken over by Chrysler, and while much of the former Rootes Group finished up in French hands as Peugeot Talbot the British Dodge finished up in the hands of Peugeot's great French rival, Renault, whose name superseded Dodge before the Dunstable factory was closed down.

It offered its first true psv chassis from its Kew factory in 1962. It was a lightweight, aimed at the market dominated by Bedford and Ford, though it had the advantage over the other two of offering a true front entrance on a 31ft chassis; at this stage Bedford only offered this feature on its 36ft three-axle VAL. The S306 had a front-mounted Leyland O.370 engine, while the S307 used a Perkins 6.354. It sold only in small numbers; the most significant order was for six S307s with Strachans bodywork for London coach operator Rickards. It was withdrawn from the market in 1967.

Chrysler took an interest in the Rootes Group in 1964, and gained control in 1973. Three years later the Commer range was rebadged as Dodge. By this time the only Commer psv was a minibus, on which the Post Office had standardised for the Postbus services. It also used the same vehicle as its standard van for telephones in the days before British Telecom had been invented. In bus form it was known as the PB1500, and it was as late as 1984 that the last of these entered service, despite the design dating back to the early 1960s and being considered decidedly obsolete in any other market.

Dodge also gained a range of larger vans and trucks

from Commer, and these too were available as minibuses and buses. What had begun life as the Commer Walkthru van had developed into a chassis cab, and sold in small numbers as a minibus, later becoming the Dodge 50-series. At one time it was also sold as a Karrier, though bearing little resemblance to traditional Huddersfield-built Karriers of prewar years!

Small numbers, that was, until the second wave of minibus mania struck after deregulation. This followed the realisation that the 16-seater, represented primarily by the Ford Transit and Freight Rover Sherpa, had quickly been outgrown by the volume of traffic. At first there was a little gap in the market for larger minibuses; Mercedes was revamping its range and there was little other choice until the Metrorider and Optare CityPacer came on stream, and the Dodge 50, in S46 and larger S56 variants, suddenly became popular as the rather basic chassis for a minibus. At one stage demand for 50s was so high that supplies of the optional Chrysler Torqueflite automatic gearbox were being air-freighted from the USA to keep up with demand. The chassis was especially popular amongst the local-authority sector, where political pressures meant that foreign-built vehicles were not considered to be quite the thing. Greater Manchester Buses for one took to the type in very big numbers, with Northern Counties bodywork, but other PTCs such as West Midlands Travel and South Yorkshire Transport also took to it, as did some of the former municipal operators such as Ipswich, Chester, Cleveland Transit and Eastbourne, and the Scottish Bus Group. In 1990 London Buses also bought 123 of the larger S75 which had been made available for psv operators wanting vehicles up to 33 seats, though many of the London ones have since been sold prematurely. By this time Renault had taken over Dodge and replaced the name with Renault; ironically

Right:
A rather basic Dodge S300-series.
It was originally a demonstrator and
was bodied by Mulliner.
Stewart J. Brown

those operators which were keen not to be seen to be buying foreign chassis found themselves buying Renaults!

Other vehicles from the Commer range were the Commando G08 and larger G10, with front Perkins engines. Most were built on virtually unmodified truck chassis, with the axle at the front, and became popular with the military and British Airways for crew transfer work, mainly with Wadham Stringer bodywork. However, the chassis were made available with a set-back front axle, allowing a proper front entrance. In reality the chassis was still virtually unmodified, with just an extension ahead of the front axle, and even the driver's position remained the same giving an odd sensation of driving from what seemed like halfway down the bus! The most celebrated was a small GO8 built for Strathclyde PTE for

use on Arran, with a demountable body. Thus it could be used as a bus morning and evening and swap its body for a van to deliver goods during the day. The idea did not catch on, and neither did the Dodge Commando.

Renault ended production at Dunstable in March 1993 and the range has now come to an end.

Douglas

Better known for logging and cross-country vehicles Douglas Equipment of Cheltenham launched a straight-framed, front-engined single-decker with Meadows four-cylinder engine and gearbox during the 1950s. The design was intended for both home market and export.

Duple

After the War Britain had a considerable number of bus and coach bodybuilders; best known of the latter was Hendon-based Duple, which became known throughout the country for its coach bodies on Bedford chassis, though built on other chassis in smaller numbers too. In 1960 it took over Burlingham of Blackpool and progressively moved production there, until it closed down in Hendon in 1968. In 1965 Harringtons closed down, and thereafter Plaxton and Duple were the 'big two' in British coach building, both solidly traditional and continuing to build separate bodies on others' chassis.

However, after the 1980 Transport Act liberalised coaching there was a sudden move by British coach operators towards the exotic coaches built on the Continent, including rear-engined integrals. Thus Duple began to look towards producing its own integrals, and built a single Caribbean body on a Neoplan underframe. This was not to lead very far, but for the 1984 and 1985 seasons Duple entered an agreement with Bova, the Dutch integral manufacturer, to build a special, low-height version of the Caribbean on a Bova Europa frame, which in turn was based on DAF running units. This emerged as the Duple Calypso, which enjoyed a reasonable following.

Though the Calypso never achieved huge volumes the experience was useful in the development of Duple's own full integral, the very striking and impressive Integral 425, which was announced at the 1984 Motor Show. In 1983 Duple had become part of the Hestair Group, owner of Dennis, and some Dennis expertise went into the underframe of the new Duple. It featured a rear-mounted Cummins L10 engine, though DAF was later offered as an option, driving through ZF manual or automatic transmission.

The 425 had a number of innovative features. The driving position was placed at the very front of the vehicle, close up to the nearly vertical windscreen, over which was a distinctive raked-back glass panel, strongly tinted in an attempt to prevent the driver frying in the summer. The forward mounting of the driver was combined with a special seat design in order to maximise capacity; the Duple 425 was able to seat 61 passengers, a record for a 12m single-deck coach, though fortunately most operators took pity on their passengers and used the capacity to give 57 seats at a pitch usually found in a 53-seater. A special stainless-steel frame was developed for it, and the external styling was not only impressive but was aerodynamically efficient too; the 425 designation represented its low drag coefficient. At that time coefficient of drag had suddenly become all the rage following Ford's recently introduced Sierra and Audi's 80 and 100 car ranges, whose unusual styling was justified by their low coefficient of drag; Audi even displayed a cd figure on their cars. In Duple's case the combination of good aerodynamics and the very efficient Cummins L10 engine led to excellent fuel consumption, often in the order of 12mpg or more, comparing with a coach industry standard of about 10mpg. Given its high carrying capacity it was thus a very economical proposition and it sold reasonably well.

Hestair decided to close down Duple in 1990, in the face of dwindling orders for both buses and coaches, and sold the coach designs to arch-rival Plaxton. Plaxton decided to keep the 425 going, and built it in France at the factory of French coachbuilder Lorraine, which Plaxton had taken over, though with finishing work undertaken at its Scarborough factory. It only built the design for one season however.

Foden

Fodens Ltd, based in Sandbach, Cheshire, was well-known as a high-quality heavyweight lorry manufacturer, and remains in business as such, though now in the American ownership of Paccar. However, it did also build some buses, on a comparatively small scale, and these, like the lorries, were manufactured to a high standard and embodied much innovation and refinement.

Foden's first bus had been built for its famous works band in 1933, and another 10 buses and coaches were built up to 1935. However, it restarted bus production in 1945 with a PVD6 double-deck demonstrator. The most immediately 'different' feature of the Foden was its full-width bonnet and concealed radiator, well ahead of the later fashion for such things, though there was much more innovation under the surface, such as hydraulic brakes and an unusual cab design, with the speedometer in the middle of the steering wheel. That first PVD6 had a Gardner 6LW engine, the standard unit in its double-deck output, and a Foden constant-mesh four-speed gearbox. It was followed the next year with a single-decker, the PVSC6, with a five-cylinder PVSC5 version. Most single-deck Fodens were built as

coaches, some using the tidy frontal treatment to produce a very effective full-front design. The excellent ride quality and attention to details such as engine mounting made it especially suitable for coach use.

At the 1948 Commercial Motor Show Foden unveiled its own two-stroke engine, the FD6. This was a 4.1-litre unit with a Rootes supercharger giving 126bhp at 2,000rpm, and had made its debut in what was nominally a PVSC6 coach in 1947. A similar engine was fitted in a double-deck demonstrator in that year, which later passed to Warrington, the largest operator of Foden double-deckers. It remained unique as a double-decker, though the two-stroke did appear in 53 single-deckers, which were designated PVFE6 when so fitted.

In 1950 Foden introduced a rather more revolutionary chassis. This was a single-deck coach chassis which moved to the style of the day with full-front bodywork with setback front axle, though instead of going to an underfloor engine Foden adopted a transverse rear-engine position, again offering the choice

Right:
In the days when most bus manufacturers were still using exposed radiators Foden introduced its psv range with this impressive front end.
John Aldridge collection

Below:
The single-deck Foden PVSC6 chassis was primarily a coach chassis, though a few were built as buses, such as this 1948 vehicle for the West Mon Board. When new it had a secondhand Dodson body off a Leyland Lion, but this Willowbrook 31-seat body was fitted in 1953. West Mon used these rugged vehicles on its notorious Bargoed Hill route.
M. A. Sutcliffe

of Foden's two-stroke engine (PVRF6) or the Gardner 6LW, though retaining the constant-mesh gearbox. A Foden-engined chassis appeared at the Festival of Britain in 1951 before being exported to Spain and bodied by Ayats. The rear-engined Fodens were not a great success, although 54 were built for the home market by the time production ended in 1954, a surprising number of them with Foden engines, and several more were exported. The last did not enter service until 1958, with Toppings, Liverpool, having been used as an experimental chassis by Fodens.

Top:
Foden chassis often carried rather exotic coach bodywork; Salopia of Whitchurch, Shropshire, had a number of Fodens; this 1950 two-stroke PVFE6 had splendid observation bodywork by Whitson, with stylish faired-in rear wheels.

Above:
Smiths Imperial of Birmingham built its own bodywork on this 1949 PVFE6; the distinctive frontal styling disguises what was otherwise quite a conservative style.

Top:
A number of Fodens had Crellin Duplex-style half-deck bodywork; this one for the Dutch airline KLM was built by Lincolnshire Trailers in 1951. It was possible to cram anything up to 52 seats in such bodywork.

Above:
Whitson managed a classically understated style of bodywork for this Foden PVRF6, built for Nottinghamshire-based Netherfield Coaches in 1951.

Left:
This Foden PVRF6 was exhibited on Associated Coach Builders' stand at the 1952 Earls Court show.

Bodywork was usually by Whitson, Gurney Nutting, Bellhouse Hartwell or Plaxtons, and Lawton — a bodybuilder generally associated with Foden — also offered a bus body. In the event though all but one of the home-market ones were bodied as coaches.

Meanwhile conventional Foden production continued, the last being five PVD6 double-deckers with East Lancs bodywork for Warrington in 1955/56. Some 450 chassis had been built in 10 years, including about 75 exports, mostly to Australia.

That was not quite the end of the story however. Leyland's decision to drop the Fleetline in the mid-1970s meant the end of any Gardner-engined double-decker on the market, prompting one or two other manufacturers to have a go at this gap in the market. Foden developed a semi-integral rear-engined double-deck chassis with transverse Gardner 6LXB engine and Allison transmission, which was launched in 1978. It was built in conjunction with Northern Counties as the Foden-NC, and two were built for Greater Manchester PTE. One-off Northern Counties-bodied vehicles were built for West Yorkshire PTE, West Midlands PTE, Derby City Transport and PMT, which evaluated the design against a Bristol VRT and a Dennis Dominator on behalf of National Bus Company. Another was bodied by East Lancs for South Yorkshire and the last chassis was never bodied. Foden decided not to proceed with the project.

Ford/Thames

Ford Motor Co is so well-known throughout automotive circles that it is surprising how recent a newcomer it is as a builder of psvs. It was in June 1957 that it first announced its intention to enter the market — although there had been Ford-based psvs before, not least on Model Ts in the early days of motorbuses, especially in rural areas.

Traditionally Ford had used other names for its commercial vehicles, such as Fordson or Thames, and the new entrant, based on the Thames Trader lorry range, was marketed as a Thames. It was a seven-ton chassis, almost identical in concept to the Bedford SB with which it competed head-on. Indeed with identical body styles it took a keen eye to tell a Thames from an SB. The front-mounted engine, over the front axle, just like an SB, was a new Ford 5.4-litre unit developing 100bhp at 2,500rpm driving through a four-speed synchromesh gearbox, and brakes were servo-assisted hydraulic. There was also an option of a 4.9litre petrol engine.

The Thames was an instant success, leaping into second place behind the Bedford SB in its particular market segment, with nearly 500 sold in the first year. Although Fords were very much in the lightweight sector the manufacturer was keen to stress the fortitude of the design, and a prototype ran from London to Moscow and back, in under 45 hours, and down the years Fords went on a number of mammoth journeys, ostensibly for proving but doubtless more for publicity.

Ford stole something of a march on Bedford in 1963, when it introduced a 36ft two-axle chassis; Bedford of course had gone down the unconventional three-axle road for its 36ft VAL. The new chassis was the Thames 36; it used the same engine as the shorter chassis, now named Thames 30, though with a five-speed gearbox and air brakes. The engine remained at the front, though now ahead of the front axle. However, it was somewhat underpowered and was replaced in 1965 by the much more successful R-series. This increased the power output up to a maximum of 150bhp by introducing turbocharging, rather a rare thing to do, especially in a lightweight chassis, at this time.

Two versions were available, the R192, a direct competitor for the Bedford VAM, and the R226, a direct replacement for the Thames 36. Both designations implied the wheelbase in inches, and were metricated as the R1014 and R1114 respectively in 1971. The Thames name was also dropped, and the new chassis proved much more successful. They now

Above:
Ford's first 36ft coach was the Thames 36; unlike Bedford's VAL Ford was able to build to the new maximum length on two axles. This prototype, seen in France on a proving run, carried Duple Marauder bodywork.

Left:
Ford's R-series was popular amongst independent operators for bus use as well as coach use; bus grant enabled them to buy new lightweight service buses very cheaply. This Willowbrook-bodied R1014 was operated by Osbornes of Tollesbury.
Kevin Lane

became a close second to Bedford in the market place, rather than trailing behind, the turbocharged engines giving a livelier performance than the contemporary Bedfords.

Surprisingly the National Bus Company was to become a major customer for the Ford R-series, and there was a vogue for them to replace heavyweights, even turning up in fleets like Southdown for long-distance work previously the preserve of heavyweights like the Leyland Leopard, while operators such as United Counties and South Wales used them for service bus work. Scottish Bus Group was an even more enthusiastic user, with bus and dual-purpose version of the Alexander Y-type body and Duple Dominant coach bodywork too.

The manual gearbox was something of a hindrance for bus work, and in 1974 Ford announced an innovative, semi-automatic control for its six-speed synchromesh gearbox. This was electronically controlled and although manufacturers such as Scania and Volvo were to adopted similar solutions a decade or so later it never went into production at this stage. However, Ford announced an Allison automatic option for the R-series in 1976 which increased its appeal for bus work.

The chassis was modified in 1977 by inclining the engine 45° to the nearside, to provide a better entrance and to reduce intrusion and noise, while six-speed gearboxes were offered. At the same time the Turbo II engine was fitted, a six-litre 141bhp unit from the contemporary D-series lorry, and a modified radiator was fitted allowing the chassis to take the Duple Dominant II body for the first time.

The last version was the R1015/R1115 with improved Dover engines, which came from the new

Above:
Later the Ford Transit was to become familiar nationwide on local bus services. The revolution can be said to have started in Exeter, with Devon General; this is one of many hundreds bodied by Carlyle for National Bus Company.

Cargo range replacing the D-Series lorries. Still a six-litre unit, power was now up to 153bhp, and gross vehicle weight was increased to 12.6tonnes on the R1115. However, like Bedford Ford was feeling the cold from the new wave of coaching, requiring much harder work from vehicles and higher standards for passengers, which favoured heavyweights. Production slumped during the 1980s and finally ended in 1985, when Ford announced it would not build a successor to the R-series. This left the lightweight sector to Bedford, to which Ford had always been No 2, but Bedford was not to stay the course much longer either.

In 1973 Ford announced a new medium-sized chassis, the A-series. This fitted into its commercial vehicle range between the D-series and the Transit. In appearance it was like a big version of the Transit, with a short bonnet and was designed for gross vehicle weights from 3.5 to 6.5 tons. It offered a choice of two-litre V4 and three-litre V6 petrol or four-cylinder 2.4litre or six-cylinder 3.6litre diesel engines and four or five-speed synchromesh gearboxes and immediately Strachans made a 20-seat bus version available. Other builders also built on it, while Alexander (qv) built an integral midibus on Ford A-series units. Although Ford had high hopes for the A-series it had a limited appeal and production ended in the early 1980s.

The end of the R-series and A-series did not, however, spell the end of Ford in the psv market; the Transit was about to come into the ascendancy. The Ford Transit had become virtually the standard minibus for the limited amount of minibus work which was required prior to bus deregulation. However, in 1984, in the run-up to deregulation, Devon General placed a number of Transits in service in Exeter, replacing large buses on wide headways with a fast, frequent hail-&-ride operation. The rest, as they say, is history; the Ford Transit was to revolutionise the provision of local bus services and soon became a familiar sight on bus services nearly everywhere. Perhaps a bit basic, with a slightly raucous 2.5litre direct-injection diesel engine, the smallest di engine available at the time, it proved a terrific workhorse with capacity for much harder work and longevity than anyone had imagined. Some of those early Devon General ones clocked up 10 years' service, and intensive urban bus work was probably the harshest environment the versatile Transit was to encounter. Most were 16-seaters, though it was found possible to increase capacity to 20. This proved counter-productive; as the Transit was so close to its design weight at 20 seats, no standees could be carried, so the 20-seater actually had less carrying capacity than the 16-seater.

A new, more stylish VE6 model was introduced in 1986, though NBC took large quantities of the old model as Ford ran out the last ones, such that the

Above:
A Carlyle-bodied Freight Rover in service in Luton. It
began life with the Bee Line Buzz Company.
Kevin Lane

VE6, though very common in other applications, was
never to became so familiar as a psv; by the time it
came on stream for psv work the Transit had become
a victim of its own success; 16-seaters were now too
small. Only the Badgerline and Transit Holdings
groups took to the new model to any extent, in the
case of the latter with a purpose-built body by Mellor,
which with its rather tall dimensions looked ungainly
but was remarkably practical and gave probably the
best passenger environment of any Transit body. The
Transit is of course still very much available, and
increases in sophistication all the time. It now boasts
independent front suspension and fancy electronic
engine controls are available. However, as a minibus
it is back in its traditional rôle for welfare and
specialist psv applications.

Freight Rover/LDV

Perhaps a slightly unusual entry, Freight Rover enjoyed
a brief vogue as a major supplier of minibus chassis as
an alternative to the much more successful and reliable
Ford Transit in the mid-1980s. The Freight Rover Sherpa
began life as one of the British Leyland Group's less
auspicious products, the successor to a number of
different Austin and Morris models, introduced in 1971.
It was built in what had been the BMC van plant in
Birmingham, a stone's throw from the MCW plant at
Washwood Heath.

It was not used to any great extent as a psv chassis
until the time of deregulation, when the National Bus
Company, in particular, needed large quantities of 16- to
20-seat minibuses, and when Ford and Mercedes-Benz

were about to introduce new models. This provided an
entry into the market for Freight Rover, and over 1,000
Sherpas went into NBC service in 1986/87, mainly with
Carlyle bodywork. Indeed, following the parcel-van
style of body, Carlyle developed its rather more stylish
Carlyle II specifically for the Sherpa. Other customers
included Yorkshire Rider, which took it in a form
converted from the panel van by Optare, and a
deregulation newcomer, Bee Line Buzz, which launched
a fleet of 160 of them into the Manchester area in
January 1987. The Sherpa was never as reliable as the
Transit, and both were quickly superseded on minibus
work by larger vehicles. Some operators, notably
Lincolnshire Road Car, got round the reliability problem
by fitting Ford Transit engines and gearboxes.

Freight Rover went with Leyland Trucks to DAF and
became Leyland-DAF Vans. Following the collapse of
the Leyland-DAF company a management buy-out was
undertaken, and the company continues as LDV; the
larger versions of the Sherpa, by now called the 400,
used Peugeot engines. A replacement for the Sherpa,
jointly with Renault, was lost in the process, but the 400
was revamped as the Convoy, which still soldiers on and
is used by Royal Mail as the standard postbus. It also
crops up in small numbers as the basis of minicoaches,
and now has an engine built by Ford. A replacement,
designed in conjunction with Korean manufacturer
Daewoo, is now on the cards.

Guy

Wolverhampton-based Guy Motors had not been a significant bus producer before the war, though in 1941 it and Leyland were appointed to build a range of standardised Utility double-deck buses, initially 500 apiece. In the event Leyland concentrated on other military work, leaving Guy to produce its 500 Arab Is, before Daimler was appointed as the other wartime supplier in 1942. Bristol followed on later. Daimler's CWG5 and CWA6 were based on its prewar models, and also built in a factory allocated to it in Wolverhampton. The Arab I in standard form was powered by the Gardner 5LW, though a small number had 6LWs requiring the front end to be extended — and in fact putting the bus over the legal length at the time. Nonetheless the Arab II adopted the extended front end, regardless of which engine was fitted.

Guy's experience of wartime production meant that it emerged into the postwar period as one of the major players in the bus business, and indeed the Utility Arab II continued in production until early-1946, despite the fact that other manufacturers had already been given the go-ahead for their postwar ranges. However, by this time the wartime specification was

Right:
London Transport specified its own version of the Guy Vixen for lightly-used country area services. GS13 is still in service with London & Country, one of the successors to London Transport's Country Bus & Coach division. They had ECW bodywork.

Below:
The concealed radiator is more readily identified with the Guy Arab IV; this 30ft model with Northern Counties bodywork was new to Lancashire United in 1958.

relaxed a little, allowing some light alloys to be used in its construction, and a polished aluminium radiator surround in place of the austere painted unit of the true Utilities. The rather basic Arab proved a reliable and durable chassis and many were rebodied or at least refurbished after the war and gave 20 or more years' service. Over 2,500 had been built during the war.

Guy's first postwar model was the Arab III, introduced in 1946. It continued the theme of the wartime Arabs, though was available as a single-decker as well as a double-decker, and featured a lower bonnet and radiator line. A new engine alternative was offered from 1948, the 10.35litre Meadows 6DC630, though despite offering larger capacity than the 8.4litre Gardner 6LW it was something of an unknown quantity, and found few takers. It was deleted in 1951. One user was London Transport, which specified the engine in a one-off Arab III with Guy's own bodywork to a sort of pseudo-RT style. This also had the preselective gearbox offered as an option from 1948. The same gearbox, though with Gardner 6LW engine, was specified by Birmingham City Transport in a new model built initially to Birmingham's specification, the Arab IV. Birmingham's first ones arrived in 1950, with concealed radiators; Birmingham was multiple sourcing identical-looking buses from Daimler, Guy and Crossley at this time, and took 301 Arabs. Like the wartime Arab these too proved very long-lived, lasting up to 25 years and being used by West Midlands PTE to see off rather newer trolleybuses in Walsall.

The Arab IV was offered generally from 1951, with a new constant-mesh gearbox and an option of an exposed radiator, while the Arab III remained on the market until 1953, partly — though by no means exclusively — to fulfil requirements for halfcab single-deckers. Guy had come from nowhere before the war to being the standard bus for a good many operators, notably smaller municipalities such as Chester, Darlington and Blackburn, though it was also taken up enthusiastically by larger operators such as Belfast, Southampton and its home town, Wolverhampton, while company operators taking to

the type included East Kent, Lancashire United, Southdown, Northern General and some of the Scottish Bus Group companies. Most Arab IVs had Gardner 6LW engines, though Moores of Kelvedon for one specified 5LWs in 30ft vehicles, which must have been decidedly slow, but in 1958 the Arab IV became the first to offer Gardner's new 10.45litre 6LX.

Meanwhile Guy offered quite a wide range of single-deckers, including a range of lightweights, some normal control. Perhaps the most famous of the latter were the 84 Vixen Specials built for London Transport in 1953, with ECW bodywork and Ford-styled fronts, which formed the GS class. However, before the war Guy had offered two small single-deck models, the normal-control 20-seat Wolf and forward-control 30-seat Vixen, production of which, with a new radiator resembling that of the Arab, resumed in 1947. A heavier 30-seat Otter was offered from 1950, with a choice of Gardner 4LK or, later, Perkins P6, as options to the 58bhp 3.7litre petrol engine also fitted to the Vixen. The Wolf had a smaller, 3.3litre 50bhp petrol unit.

Underfloor-engined versions of the Arab for single-deck use appeared in 1950, offering a horizontal Gardner engine and preselector or constant-mesh gearbox, with a lighter-weight LUF replacing Arab III single-deckers from 1952. The LUF remained in production until 1959, though did not sell in large quantities. Meanwhile a new front-engined chassis, the Warrior, was built for overseas markets as a replacement for the Arab III single-decker, and an underfloor-engined version of this was developed which sold a few in this country. It offered a wider range of engines than the Arab LUF, including AEC and Meadows.

It was unfortunate that Guy, with its origins in straightforward, robust engineering should stray from that path when it came to developing a vehicle for the new vogue of front-entrance double-deckers heralded by the Leyland Atlantean. The placing of well-tried components in a package across the back of the bus, with recourse to angle drives, was not an immediate or universal success, so there was some logic in developing an alternative with a more straightforward drive line. The idea was the brainchild of West Riding's chief engineer, Ron Brooke, who was also keen to try different suspension systems to counteract the problems of rough roads in his company's operating area. Other manufacturers had turned down the idea, but Guy agreed to develop it.

The Wulfrunian appeared in 1959. It featured a Gardner 6LX engine mounted ahead of the front wheels with the entrance alongside it. It also had other advanced features for the time, all items from which Leyland had fought shy with the Atlantean, such as air suspension, independent at the front, and disc brakes. Maybe a more conservative design utilising the same basic concept might have worked, though even that is doubtful; the Gardner 6LX owed much of its reliability to solid construction and generous specification, and as a result was a big beast which took up too much room on the platform, resulting in a cramped entrance, compared with Leyland's excellent entrance arrangement on the Atlantean, necessitating a nearside staircase which was also cramped, and an equally cramped cab. Originally Guy had intended to offer the Gardner 6LW, Leyland and AEC engines in the Wulfrunian.

The front-mounted engine also gave the bus very poor weight distribution (emphasised by the strange toe-out attitude afforded to the front wheels by the independent suspension). In later years West Riding had to take out the upstairs front seats to alleviate the problem of tyre wear.

The Wulfrunian took up a huge amount of sparse cash reserves in its development and did not sell, other than to West Riding, which took 127 from 1960 to 1965. Only 10 others were built, for Bury, Lancashire United, County Motors, West Wales, Accrington — which oddly had them with rear entrances and a short front overhang, rather negating the whole purpose of the Wulfrunian, and Wolverhampton, which also had one with a short overhang though forward entrance. By 1961 the company was bankrupt, and was bought by Jaguar, now the owner of Daimler.

Under Jaguar ownership a new version of the Arab emerged in 1962, the Mark V, available in 27ft or 30ft versions. It had a lower chassis frame than the Arab IV and was thus better suited to forward-entrance applications than its predecessor, though it appeared in both forward and rear-entrance forms.

Although a conservative design, it remained in production, apart from a short break in the 27ft model when Daimler's CCG6, with a Guy constant-mesh gearbox, was offered in its place, until the end of half-cab bus production in this country; the last went to Chester in 1969, one of a only a handful of H-registered half-cab buses.

Guy, by now owned by British Leyland, continued in the export market, but production was transferred to Leyland in 1982 and the Wolverhampton factory was closed.

Harrington

Hove-based Harrington was one of the most highly-respected coachbuilders in postwar Britain, with a fine range of bodies bought particularly, though by no means exclusively, by the BET Group companies. It also built a smaller number of competent bus bodies, and like Beadle, Harrington, which had a Rootes car dealership in Hove, saw the opportunities presented by Commer's underfloor-engined concept for an integral single-decker with the entrance ahead of the front axle. Thus in 1953 it produced an integral coach, the Contender, using the petrol engine from the Avenger. However, later ones used the two-stroke TS3 diesel. BOAC bought 12 Contender coaches between 1953 and 1958, the last three with Rolls-Royce petrol engines and automatic transmission. It did not sell in large numbers, though Maidstone & District bought 11 with 42-seat bus bodywork and TS3 engines in 1955.

Harrington also built integral minibuses based on Ford 4D running units. They had up to 19 seats, but many went to BOAC as 12-seaters.

Right:
A Commer-powered Harrington Contender coach of 1953.

Jensen

This West Bromwich firm is generally remembered for its exotic sports cars, and the Interceptor of the late 1960s was one of the all-time classics in British sports cars. Nevertheless it did dabble into the commercial vehicle business in the late 1940s/early 1950s, under the JNSN tag which came from the characteristic use of these initials as a cut out for the radiator. Its specialism was integrally-built vehicles, mainly pantechnicons. However, it did branch out in a small way into passenger vehicles, with a lightweight 40-seater using a Perkins P6 engine and David Brown five-speed gearbox. It was introduced in 1949 and had a body structure by Sparshatts. A 38-seat luxury version came out at only 5tons 3cwt unladen, but it failed to catch on.

Jensen made another attempt in the psv market in 1958, with a remarkable 13-seat minibus, the Tempo 1500. This was built under licence from a German manufacturer, Tempo, but for this UK application was fitted with a BMC 1.5litre B-series petrol engine mounted back-to-front under the floor at the front and driving the front wheels via a ZF four-speed gearbox. The vehicle was also available as a van.

Below:
A Jensen integral bus, showing the Sparshatts tubular construction for the body. Note the 'JNSN' emblem forming a grille.

Bottom:
The Jensen Tempo 14-seat minibus with Austin petrol engine, seen at Earls Court in 1958.

Karrier

Karrier was best-known as a bus producer up to the mid-1930s when it was taken over by the Rootes Group, in 1934, after which production was transferred from Huddersfield to the Commer factory at Luton. Thereafter it concentrated on smaller, lightweight vehicles, effectively the smaller end of the Commer range. Its main model throughout the 1950s was the Bantam, which was available as an attractive 14-seat Reading-bodied coach, notable for its faired-in rear wheels. It had a four-cylinder 48bhp engine.

A few Commer Walkthru van derivatives used as minibuses were sold as Karriers.

Leyland

It still seems incredible that Leyland is no longer with us. At one time, when Volvo was still an insignificant Swedish also-ran, it was the world leader in bus and coach production. It had markets all over the world and by the end of the 1960s had mopped up the entire heavyweight bus production of this country. Yet by 1993 it had all gone, with just vestiges of it showing in certain Volvo models. If one discounts the engineering legacy which can be found in the products of numerous manufacturers throughout the world, that is.

But before we get too gloomy about the present we must return to 1945, when Leyland was just returning to bus production after an enforced rest. A rest that is from building buses; instead Leyland was a major producer for the war effort and as mentioned above, although it was intended that Leyland should build buses during the war that didn't come about, once it had finished assembling chassis for which it already had parts.

Its postwar range was launched at the end of 1945, and comprised two solid but unremarkable models, the Titan PD1 double-decker and mechanically identical Tiger PS1 single-decker. They followed on from prewar models, though with the 7.4litre E101 engine that had been developed for military use during the war and a redesigned front end which was to set the standard for postwar production. They had four-speed constant-mesh gearboxes, vacuum brakes and were quite conventional. They were followed in 1947 by the PD2 and PS2 models, which were undoubtedly Leyland's most successful models ever. These used the new 9.8litre 125bhp O.600 engine, on which much of Leyland's postwar success was built, coupled to a synchromesh four-speed gearbox, which was less successful. Indeed this had to be reworked, with a new version with synchromesh only on the top two gears, which settled down to be Leyland's standard gearbox for the next 20 years, and some PD2s reverted to crash gearboxes while this was being undertaken.

The PD2 was to remain in the catalogue for 20 years, and appeared in numerous guises, 7ft 6in and 8ft wide, with vacuum brakes or air brakes, with manual gearboxes, semi-automatic gearboxes and even preselectors, with conventional exposed radiators or with two types of concealed radiator. It was developed into the slightly heavier export version, the OPD2 (also sold in Ireland), up till 1954 it could be obtained as a complete vehicle with Leyland's own competently-styled body or bodied by other concerns, and it even spawned a special version for London which was virtually a Leyland-built RT chassis, in 7ft 6in wide RTL form or 8ft wide and bodied by Leyland as the RTW. Nominally these were respectively PD2/1 and PD2/3 versions, although they shared little in common with provincial versions of the same chassis, other than the O.600 engine and the axles. They had AEC preselector gearboxes, air brakes and a low bonnet and radiator style which was virtually the same as the AEC version, though without the famous Blue Triangle, of course.

In 1956 the PD2 was joined by the mechanically identical PD3, which was 30ft long, and shared all the same variants as the PD2. The Titan sold in huge quantities mainly to municipal and BET fleets in this country, though PD1s had also appeared with THC fleets before they were tied too securely to Bristol, and also sold well abroad. The Tiger PS2 was no less competent, but was rendered obsolescent, not least by Leyland's own other endeavours in the single-deck department.

Meanwhile Leyland had been looking at underfloor-engined single-deckers. It had produced a batch for London Transport before the war, though still with the front axle in the normal position. A horizontal version of the O.600 engine was shown at the 1948 Commercial Motor Show, and details also emerged of an integral frame by MCW for an underfloor-engined Leyland. This appeared in 1949 as the HR40 Olympic, 40 designating the seating capacity. When length regulations were relaxed in 1951 to allow 30ft single-deckers on two axles it became the HR44, a 44-seater. However, the market was still reluctant to accept integral buses, and the Olympic was a pretty heavy bus anyway so showed little advantage as an integral, so the same components were fitted into a separate chassis, the Royal Tiger, from 1950. In the event all home-market ones were 30ft long, though there was a choice of 7ft 6in or 8ft width, air or vacuum brakes and a rear extension to support the boot on coach versions. Like the Olympic, it was a heavy bus and in 1952 the lighter-weight Tiger Cub was introduced, with the smaller, 5.7litre O.350 engine, which was similar to that fitted into the normal-control Comet, basically a lorry range but available as a passenger vehicle of the Bedford OB school. The Tiger Cub had a constant-mesh gearbox and air brakes, and from 1953 the same components were available in another MCW-built integral, the

Above:
London's own version of the Leyland Titan PD2 was the RTL; RTL1176 is seen here prior to setting off to New York on a 'Come to Britain' tour in 1964.

Right:
The combination of Leyland's own bodywork and concealed radiator was a very rare one, specified by Midland Red to resemble its own products on 100 PD2/20s bought in 1953 as its class LD8. Two are seen in Coventry in 1955.
W. H. R. Godwin

Above:
Seen when newly delivered to SMT in 1957 is a Park Royal lowbridge-bodied PD2, in St Andrew Square, Edinburgh, shortly before the new bus station opened there.

Above right:
When Leyland Tiger PS1s and PS2s became outmoded a number of operators had them rebuilt as double-deckers; this Yorkshire Woollen vehicle is a rebuilt Tiger PS1.
Kevin Lane

Olympian, though this met with rather less success than the Olympic had enjoyed. The Tiger Cub however, sold very well, and later larger O.375 and O.400 engines were offered, as were Albion five-speed gearboxes.

The heavier single-deckers were effectively phased-out; although the Tiger PS2 continued for export as the OPS2, home-market production ended in 1954, and in the same year the Royal Tiger became the Worldmaster, also intended for export though some were sold in this country. The Olympic too was developed as an overseas model.

The next single-deck chassis with the O.600 engine was the Leopard L1, which was shown at the 1959 Scottish Motor Show. This was rather lighter in weight than the Royal Tiger, though mechanically similar. However, it was built as standard with air brakes. The L2 was a coach version, with a more powerful, faster-revving version of the same engine and a rear frame extension. 36ft versions became available in 1961, as the PSU3, and the Leopard steadily developed as Leyland's main coach model, gaining Pneumocyclic semi-automatic transmission and the larger O.680 engine over the years. As Leyland took over various other heavyweight manu-facturers it was to become the only British heavy-weight coach, available in 12m form as well as 11m and 10m, and became the standard National Bus

Company and Scottish Bus Group coach. Ulsterbus too standardised on it for bus and coach work. Production was finally replaced by the Tiger in 1982, by which time the Leopard was showing its age quite seriously. A hybrid model, heavier than the Leopard but less heavy than the Worldmaster was the 33ft-long Royal Tiger Cub. Intended for export it was also bought by Doncaster Corporation.

Returning to the 1950s, Leyland was looking at alternatives for double-deckers, largely with a view to increasing seating capacity. The first rear-engined double-deck prototype was built in 1952. Named the Lowloader it had a body by Saunders-Roe, showing distinct similarities to the body developed by that

company for the Tiger Cub. A turbocharged O.350 engine was fitted on the rear platform; apart from a trolleybus-style full front the layout of the bus was entirely conventional, with open rear platform, and the O.350 was chosen for its small dimensions. The structure was semi-integral, with an underframe incorporating wheelarches etc and it had independent front suspension. A second prototype, using a similar underframe though bodied with a half-cab body by MCW followed two years later. However, the third prototype was built in 1956, by which time 30ft double-deckers could be built on two axles. Thus the entrance was moved to the front, ahead of the front axle, which not only gave driver supervision of the platform but also left more room for the engine at the rear, so the trusty O.600 could be used instead. The integral, low-height prototype still used independent front suspension, and the underframe included the entire floor structure. The body was built by MCW and the whole was named the Atlantean.

However, the complex construction of the Atlantean was found to create various drawbacks, and there was customer resistance from the likes of BET, which didn't like to be tied to one bodybuilder, so when the production Atlantean was launched in 1958 it reverted to a conventional chassis frame, beam front axle and a straight rear axle dictating a normal height. Bodywork was initially by MCW, though other

builders were soon able to build on it and despite the fact that its main advantage over a PD3 was an increase in capacity of only five seats at the most it sold remarkably well. Within 10 years it had seen off the conventional front-engined chassis, though by this time one-person operation of double-deckers had been legalised, so it offered obvious advantages. Indeed during the early 1960s there was something of a backlash against the concept; early operators got their fingers burnt with unreliability and found little advantage, so returned to conventional buses. Ironically many of those early Atlantean users worked hard to get their vehicles working properly and eventually got very good, long service out of them.

As one-person operation became the norm, so improvements were necessary for the Atlantean, and an improved AN68 version was introduced in 1972. This used the O.680 engine as standard (it had been an option on the earlier, PDR-series), and also had standard power steering, spring brakes etc as well as a lengthened rear overhang to accommodate back-to-back seating over the rear wheelarch as had become popular. In this form the Atlantean was a remarkable success, overcoming most of the unreliability of early models. It remained in production until 1984, outlasting later newcomers, the Daimler Fleetline and Bristol VRT. Although Leyland had had plans to replace its entire double-deck production with a single

Left:
A Ribble Leyland Royal Tiger coach with Leyland's own bodywork, seen in Rochdale.

Centre left:
The Comet was a popular medium-weight lorry, though appeared sometimes in bus and coach guise too, like this one for Mulleys, Ixworth.
M. A. Sutcliffe

Below:
Following the Royal Tiger was the lighter-weight Tiger Cub, suitable as both a bus or a coach. This Ribble one has Burlingham Seagull bodywork.

Right:
Leyland produced the first successful rear-engined double-decker, the Atlantean. Earlier ones had plain front ends, though by the time this one was bodied by MCW for Bournemouth in 1964 more style was being put into bodywork for them.

new model in the 1970s, as we shall see, it was European regulations which finally ended the Atlantean's 26-year run — with that O.680 engine it was just too noisy — by which time some 15,000 had been sold. It was the best-selling double-decker of all times.

Leyland's forays into rear-engined single-deckers were less successful. In 1962 Leyland had merged with ACV, and the same chassis was used as the basis of the Leyland Panther and the AEC Swift. Neither did much credit for their manufacturer, though oddly enough both types were highly regarded in Australia. The Panther and the Panther Cub were both launched in 1964, the former a 36ft chassis with the O.600 engine mounted horizontally at the rear, the latter 33ft with the O.400. The Panther was available with a stepped chassis frame as the PSUR1/1, for bus use, offering a very low entrance, or with a higher, straight frame as the PSUR1/2 for coach use, with the advantage of useful underfloor locker space. Most were built as buses however. Neither type was hugely successful, and once one-man operation of double-deckers was legalised from 1966 few operators persisted with it.

Much was about to change for Leyland. It had already acquired ACV, then in 1965 took a 25% stake in Bristol. In 1968, however, it was merged with the ailing British Motor Corporation to form British Leyland. BMC had acquired Jaguar two years earlier, so Daimler and Guy also joined the Leyland stable. Problems now really began, as the car and commercial vehicle businesses did not coexist terribly happily. Both needed to invest in new models, and the commercial vehicle business lost out as money was invested in new car ranges; and even these were hardly the cream of the European automotive industry, resulting in models such as the Austin Allegro and Morris Marina. Another effect was that production of Daimler's last model, the Fleetline, was moved from Coventry to Leyland in 1973 to make room for increased production of Jaguar cars. The name was changed to the Leyland Fleetline at the end of 1974 and production ended in 1980.

A joint venture was set up with the new National Bus Company in 1969. Leyland and NBC became equal partners in Bristol, and also set up a whole new organisation, Leyland National, to build a brand new integral rear-engined single-decker on mass-production lines in a brand new factory at Workington. The integral construction was such that many of the structural problems which had bedevilled the first generation of rear-engined single-deckers were overcome, especially as the new structure was jig-built, allowing semi-skilled labour to produce a precision job.

Leyland had been working on a radical four-axle Commuterbus, which might have brought low-floor buses in by the 1970s rather than the 1990s, and while the Leyland National stopped short of that it was still quite radical. Leyland had developed a new fixed-head engine, the 500, and a horizontal, turbocharged version of this 8.2litre unit was used in the new bus. Although its 200bhp plus output was impressive, as was its free-revving character, it was not to be the most reliable of units and the installation in the Leyland National meant it was rather prone to smoke too. However, the corrosion-protected steel structure of the bus was rather more successful and proved to be remarkably strong and durable. Being mass-produced there was little operator choice; features such as destination boxes, seats etc were all standard-ised, though there was a choice of single or double doors and 10.3m or 11.3m length. Air suspension was standard as was a five-speed Pneumocyclic gearbox, with semi- or fully-automatic control.

National Bus Company adopted it as its standard single-decker and quickly took large quantities, which was just as well; once one-person operation of double-deckers was unexpectedly legalised in 1966 the writing was on the wall for rear-engined single-deckers. However, the bus industry was falling into a very bleak period, with long delays in fulfilling orders and many operators took readily-available Leyland Nationals rather than wait for something more to their liking. Nonetheless ambitious production forecasts

needed to offset the high capital cost in setting up the highly automated factory were never met. The Leyland National was first exhibited at the 1970 Commercial Motor Show, and soon started appearing in large numbers on the roads. It went through a number of modifications before a Mark 2 model was introduced in 1979. This used the O.680 engine and moved the radiator to the front, extending the bus by 0.3m and giving rise to a rather bulbous snout, which spoilt the clean lines of the original design. Options of Gardner and Leyland TL11 engines were offered later, but the days of large-scale purchases of new buses were over and the National 2 never reached the sort of volumes enjoyed by the earlier model. They drifted downwards until production ground to a halt in 1984.

Leyland also had similar ideas for the double-deck market. With the Leyland National it had virtually wiped out all opposition in the single-deck citybus market, and during the 1970s plans were hatched for a new integral double-decker to do the same. A highly-sophisticated new bus emerged as the B15 in 1975, at a time when British Leyland was struggling to such an extent that the Government had had to step in to rescue it in 1974. When the B15 eventually got into production it was named the Titan. Though proto-types had the Leyland 500-series engine and it was then expected that the replacement for the O.680, the TL11, would be used, the Gardner 6LXB engine became standard with a hydraulically operated auto-

Left:
The AN68 version of the Atlantean was produced from 1972. This Alexander-bodied vehicle began life with Grampian but later passed to Midland Bluebird, after it came into Grampian ownership.

Right:
The Leyland Leopard was a popular choice for coach work from its introduction in 1959, and it was one of the first types available for 36ft-long coaches. This early 36-footer has Plaxton Panorama bodywork for Yorkshire Woollen District.

Centre right:
The Leopard also made a popular high-capacity single-deck bus, especially with BET companies. With typical BET-style Willowbrook dual-purpose bodywork is Midland Red 6398, one of that operator's class S24 of 1971.

Below:
The combination of Leyland Leopard chassis and Plaxton Panorama Elite bodywork was probably the classic coach of the early 1970s. This one, new in 1974, belonged to Lancashire United.
R. L. Wilson

Top:
ECW produced its rather unsuccessful B51 coach body for the Leopard and Tiger in the early-1980s. This Leopard was new to Hants & Dorset, remaining with Hampshire Bus and passing with it to Stagecoach South's Coastline operation.

Above:
The rugged construction of the Leopard meant that it became a popular basis for rebuilding as service buses once it had become outmoded for coach use. Willowbrook did a brisk trade in such rebuilding, with its functional looking Warrior body.
Kevin Lane

Top right:
However comprehensive a manufacturer's catalogue was, someone always wanted something different. So when Leyland introduced the Panther Manchester Corporation wanted something smaller. Regulations governing the relationship of overhangs to overall length meant that the O.600 engine was too big, so the Panther Cub used essentially Tiger Cub running units in a Panther-style rear-engined chassis. They had attractive Park Royal bodywork of a style also supplied on Panther chassis in some quantity to Stockholm.

Right:
One of the first of several thousand production Leyland Nationals was this one for Crosville.

Above:
The Leyland 500-series engine in the Leyland National was often considered its worst feature, so Leyland introduced the National 2 in 1979, with an O.680 engine, which necessitated moving the radiator to the front. This resulted in a 0.3m bulge at the front, detracting from the clean lines of the original design. This one went to Eastern Scottish; Scottish Bus Group had been a less than enthusiastic user of the original Leyland National. Mull is an area of Airdrie, rather than the better known island.
Iain MacGregor

Left:
Carrying Leyland decals is a late-model Fleetline of Chester, running on hire to Maidstone in 1986.
David Jenkins

Below left:
A Workington-built Leyland Titan working for London Coaches. It was new to London Transport.

matic gearbox, the Hydracyclic, air suspension, independent at the front, and a low, flat floor. Small numbers were built with Leyland TL11 engines. The Bristol VRT had been used in its Mark 3 form as a proving ground for an advanced cooling system which enabled the engine to be encapsulated for very low noise levels, and in terms of noise and ride quality it was an impressive performer.

However, Leyland's plans to make the Titan the sole, standard double-deck bus were thwarted. Industrial relations problems surrounded its efforts to get it into production, such that large orders outside London were lost, and the threat both to bodybuilders, faced with starvation of chassis, and dismay amongst operators being denied their traditional element of choice led to a rise in new rival manufacturers. Production eventually got going at Park Royal, which

had become part of the Leyland empire through the merger with ACV, but further industrial problems there led to the closure of the plant after 250 London Titans, plus smaller numbers for Greater Manchester, West Midlands and Reading, had been built and production continued at Workington, where there was excess capacity. It too ground to a halt in 1985 after less than 1,200 had been produced.

Leyland also saw that it needed to offer a double-deck chassis, so Titan components were arranged in a separate frame, similar in many respects to the Bristol VRT, to produce the Olympian. Unlike the Titan this had a beam axle at the front, with a clever arrangement of outboard air bellows to give a low entrance, and a dropped-centre rear axle to enable low-height bodywork to be built on it. It had a bolted perimeter frame chassis and engine options at this stage were

Above:
Leyland launched the Tiger in 1981 in grand style in Morocco, hence the exotic background to this Eastern Scottish coach with characteristic Duple Dominant III bodywork.

Right:
Ulsterbus was a keen user of Leyland Tigers for service bus work; indeed for several years it was the standard Northern Irish bus. This one has Alexander (Belfast) Q-type bodywork.

Left:
London Country took Leyland Tigers with high-floor Berkhof bodywork for Green Line use in 1985. The first is seen at the official launch at Gatwick Airport.

Centre left:
Leyland's response to the influx of Continental integral coaches was the stylish rear-engined Royal Tiger Doyen. Reliance of Gravesend is a keen user of the type.
Kevin Lane

Below:
The Royal Tiger was also available as a separate underframe; this one, delivered to Jacobs, Southampton, in 1984, has Van Hool bodywork.

Above right:
The Cub was a small, front-engined chassis based on the Terrier truck. Though used extensively for welfare and local-authority work some were used as psvs; Southdown used this one with Reeve Burgess bodywork on County Rider services in East Sussex. They had wheelchair lifts at the rear and combined local bus operation with various social services and health service functions.

Right:
With typical ECW bodywork is a Crosville Wales Leyland Olympian, seen in Chester in 1987.
Kevin Lane

the Gardner 6LXB or Leyland TL11. Production began at the Bristol factory in 1981, and was moved to Workington when Bristol was closed the next year. Some production went to Leyland in 1985, and by 1987 all Olympians were being built there before production moved back to Workington in 1990.

Meanwhile Leyland had had to address the coach market, where the aged Leopard was losing ground to the importers. It was replaced from 1981 (though production continued until the next year) by the Tiger, which had a more powerful turbocharged TL11 engine, giving 218bhp, coupled to a choice of Hydracyclic or ZF manual gearboxes, and full air suspension. It was an impressive chassis compared to the Leopard, and in later life 245bhp and 260bhp versions of the TL11 engine were offered. The next year an even more impressive coach was launched, resuming the Royal Tiger name, and this was built at the Charles H. Roe body plant. It used similar compo-

nents to the Tiger but with the engine at the rear and employing a complex space frame which could be bodied by other builders or take Roe's own Doyen body, which featured bonded glazing and styling which was completely up to date with the rear-engined integrals coming in particularly from Germany. Whereas the Tiger quickly settled down as a reliable workhorse the Royal Tiger was a bit more temperamental and certainly didn't match its German rivals for build quality. Only 60 Royal Tigers were built at Roe, 41 of them bodied there, before production moved to Workington in 1984.

Development work had been progressing only slowly on the replacement for the Leyland National; as single-deck volumes were so low it was hardly a pressing priority. A prototype underframe had been built in 1983, and a few more were built in 1985/86, including a small batch to be bodied by Alexander (Belfast) for Ulsterbus and Citybus. The Lynx offered

Top:
The Stagecoach Group standardised on long-wheel-base Olympians with Alexander bodywork. This early example is seen in Chichester.

Above:
Stagecoach also took three Hong Kong-style three-axle Olympians.
G. H. F. Atkins

a choice of TL11 or Gardner engines with ZF automatic transmission, and later the Cummins L10 was also offered. Meanwhile a very box-like body with flat bonded glass was developed for it, lacking much of the style of the Leyland National and also the structural competence of it. Nevertheless sales did pick up by the end of the 1980s, largely through large orders from West Midlands, Badgerline and Caldaire.

By now Leyland was into a new regime. Margaret Thatcher's Government which had come to power in 1979 was determined to take organisations like British Leyland out of the state sector. As a result the company was split into various separate businesses and Leyland Bus was finally sold to its management on 13 January 1987. This could scarcely have been a worse time for its new owners as bus orders had slumped nationwide in the wake of the restructuring of the operating industry. However, they managed to introduce one new model, the mid-engined Swift midibus, based on the Roadrunner lorry chassis, though this provided a much less suitable urban midibus than the Dennis Dart, which was mechanically very similar with a Cummins B-series engine, Allison transmission and parabolic steel suspension, was later to prove. The Swift had replaced a rather less acceptable, similar-sized front-engined chassis, the Cub, which had a Perkins engine and was used primarily for welfare and schools use. The Inner London Education Authority was a particularly large user, though some were built for psv use.

The Lynx was now established and the Olympian had always enjoyed a good reputation while the Tiger was holding its own, especially since the splitting up of Leyland, leading to the phasing-out of Leyland's engine production, meant that Leyland Bus was now fitting the well-respected Cummins L10 engine and giving it power outputs up to 290bhp. The L10 also became the standard power unit for both the Olympian and the Lynx, using ZF automatic transmission; Leyland by this time was producing parts for ZF. However, longer-term investment in research and development was going to be difficult with such low volumes and lack of major backing, and so on 30 March 1988 Leyland Bus was sold to Volvo.

Volvo had great plans for Leyland, including the development of the Lynx for world markets and production of the B10M at Workington, although it promptly ended production of the Royal Tiger. A new joint sales organisation, VL Bus & Coach, took over Leyland's sales from 1 January 1989, but by 1 July 1991 further integration took place under the Volvo Bus Ltd name. By the end of that year Volvo decided enough was enough and having sustained substantial losses over the Leyland business pulled the plug on 6 December 1991. The closure of Leyland's last manufacturing plant, Workington, was announced as was the end of the Tiger and Lynx, with only the Olympian to continue as a Volvo. However, it took until July 1993 to close down Workington, as there were large run-out orders for the Leyland Olympian.

Left: Newly-delivered to Maidstone & District in 1990 is a Northern Counties-bodied Leyland Olympian.

Below: Ulsterbus and its associated Belfast-based Citybus were late recipients of Leyland Tigers, on which it had standardised for bus use. A special Volvo-powered version was built for Northern Ireland use after Leyland engine production ceased. 1400 (WXI 1400) is a Volvo-engined Tiger with Alexander (Belfast) Q-type bodywork on CityExpress work — a limited-stop commuter service to Belfast from Newtownabbey, a satellite town to the north of the city.

Above:
The Leyland Swift was developed from the Roadrunner truck chassis, though with mid-underfloor engine, the Cummins B-series in vertical format, during Leyland's independent period. It was soon eclipsed by the Dennis Dart, using the same driveline components in a more 'user-friendly' form. Many Swifts were bodied by Wadham Stringer, such as this Luton & District vehicle.
Kevin Lane

Below:
Leyland valediction. Two of the last Leylands built are this United Olympian with Alexander bodywork and Cleveland Transit Lynx 2, which, like the National 2, gained a bulge at the front to accommodate the radiator, in this case to fit in the intercooler for the Volvo engine which was later offered as an option. They are seen together in Stockton in August 1994.
Kevin Lane

Marshall

Though a bodybuilder of some repute, which really rose to prominence in the 1960s, Marshall's sortie into complete vehicle building was scarcely covered in glory. Marshall is a diverse family-owned business, involving interests in engineering for the aviation business, car and commercial vehicle dealerships and ownership of Cambridge Airport, where it is based. Commercial vehicle building included taking over the former Bedford range from AWD to which it was sold, though neither AWD nor Marshall saw fit to revive Bedford's psv range.

Marshall's contribution to complete buses started off as a good idea which turned rather sour in the implementation. Having taken over the former Duple Dartline body, which had been developed for the Dennis Dart, it developed the body into its own style. As low-floor Darts and Volvo B6s rather left behind the original concept of a small vehicle, Marshall saw a gap in the market opening up, and in 1995 announced its Minibus.

The Minibus was a stainless-steel-framed, rear-engined, low-floor, integral vehicle, 8.5m long and 2.37m wide, with up to 30 seats, a low-floor front end, air suspension and air-over-hydraulic disc brakes. It was powered by a four-cylinder Cummins B-series engine, the 135bhp 4BT, with an Allison automatic gearbox, and had a big-bus-style front entrance ahead of the front wheels. It made its public debut at Coach & Bus '95.

It would appear to have been just what the market wanted, with the Dennis and Volvo having grown bigger and there consequently being no suitable low-floor minibus. The design was well-executed, but the type was problematic and the little four-cylinder Cummins was sadly lacking in refinement.

It was destined to be primarily a London model, but the first two went to Chester City Transport in the summer of 1996, while Derbyshire independent Glossopdale took four in early 1997. MTL London took a pre-production bus, unusually fitted with two child seats, in November 1996 for a service in Potters Bar, and London General took its first six at about the same time, which it followed with a further nine before the end of 1996. Meanwhile CentreWest ordered 16, which did not materialise until Marshall had tried to address noise and cooling problems and launched a Minibus 2 at Coach & Bus '97. This also offered Multiplex wiring, but the modifications were obviously not enough.

London General disposed of its Minibuses on loan to Limebourne as soon as it could, and when it got them back all 15 returned to their maker. A similar number of Marshall-bodied Dennis Darts arrived to replace them. The story was the same at CentreWest, which had sent all its Mk2s back to Marshall by 1999, and also received Darts instead. Even Glossopdale sent its Minibuses back. Production barely reached 50, and nearly all finished up back with their maker. Four of the Mk2s came back into service with Buzz Co-operative of Harlow, and three of the London General buses reappeared with Avon Coaches for services on the Wirral.

Marshall subsequently sold its vehicle business to ERF, which has been active in African markets, offering a range of basic, rugged high-floor bus models and a sophisticated rear-engined coach for South Africa; it also contended for the Maltese market when it looked as if that was opening up to new models. ERF indicated an intention to enter the UK bus business with a low-floor model, although Minibus production did not resume. Latterly owned by American company Western Star, ERF was acquired by MAN in early 2000. The bus side did not go to MAN, however, but passed to American builder Orion, which also produces rather specialist low-floor buses.

Left:
The Marshall Minibus at Expocoach '96.

Maudslay

Maudslay was a very old-established engineering firm based in Alcester, Warwickshire. Some of its prewar bus and coach designs showed some interesting innovation, but its postwar Marathon II and III single-deck coach chassis were highly conventional. The Marathon II was announced in 1946, and very quickly found a good following from independent coach operators in the main. It was conservative to the point of having a petrol engine, a rare example of a postwar heavyweight being so fitted, but sold 120 in about two years. It had a 7.4litre six-cylinder petrol engine with a unit-mounted five-speed gearbox, with direct-drive top, and was noted for its smoothness, with the combination of petrol engine and a high-geared rear axle.

The Marathon III was introduced at the beginning of 1947, with a diesel engine, though rather than develop its own suitable diesel Maudslay fitted the well-tried AEC 7.7litre diesel engine (actually 7.58litre, but always known as the 7.7) coupled to a four-speed AEC sliding-mesh gearbox. Production of both models continued side by side, though the Marathon III was by far the most successful postwar Maudslay. Again it was popular with independent operators, and sold around 600.

AEC was in something of an expansionist phase after the war, and in 1948, as it was already a supplier

Above:
Full-front Metalcraft 37-seat bodywork was fitted to this 30ft-long, 8ft-wide Marathon III of Churchbridge Luxury Coaches, Cannock. It was new in 1951.

of components to Maudslay, it bought the business. This was the same year in which AEC bought Crossley, and Associated Commercial Vehicles was established as a parent company. Production of the Marathon III continued until 1950.

That was not quite the end of the story for Maudslay; AEC rather shamelessly performed 'badge engineering' up to about 1956, largely to collar more space at Commercial Motor Shows, and Regal IIIs, Regent IIIs and even Reliances all appeared with the Maudslay name, while some Regal IVs were built as Maudslay Marathon IVs. Most were pure Southall products, although a batch of nine Regent IIIs was built for Coventry at the Alcester factory in 1950 and were suitably badged. They entered service the following January. Maudslay then became an axle plant and also built AEC's dump trucks. It was sold by Leyland in 1972 to the American-owned Rockwell International as an axle manufacturer, and Rockwell still builds axles and brake systems in Alcester.

Metro Cammell Weymann

Metro Cammell Weymann was originally the sales organisation set up in 1932 to handle the separate bodybuilding activities of Metropolitan Cammell, based in Birmingham, and Weymann, of Addlestone, Surrey. The two later joined forces as a single entity

and the Weymann factory closed in 1965. Although a leading builder of separate bodywork, and a pioneer of all-metal construction, MCW also had a long history of building integral vehicles in conjunction with Leyland; the Olympic came out in 1949, and MCW also produced integral bodywork for the prototype Atlantean.

When it became apparent that Leyland was aiming to produce its own integral vehicles for the 1970s, effectively shutting the doors on the mainstream bodybuilders, MCW decided to look for a partner with which to build its own range of integral vehicles. At the same time Swedish builder Scania-Vabis was keen to break into the UK market, and so the two agreed in 1969 for MCW to build the body structure for what were effectively UK-market Scania CR111 integral vehicles. The Metro-Scania was something of an advance for the UK, with full air suspension, Scania's unusual two-speed fully-automatic transmission and performance which was rather more potent than the norm for buses in Britain.

It gave the new Leyland National some competition, and actually got into the market before Leyland's new products, in 1971. The Metro-Scania remained in production only until 1973, by which time 133 had been built, but MCW had developed a double-deck version, the Metropolitan, which made its debut at the 1973 Scottish Motor Show. This sold rather more strongly; major orders were won from some of the PTEs and London Transport, and 663 had been sold by the time production ended in 1978. MCW also built a one-off Scania-based coach in 1972, the Metropolitan 145, based on the V8-powered Scania CR145.

MCW had been considering building its own

Above:
A typical London Mark 1 MCW Metrobus, M918, in Wimbledon in 1994.

Below:
A Mk 2 Metrobus in service with Maidstone & District at Tunbridge Wells in 1984.
John Marsh

integral since 1975. The Scania engine, for all its power, was considered thirsty, and there had also been problems with body corrosion. MCW had an agreement to build on Scania running units until 1979, but began serious work on its own integral in April 1976. It was to be a mainly alloy, semi-integral structure based on well-proven mechanical components, which involved the use of the Gardner 6LXB engine and Voith transmission, and full air suspension was used. The new vehicle was named Metrobus, and a demonstrator appeared in October 1977, followed by the first production bus, for West Midlands, which emerged the following January. This was closely followed by four more and five for London Transport. Both operators adopted it as a standard double-decker, almost exclusively so in the case of West Midlands, and dual-sourced with Leyland Titans in the case of London Transport. Between them they took more than 2,500 Metrobuses. It sold well both on the home market and overseas, and a Rolls Royce engine option was offered.

A new three-axle version was built for Hong Kong from 1981, and this had a revised body structure which was adapted to form the Mk 2 Metrobus for the home market from 1982. This superseded the original version, with its characteristic asymmetric windscreen (a feature it inherited from the Metro-Scania), although London Transport still specified the more expensive Mk 1 until it received its last in 1985.

MCW also branched out into other markets in 1982. At the Motor Show that year it showed an exotic three-axle double-deck coach in Scottish Citylink livery. It was the first time the new Citylink livery had been seen and it was also the first application in a British psv of the new Cummins L10 engine. Cummins had gained rather a bad reputation in the British bus industry which couldn't get on with the V6-200 fitted in the Daimler Roadliner (despite it faring rather better in other markets), though the new 10-litre L10 quickly gained a reputation for reliability, good performance and low fuel consumption, and was later to knock Gardner off its perch. The new coach, the Metroliner, used a 290bhp version of the engine, coupled to a Voith automatic transmission in a structure based on the Hong Kong Metrobus, though with bonded glazing and a much more stylish appearance. The standard of interior finish was impressive too, and for a manufacturer steeped in buses it stood up well against more established coach manufacturers. A single-deck version was also shown, again with the Cummins L10, though mounted in-line at the rear and driving through a ZF manual gearbox. Styling of this was rather more restrained, even uncompromisingly square. The single-deck version never caught on as well as the double-decker, despite a much-needed facelift, following the launch in 1983 of a high-floor Hiliner. Unlike the original single-deck Metroliner, this was fully integral; the original single-decker had a conventional chassis frame which intruded into the luggage space.

Above left:
East Kent was the largest user of the single-deck MCW
Metroliner. Two are seen at Victoria Coach Station, in
National Holidays livery, when new in 1982.

Above:
One of the first double-deck Metroliners for National
Express work. This one was new to National Travel
West in 1983.

National Express had a large requirement for
double-decker coaches at this time. The Metroliner
had the drawback of being over 4m high, and therefore not suitable for Continental operation, which was
what most operators used double-deck coaches on.
National Express however, required the capacity of
the double-decker without needing it to go abroad,
and quickly ordered 39. It went on to order plenty
more and altogether 127 were built, all but 25 for
National Express. The single-decker only made it to
41, and ironically when MCW did get round to
producing a 4m double-decker, the Metroliner
400GT, with attractive styling and an in-line
Cummins 14-litre or Gardner 6LYT 15.5litre unit, it
sold only three. ·

MCW was developing a knack of producing new
products quickly to meet the demands of the market.
This had the drawback that they were not as reliable
as they might have been had a little more time been
spent getting out the bugs before production began.

This knack was also evident at the 1986 Show, when
MCW showed its first midibus, the 25-seat front-
engined Metrorider, the first integral vehicle aimed at
the post-deregulation minibus revolution. It offered
the choice of Perkins Phaser or Cummins B-series
four or six-cylinder engines of around one litre per
cylinder capacity, with a ZF manual or Allison automatic transmission. In the end virtually all orders
favoured the six-cylinder Cummins/Allison driveline.
Manual versions offered a new ceramic-lined clutch,
which wore well but took up too sharply for bus use.
Despite being pushed into production too quickly the
Metrorider sold like hot cakes, leaving some operators to repent at leisure when structural weaknesses,
especially round the back end, showed up.

It seems sales were also being gained rather too
cheaply at a time when the bus market was badly
depressed, and MCW's parent Laird Group was
concerned at the lack of profits coming in from
MCW. The Group considered that if it bought
Leyland Bus, which had come on to the market, with
the Government's desire to get British Leyland out of
the public sector, it would make a viable British bus
manufacturing business. In the end the Government
favoured Leyland's management buyout bid, and so
Laird Group decided to sell MCW at the end of 1988.
It proved a difficult business of which to dispose, and
it finished up, bit by bit, in the hands of Optare, which
reworked the Metrorider very effectively and reintroduced the Metrobus in a very different form.

Left:
The impressive Metroliner 400GT at the 1986 Motor Show. Only three were built.
T. W. Moore

Below:
Cardiff Bus is a big user of both MCW and Optare Metroriders. This is an early 25-seat one.
Kevin Lane

Bottom:
Longer, wider Metroriders were also made available, with up to 33 seats. Seen in Chichester is a wide, long-wheelbase example of Stagecoach South.

Morris-Commercial

Morris was another manufacturer based in Birmingham. Before the war it had produced a range of purpose-designed heavyweight psvs, though it built no psv chassis from 1935 to 1948. Again that 1948 Commercial Motor Show was the venue for the launch of a 32-seat Morris-Commercial coach. It was a lightweight, though offered forward-control, and was powered by a Morris 4.25litre six-cylinder diesel engine, designed by Saurer, with the option of a 3.75litre four-cylinder petrol unit, driving through a four-speed manual gearbox. With the diesel engine it was known as type OP, and the petrol version was type PP.

It was largely an export chassis, though also sold in small numbers in this country. Thereafter Morris psvs were based on goods chassis, and the J2 of the late 1950s/early 1960s particularly sold, in both Austin and Morris forms, as a minibus.

Below:
A typical early postwar Morris-Commercial bus, of which little is known; it appears to be an export vehicle, probably a 1947 CVF13/5 with Wadham bodywork for Bermuda.

Bottom:
This rather attractive Mulliner-bodied Morris-Commercial was built in 1951 for the Morris Motors Band.

Moulton

Some time after Austin and Morris merged to become BMC it was decided to design a full-sized coach chassis to augment the large range of trucks. Work proceeded slowly, and was overtaken by events; BMC had become part of the enlarged Leyland empire and there was no longer any need for it.

But Moulton Developments subsequently completed and bodied a vehicle and put the design on the market in the early 1970s in the (unfulfilled) hope of finding a maker to buy the designs. The coach was an eight-wheeler, with twin steering axles at the front. Alex Moulton, of Hydrolastic suspension and Moulton Bicycle fame, was responsible for the design which provided superb riding and handling. The chassis had a Perkins 6.354 engine at the front, was of welded tube construction and weighed only 7,360kg when bodied. Most chassis parts came from the BMC-derived Leyland mid-weight truck range.

Northern General Transport

The major north-eastern bus operator Northern General had something of a history of building its own buses and coaches, some to very advanced design, prior to the war. After the war it built a few single-deckers using parts from prewar buses in a similar style to Beadle, in an effort to increase the number of 30ft vehicles in the fleet; Northern had probably the most intensive operation of any company operator. It was also obsessed with producing vehicles of light weight.

A bus and coach were built in 1951 to the maximum dimensions. The coach had a lengthened AEC Regal chassis, with a 7.7litre engine and preselector gearbox, and a new Picktree body, and 24 were built between 1951 and 1953.

The bus versions were probably more genuinely Northern General products, as they had 30ft x 8ft chassis frames fabricated by the company itself, and used 7.7litre engines and other components from 1936 AEC Regal IIs. Again they had Picktree bodies, designed by the operator, with an impressive 43 seats, only one less than the maximum possible in a contemporary underfloor-engined type which in the days before Tiger Cubs would have weighed considerably more than the 6ton 2cwt of the Northern vehicles. Only four were built and they were known as 'kipper boxes'.

In the 1970s Northern General also built its famous Tynesider and Wearsider double-deckers, which were heavy conversions respectively of a Leyland PD3 and a Routemaster for one-person operation. No more followed.

Below:
Two of Northern General's AEC-based 'Kipper Boxes' with a single-deck Guy Arab III.
M. A. Sutcliffe

Below right:
An Optare MetroRider in service in London.

Optare

Optare is something of a phenomenon. It was formed only in 1985, the worst time one could choose to come into the UK bus industry, and was a buyout of the former Leyland-owned Roe plant in Leeds. Leyland had closed it down in order to reduce bodybuilding capacity in the face of slumping orders nationwide.

The new company made a very good showing, combining the experience and expertise of the Roe workforce and the flair of a brand-new company. It was essentially a bodybuilder, but marketed its products as complete vehicles, with specific bodywork designs married to specific chassis types, which in some cases were not available for bodying by anyone else.

Optare's first new model in this vein was the CityPacer, built on the Volkswagen LT55 chassis, specially imported for Optare's use and modified to suit Optare's design by the Leeds firm. It was introduced in 1986 as a 25-seater, at a time when 16-seat minibuses were still in vogue. However, the company had read the market well; the 25-seater was what the industry was on the verge of requiring and, unlike the 'breadvan' style of minibus, the CityPacer had refreshing and very distinctive styling which captured the imagination. It was followed by the bigger, Mercedes-based StarRider.

Optare launched the full-sized Delta at the 1988 Birmingham Motor Show. It was based on the DAF SB220 chassis and marked the beginning of a relationship between DAF and Optare which was to have a profound bearing on the company's direction in the coming years. Like the CityPacer it had futuristic styling,

and used the Alusuisse system of bolted aluminium construction. At this stage the Delta was the only version of the SB220 available in Britain. The first went into service in February 1989 with Wigmore's (Northern Bus), Sheffield, and production thereafter averaged about 70 a year.

As mentioned above, MCW came on to the market at the end of 1988, and Optare bought the rights to produce the Metrorider. It reworked the bus to some extent, standardising on the turbocharged Cummins 6BT engine and Allison transmission. There was some restyling, and the structural weaknesses were ironed out. The interior styling came to resemble other Optare products, and the name was altered subtly to MetroRider in the style of its other midibus products. General opinion was that it was a much-improved product over the original MCW.

Optare also took over the rights to the Metrobus, but did not put it into production as such; certain features were built into a new DAF chassis, the DB250, which was identical to the SB220 at the front but had a transverse engine and a driveline/rear suspension layout based on the Metrobus. Optare developed a new, very stylish Alusuisse body for it and it was launched in 1991 as the Spectra. In the interim, Optare had also started building a smaller single-decker, the Vecta, based on the MAN 11.190 chassis.

Optare's ties with DAF had become stronger in July 1990 when it joined a new organisation, United Bus, which had been formed to build links between certain manufacturers in Europe. DAF Bus was the prime mover, but the Dutch bus market collapsed and United Bus went into receivership in 1993. Optare managed to buy itself

Above:
This Optare MetroRider for Reading Buses' Newbury operation is rather unusual in being powered by a Rover V8 engine fuelled by compressed natural gas.

Left:
Although based on other manufacturers' chassis, Optare's full-sized vehicles are marketed under the Optare name. This is the first Sigma, based on the Dennis Lance, for Ipswich Buses.

out, and regained its independence, though it lost exclusivity with the DAF DB250 chassis which was then marketed in Britain by Hughes DAF (now Arriva Bus & Coach). The Delta body was made available on Mercedes O.405 chassis as the Prisma, using Mercedes' own front end — thereby losing its distinctive front end treatment — and on the Dennis Lance as the Sigma.

With its experience of building MetroRiders, however, Optare took the decision to develop its own range of integral buses. While this increased Optare's risk, at the same time it meant a much higher proportion of the price of the vehicle went to Optare, and costs could be reduced

by having engines and other expensive components delivered on a 'just-in-time' basis rather than having complete chassis hanging around waiting to be bodied.

As the low-floor revolution began to take off around 1996, Optare was ready with a new product, the Excel. Typically stylish, it featured a deep front windscreen and was powered by a Cummins B-series engine driving through an Allison World Series gearbox. Although easily seen as a direct competitor to the Dennis Dart it used rather more 'big bus' technology, with full-sized wheels and other heavyweight components. It was also 2.5m wide, though lengths ranged from a midi-sized 9.6m

Right:
A major customer for Optare is Wilts & Dorset, operator of this MetroRider seen at Shell Bay, Dorset.
John Young

Below:
Blackpool Transport was the first customer for the low-floor Optare Excel. These first buses were later taken back by Optare in exchange for some new ones, and were refurbished and offered for sale in early 2000.

Bottom:
A short-wheelbase Excel of Springfield Coaches, Wigan.
Russell Young

through 10m and 10.7m up to 11.5m, definitely in the big league.

The first Excels went into service with Blackpool Transport in May 1996, and since then the type has been a steady seller with a number of customers. Optare was well placed to supply medium-sized customers, notably Go-Ahead Group, Trent and Reading Transport, but numerous other operators have taken it. Export was foreseen as a possibility, and an MAN engine was offered for export versions; front axles too came from MAN. So far only Malta has been supplied outside the UK.

A Mark 2 Excel was announced at Coach & Bus '99, with revised frontal treatment featuring circular headlamps rather than rectangular, and a new option of a 230bhp Mercedes OM906 engine was offered. At the same time the larger two models increased in length to 11m and 11.8m. Also shown at Coach & Bus '99 was the Irisbus (*née* Renault) Agoraline, a French low-floor suburban full-size chassis which is intended to be bodied for the UK market by Optare, using Irisbus's front and rear ends.

Optare's next new product was yet more innovative, and gained Millennium Product status. The Solo is a true low-floor minibus, available in 8.5m or 9.2m lengths. Although externally it looks as if it should be a front-engined vehicle, with no front overhang, in fact it has a Mercedes-Benz four-cylinder 4.2-litre diesel mounted in line at the rear, driving through an Allison gearbox, giving it the same driveline as the Mercedes-Benz Vario. Again, styling is distinctive, with a hint of single-deck trolleybus to its front end, and no rear window. Having the entrance behind the front wheels, where it does not affect approach angles, gives it the lowest entrance of any low-floor bus.

Optare was in two minds whether to go ahead with production, but one of its major customers, Wilts & Dorset, which wanted both to embrace low-floor technology and to replace the oldest of its large fleet of Metroriders, pledged an order for 85, so long as it was built to a full width of 2.5m. Optare went ahead and received orders for 300 before any were built. Along with Optare's usual medium-sized customers, Travel West Midlands and FirstGroup have embraced it enthusiastically. Wilts & Dorset was also one of the first customers for the low-floor version of the Optare Spectra

double-decker, and converted all of its Salisbury operations to low-floor in 1998. Travel West Midlands was another early customer for the low-floor Spectra, taking 22 (one after a spell in Dundee).

Optare's production has steadily increased over the years; in 1995 it had built 272 vehicles, nearly half of which were bodies on other builders' chassis. Expansion in 1998 saw it take over minibus builder Autobus, and MetroRider production was transferred to that firm's Rotherham factory. In 1999 most of the 400 or so vehicles Optare produced were integrals; only the Spectra remains as a body-on-chassis, other than some Mercedes-based products in the small coach sector, and Optare is known to be working on an integral double-decker to replace it. The company is also due to introduce a true minibus — a front-wheel-drive 'grown-up people carrier', aimed primarily at the welfare sector — in 2000. Meanwhile, the MetroRider remains in production, but in sales terms has proved a victim of the very rapid switch to low-floor buses.

Optare's independence ended in January 2000, when it was sold for £21.5 million to NABI, a Hungarian firm established in 1992 to take over the American production of Ikarus. NABI was active only in North America, and was seeking an entry into the European market. It is also hopeful of introducing the Solo to North America.

Quest 80

Quest 80 was another short-lived manufacturer, which flourished briefly in the 1980s. Primarily an exporter, it did build a few home market vehicles in the Telford factory which it occupied from 1979.

Much of its activity was in South Africa, so at that

Above:
One of the rather disastrous Quest 80 B-types built for Merseyside PTE. This one had returned to Merseyside and was operating on a Merseyside PTE service, though with David Tanner of St Helens, in October 1994.
S. J. Kelly

Below:
The prototype Quest 80 Model D, with Reeve Burgess bodywork, at the 1983 Brighton Coach Rally.

time when commercial activity with South Africa was frowned upon publicly little was heard of Quest 80. It developed a trolleybus chassis and the Q-Bus, which had a vertical Mercedes-derived Atlanta engine, side-mounted in the same style as the prewar AEC Q.

It was in 1983 that it entered the UK market with rear-engined bus and coach chassis, using Ford or Perkins engines. Prototypes were built with Locomotors and Reeve Burgess bodywork, and a Locomotors-bodied B-type was built for Ralphs Coaches for work at Heathrow Airport. This had a Ford 2726T six-litre engine and Allison gearbox.

The nearest thing Quest experienced to a break-through was when Excelsior of Bournemouth, a keen Ford user, wanted a more up-to-date Ford-powered chassis than Ford could provide. Excelsior managing director Vernon Maitland was a keen sailor and had found Ford diesels modified for marine use by Sabre to be effective power units, and so specified this 5.95litre 220bhp unit in his coaches, which were named after him, as type VM. They were rear-engined 12m air-sprung coaches with low driver positions, as was then fashionable, and 20 were sent for bodying for Excelsior by Plaxtons. Problems with them meant that two never entered service and a third was never bodied by Plaxtons.

Quest 80 tended to use Locomotors bodywork for bus chassis, and in 1984 Locomotors' parent UEI plc bought Quest 80, and three C-type Cummins-engined coach chassis were built at Locomotors' Andover factory before all production was transferred there that summer. A few D-type rear-engined buses, a straight-framed, leaf sprung chassis with vertical Ford 2723E or Perkins 6.354 engines and Ford synchro-mesh gearboxes were built for welfare customers, and the last vehicles completed were six B-types for Merseyside PTE with very square, oddly-proportioned Locomotors bodies. They had rear-mounted Perkins 6.354 engines, mounted on the nearside and driving through a U-drive arrangement which Quest 80 had developed to enable standard proprietary units to be used in a confined space. Again they were not a success, and Quest 80 production ended in 1985.

However, examples of another Quest type, the J-type, entered service after this. These were a shorter version of the D-type, also had Ford engines and the U-drive arrangement, and were bodied by Jonckheere, mostly with 37-seat bodies. They were heavily modified by Southampton coach operator Buddens, usually with a straight driveline using the Cummins B-series engine and 11 entered service in Britain and Ireland with independent coach operators up to 1988.

Quest 80 may have been an innovator, though something was obviously sadly lacking in its production. Of all the unusual British manufacturers this seems to have been the most disastrous, and a surprisingly large proportion of its output never reached completion.

Rowe

Another short-lived manufacturer was M. G. Rowe (Motors) Doublebois Ltd, which built a few Hillmaster bus and coach chassis in Cornwall in the 1950s. A prototype lightweight chassis was built in 1953, with a Meadows 4DC four-cylinder 5.7litre engine at the front and a five-speed Meadows

gearbox. It was bodied by Whitson with a full-front coach body, but before it was registered Rowe decided to develop underfloor-engined chassis. Thus the engine of the prototype was converted to horizontal format by Rowe itself, and went into the company's own fleet.

Meadows then produced its own horizontal version of the 4DC, the 4HDC, and the rest of Rowe's psv output was of mid-engined layout with entrances ahead of the front wheels. A Reading-bodied 44-seat bus was built for Millbrook Steamboat & Trading in 1956, followed by three for Morlais Motor Services, Merthyr Tydfil, in 1957/58. The operator built its own 44-seat bodies on Metal Sections frames. Production ended with these five, though lorry production was rather more significant, reaching three figures before the company went into receivership in 1960.

Rutland

The rear-engined Rutland Clipper was almost an exact contemporary of the first Rowe Hillmaster and was also bodied by Whitson. The 30ft coach chassis, built in Croydon by Motor Traction Ltd in 1954, had a vertical Perkins R6 108bhp engine driving through a David Brown four-speed synchromesh gearbox. In order to fit the driveline within the length of the rear overhang permitted on a 30ft chassis the drive was taken forward to a transfer box halfway along the chassis and then transmitted back into the front of the rear axle, a similar arrangement to that used on the Bristol RE in later years.

The 41-seat coach went to West Kent Motors of Biggin Hill and two more were built in 1954 and 1955, also bodied by Whitson.

SMT

Scottish Motor Traction built a 32-seat integral bus based on Albion components in 1955, though it was not announced officially until the following year. It had an aluminium alloy frame and used the same 65bhp four-cylinder horizontal diesel engine as the Albion Nimbus (also used in the horizontally-engined Claymore goods vehicle) and a four-speed synchromesh Albion gearbox. Perhaps the most interesting feature, apart from the very low unladen weight of 3tons 9^1/$_4$cwt and fuel consumption around 22mpg, was the use of rubber suspension; independent suspension was considered but ruled out because of its complication and cost. It remained a one-off.

Saunders-Roe

Saunders Roe was based in Beaumaris on Anglesey, and was best-known for its bus bodywork, particularly on Leyland Tiger Cub chassis, though it also built a sizeable number of RTs for London. However, in 1955 it built an integral bus, to a style identical to the Tiger Cub, for Maidstone & District. It had a Gardner 5HLW horizontal engine.

Seddon

The Oldham-based Seddon concern, which had moved from Salford just after the war, had built a small number of goods vehicles in the years leading up to the war. In 1946 a passenger chassis was developed, based largely on the 5-ton goods chassis, and fitted with a Perkins P6 engine and five-speed gearbox. It was a conventional, front-engined design, known as the Mark 4, and the first two were bodied by the company for a Scottish operator. It was suitable for 28-seat coach or 32-seat bus bodywork. A larger Mark 6 followed in 1950 when the maximum length limit was extended to 30ft. Quite a number were bodied by Seddon, which maintained a tradition of offering bodywork on its own chassis until virtually the end of production.

Although Bedford's Y-series chassis are sometime considered to have pioneered the use of vertical underfloor engines, Seddon was already building vehicles of that configuration by 1952, when it launched its Mark 10 and Mark 11 chassis. The Mark 10 had the Perkins P6 engine while the Mark 11 had the faster, 108bhp R6. The Mark 11 was intended for 30ft coachwork, the Mark 10 was about 3ft shorter, and both had the entrance ahead of the front axle, and quite a high chassis frame, with the engine protruding another 10in above it. The 1952 Show vehicle was a Mark 10 for West Riding, with Seddon's own 32-seat bodywork, though it was soon sold back to Seddon. Nevertheless the Mark 10 and Mark 11 remained in production until 1960, and about 100 were sold.

The Mark 19 was the next production underfloor-engined chassis, though only one, with an AEC horizontal engine, was built for the UK in 1959, and remains in service with its original operator, Thorne of Bubwith. It has an attractive Harrington body. All other Mark 19s were exported, and for much if its life as a bus producer Seddon was more active overseas than it was on the home market.

In 1958 Seddon bodied a batch of non-Seddon vehicles, six Albion Aberdonians for Manchester, and later renamed its bodybuilding organisation Pennine, to distance it from Seddon itself in order to build more on other manufacturers' chassis. The Pennine name was also applied to later chassis, and the Pennine 4 emerged in 1967. This was primarily a coach chassis in similar vein to the Ford R226, though available in lengths from 30ft to 36ft, with a Perkins 6.354 engine alongside the driver, ahead of the front axle, and driving originally through a five-speed constant-mesh gearbox, though later chassis had synchromesh. The 170bhp 8.5-litre Perkins V8.510 was also offered later, which gave it rather more performance than was usual from a lightweight chassis. An unusual customer for the type was SELNEC PTE, which adopted it as its standard coach chassis, some fitted with V8s, though one of the first operators was Gosport & Fareham which had some as service buses with Pennine bodies.

From the Pennine IV was developed what was reckoned to be the first midibus chassis. With no major mechanical components within the wheelbase it was quite a simple matter to produce a short version of it from 1972, which was sold as the Seddon Pennine 4.236, with a Perkins four-cylinder engine of that designation and either manual or Allison automatic gearbox. The most famous were the SELNEC Manchester Centreline vehicles, though others were sold to Edinburgh and Doncaster. All had Pennine bodies. By this time the full-sized Pennine had reached the Pennine VI, which was still front engined

Above:
An unusual Beadle-bodied, Perkins-engined Seddon Mk IV of Western National.
A. R. Packer

Left:
This Seddon Mk 10 appeared at the 1952 Commercial Motor Show. It had Seddon's own bodywork and carried West Riding livery. It is seen during the short period in which it actually worked for West Riding.
G. Holt

but available in lengths up to 12m. The engine was mounted very low in the frame to give a flat floor in the entrance area, though resulting in a very high floor level.

However, Seddon was not to remain just a lightweight producer; in 1969 it announced a rear-engined service bus, the Pennine RU. This was to be available in 33ft and 36ft form, with a horizontal Gardner 6HLX engine and five-speed Self-Changing Gears semi-automatic transmission. It was kept rather simpler than other rear-engined chassis of the 1960s, and had a straight chassis frame rather than one

Below:
Most Seddon Pennine RUs had Pennine bodywork, built by Seddon, though Lancashire United used this rather attractive Plaxton body instead. This one is seen operating on hire to SELNEC in Stockport on a former Stockport Corporation service.

Bottom:
Crosville was a major operator of RUs, this time with Pennine bodywork. EPG704 is a dual-purpose example, seen on the Rhyl-Ruthin service on 27 July 1971.
J. G. Carroll

Top:
Also operated by Crosville, though built as a demonstrator, was this Seddon Pennine VII with underfloor Gardner engine and bodywork to RU style, though with a flat floor.
R. L. Wilson

Above:
The Seddon Pennine VII was more readily associated with Scottish Bus Group; this 1975-built vehicle for Eastern Scottish had one of the first Alexander T-type bodies.

Right:
Another Eastern Scottish Seddon Pennine VII, this time with Plaxton Supreme bodywork, in Taunton on a tour to Torquay in 1978.
Ray Stenning

Below:
The midi version of the Seddon Pennine IV, the 4.236, in service in Manchester.
John Robinson

cranked over the rear axle; however, the chassis was inclined from front to rear so it still had the advantage of a low entrance, with a step-free interior too. The radiator was mounted on the side, and Seddon developed quite a stylish body for it. Darlington Transport was one satisfied customer, while other operators of it included Huddersfield and Doncaster Corporations, and most surprising, in view of its traditional Tilling loyalty to Bristol was Crosville which took 100 in bus and dual-purpose forms in 1971-72, when it was unable to obtain Bristol REs quickly enough. Another major customer was Lancashire United Transport, which took 50 with Plaxton bodywork. Production ended around 1974. Although Darlington was well-pleased with its RUs, and, as noted earlier, had the Ward Dalesman GRXI built as a replacement, others found it less reliable; all of Crosville's had to have their engines moved to permit a longer propshaft at a less sharp angle.

However, this wasn't to be Seddon's last heavyweight effort. Spurred on by the Scottish Bus Group, which required something resembling a Gardner-engined version of the Leyland Leopard, it built the Pennine VII, which had a mid-mounted Gardner 6HLXB engine and a choice of ZF four-speed or five speed synchromesh, favoured by SBG, or Self Changing Gears semi-automatic transmission. It was the first application of the horizontal version of the Gardner 6LXB, and the prototype appeared at the 1973 Scottish Motor Show with an Alexander Y-type dual-purpose body in Eastern Scottish livery, and most were built for the Scottish Bus Group with Alexander Y-type bodywork in bus or dual-purpose form or the later T-type. However, there were some full coach versions for SBG, including 12m vehicles

with the impressive Alexander M-type motorway coach body for its London services and with Plaxton Supreme bodywork. SBG's requirement for a simple, straightforward vehicle meant that it had a mechanical handbrake, rather than the spring-type which was standard on most types by then, though spring brakes were available for less conservative operators. A few others were built for independent coach operators, again with Plaxton bodywork, while Crosville took an ex-demonstrator with a Pennine body, of very similar style to the body for the RU. Production ended in 1982. SBG had had some 500 Pennine VIIs. By now Seddon and Atkinson had merged and concentrated entirely on goods vehicles.

One small diversification worth mentioning was into electric vehicles. A battery-electric midibus based on a 4.236 was built in 1974, and a larger RU-based vehicle was built at the same time. Both were built for SELNEC PTE, the midibus putting in some useful service on the Centreline service, where its lack of range — despite holding records for battery vehicle range — was not a problem. The RU saw little service however.

Sentinel

It was only after the war that Shrewsbury-based Sentinel became known as a bus builder, and then only for a comparatively short period. It was better known before the war for its steam vehicles, both for road and rail, and although by the late 1930s steam power was very much outmoded for road transport Sentinel nonetheless built highly-sophisticated steam lorries. The relevance of these to our story is that Sentinel had developed horizontal steam engines that

Left:
Ribble's first Sentinel STC4 of 1949. This particular bus was bodied by Beadle, though subsequent ones were bodied by Sentinel to the same style.

Top:
The STC6 was rather more of a heavyweight; this one was built in 1951 for Boyer of Rothley, Leicestershire.

Above:
Sentinel also built a conventional coach chassis version of the STC6; this one was fitted with a Plaxton Venturer body for Warners of Tewkesbury in 1952.

could be tucked under the chassis of a lorry out of the way. Thus when it came to produce diesel engines Sentinel was able to adapt its steam engine technology and get ahead of the field to produce a workable underfloor-engined bus.

Sentinel caused something of a stir at the 1948 Commercial Motor Show at Earl's Court, by showing the first production underfloor-engined bus for the British market. Leyland was only able to show the horizontal engine for its forthcoming integral Olympic; Sentinel had got in ahead of Leyland, AEC and Bristol which were all developing underfloor-engined single-deckers. The Beadle-Sentinel at the 1948 show, for Western National, featured a four-cylinder, 6litre 90bhp indirect-injection engine with

five-speed overdrive gearbox and weighed in at only 5tons 8cwt, despite being a 40-seater. It had Sentinel's running units arranged in an integral structure by Beadle. Apart from a demonstrator and the first of a batch of six for Ribble, thereafter Sentinel built the bodywork itself, to Beadle's style, for service buses, though Beadle continued to body the SLC4 coach version. Ribble took its batch of six in 1949/50, though most STC4s were built for independent operators; the show exhibit was billed as 'one of

a fleet ordered for Western National', but remained a one-off.

When the dimensions regulations were relaxed to allow 30ft vehicles Sentinel moved on to a 30ft vehicle with a six-cylinder 9.12litre 135bhp indirect injection engine, the STC6 integral bus, with a four-speed constant-mesh gearbox. The coach version was a conventional chassis, the SLC6 with a five-speed overdrive gearbox, which with 135bhp on tap must have made for excellent performance. The same must have been true of the STC6, with a most impressive power to weight ratio, as it weighed only 5ton 15cwt. The STC4 and SLC4 remained in production, however. Ribble too was the most significant customer for the STC6, with 14 44-seat buses built in 1951, despite the fact that the Olympic was now available from Ribble's usual supplier, Leyland. The SLC6 was bodied conventionally by firms other than Beadle, and the SLC4 was also made available as a chassis; Adams of Barry took a Gurney Nutting-bodied SLC4 in 1951, while three SLC4s were bodied by Plaxtons with 37-seat centre-entrance bodies in 1952/53 and Bellhouse Hartwell bodied two SLC6s for Blue Cars, a London operator, in 1952/53.

From 1953, by which time 104 Sentinel psvs had been built, including 10 for export, all production was on separate chassis, the SLC6/30, which introduced a direct-injection version of the 9.12-litre six-cylinder engine, reducing the power output to 120bhp. Production was hardly rapid, however, and less than 30 were built for the home market before the company sold out to Rolls-Royce in 1956 and road-

vehicle construction finished. The majority were coaches with a variety of bodybuilders, including Plaxton, Duple and Whitson. Burlingham bodied nine of them as coaches, four of them for Schofield, Marsden. But four were bodied as buses, two unusually by Whitson, one by ACB, a dual-door demonstrator, and there was a particularly handsome one by Burlingham in 1955 which went to Green Bus, Rugeley, but ended its days with Yorkshire Traction.

Shelvoke & Drewry

Shelvoke & Drewry has always been a very specialist vehicle builder, particularly associated with refuse disposal, and came up with some highly innovative designs in the 1920s, some of which were built as buses mainly for seafront work.

It built only one bus postwar. In 1982 it was developing its SPV range for a whole host of highly-specialist applications, and this included a bus for airport transfer work. It had a front-mounted Ford engine and Allison automatic transmission. The chassis frame then cranked down behind the cab to give low access for passengers via a centre entrance. It had a full-width cab with no seating alongside the driver and received a Reeve Burgess body. It worked at Heathrow and Gatwick. It terrified the author when he drove it, so the less said about it the better.

Talbot

The rather complicated history of the Rootes Group ended up with a British offshoot of Peugeot called Talbot, which ceased building cars around 1985. One

Top left:
This splendid-looking 1952 SLC6 had stylish Bellhouse Hartwell bodywork for Blue Cars of London.

Left:
The Shelvoke & Drewry SPV airport bus with Reeve Burgess bodywork, built in 1981. It remained a one-off.

Below:
A TBP-built Talbot Express Pullman on an Essex County Council contracted service at Epping station.

Left:
A 1949 Tilling-Stevens K6LH7 with Dutfield bodywork. It was new to Kemps Motor Services, which was bought out of receivership in 1955 to become Chiltern Queens. It is seen, with a Leyland Comet behind, at Theale in 1960; it remained in service until 1964.
M. A. Sutcliffe

Below:
A 13-seat Trojan minibus at Outwood Mill, Surrey.
John Aldridge collection

product did remain however, the Italian-built Talbot Express, which was a van of Ford Transit dimensions which was also built as a Fiat and a Citroën. Unlike the Transit it was front-wheel drive, and as the front end was thus fully self-contained it was possible to get a proprietary-built aluminium-framed chassis extension with two pairs of wheels. This made the basis of a very useful minibus; with no driveline to get in the way a truly low-floor minibus could be produced, with no interior steps. The Talbot Express Pullman resulted in 1986.

Although used largely as a welfare vehicle it has excellent psv applications too, and was bought by a number of operators, not least Barrow Borough Transport, Kentish Bus and BET's short-lived Zippy operation in Preston. It is also often used on County Council tenders requiring a low-floor vehicle; the Talbot is a much cheaper alternative to much more expensive low-floor buses and just as effective where high capacity is not required.

Production was too small for a volume manufacturer, so in 1990 it was taken over by TBP of West Bromwich, which announced a successor based on the new Peugeot Boxer which finally replaced the Talbot in 1994.

Thornycroft

Most of Basingstoke-based Thornycroft's output of buses was prewar, though it also built a few of its Nippy HF lorry chassis for psv use, with small bodies with up to about 20 seats, between 1946 and 1950. MacBraynes was a user, which also took a specific psv chassis which Thornycroft introduced in the late 1940s. The Nippy had a four-cylinder 3.9litre petrol engine and four-speed gearbox.

Thornycroft built two new double-deck chassis in 1947, with its own 7.8litre diesel engine, fluid flywheel and an unconventional design of gearbox. Five similar single-deck chassis were built; bodied as coaches they operated for some years for the Bristol Co-Operative Society. Thornycroft was taken over by AEC in 1961.

Tilling-Stevens

Tilling-Stevens of Maidstone is another manufacturer which was best-known for its prewar products and is especially associated with the early days of motorbuses for its unusual petrol-electric concept. By the time World War 2 broke out it was a spent force, although it built a small number of coaches after the war. Unlike those pioneering efforts its postwar vehicles were entirely conventional, even conservative, in their approach, and despite Tilling-Stevens' involvement in the development of what became the Commer TS3 horizontal engine, they all had conventional vertical front engines.

Its first postwar models were the K5LA7 and K6LA7, which were introduced in September 1947. The K5LA7 was intended primarily as a half-cab single-deck service bus, though some were fitted with coach bodywork, and this had a Gardner 5LW five-cylinder 7.0litre engine and five-speed David Brown constant-mesh gearbox. The K6LA7 was a coach version with the larger six-cylinder, 8.4litre Gardner 6LW. The next year it made a version available with a larger Meadows 6DC.630 130bhp 10.35litre direct-injection diesel, the K6MA7. It appeared at the 1948 Commercial Motor Show with a Dutfield body featuring a radio and fluorescent lighting.

The various K-series models sold only to independent operators; no orders were forthcoming from the major operators, and in 1950 Tilling-Stevens had a go at the lightweight market with the Express Mark II. This was a full-fronted front-engined 30ft-long chassis, aimed at a similar market to the Bedford SB, introduced at the same time, and had a small four-cylinder Meadows 4D.330 5.4litre 80bhp diesel engine and five-speed constant-mesh gearbox. Despite a very low selling price and simple specification it too was destined not to sell very well and in 1953 Tilling-Stevens sold out to the Rootes Group. Its factory was turned over to production of the Commer TS3 engine.

Trojan

Trojan of Croydon was well-known as a lightweight van manufacturer in the 1950s. The bonneted one-ton model and the $1^1/4$ ton forward control model were offered as 13-seat psvs, and often marketed as a complete vehicle. All were unusually fitted with the two-stroke three-cylinder Perkins P3 engine. The forward-control chassis was also said to be bodied by Trojan itself; two all-Trojan coaches were at Earls Court in 1960, one for Scotts Greys of Darlington, the other for Edinburgh Corporation.

Volvo

During the 1980s there was much argument as to whether Volvo should be counted as a British manufacturer or not; it sourced some of its components in Britain and, although based in Sweden, built lorries in large numbers at its Scottish plant (see 'Ailsa').

For our purposes we will examine only those Volvo models built in Britain, which excludes Volvo's first model offered in Britain, the highly-regarded B58 mid-engined coach chassis. As noted earlier there was a close tie-up between Volvo and Ailsa — which was a British marque — in those early days, and the former Ailsa factory has at different times been used by Volvo for psv production in Britain, though was facing closure in mid-2000.

Volvo replaced the B58 with the yet more successful B10M in 1980. This again was a Swedish chassis, though B10M parts were assembled into British-built

Citybus double-deckers for a time.

However, Volvo was to become very much more significant in the history of the British bus. Leyland Bus had been sold to its management on 13 January 1987, during a very difficult time in the British bus market. In 1988 Volvo made a very generous offer to buy Leyland from its management, and on 30 March 1988 Leyland Bus was sold to Volvo. Volvo had great intentions for Leyland and, as part of its strategy for the company, began production of the B10M at Workington in 1990. The idea was that all UK market production would take place there, as well as some for certain other markets. VL Bus & Coach took over Leyland's sales from 1 January 1989, but on 1 July 1991 the Volvo Bus Ltd name replaced it; despite this, the Leyland name remained on the remaining Leyland-designed models.

In a shock announcement on 6 December 1991 it became known that Leyland's last manufacturing plant, Workington, was to close, spelling the end of the Tiger and Lynx. The Lynx was replaced in the UK market by the Swedish-built Volvo B10B chassis, and B10M production was once again concentrated in Sweden. However, this was not the end of the story for Volvo production in Britain. The Leyland Olympian was to continue, albeit revamped as a Volvo, and 60% of its components were sourced from Volvo. The Gardner engine option was dropped in favour of Volvo's own TD102KF 9.6litre engine, alongside the Cummins L10 which remained available. Production was moved to Irvine, which became partly a bus factory again, and the first Olympian was driven off the production line there on 22 March 1993.

Volvo had announced a new rear-engined midibus in 1992. When it had acquired Leyland, Volvo was keen to use some of the engineering expertise there, and there was some Leyland influence in the design of both this and the full-size B10B, while the B10L low-floor bus also owes some of its design to Leyland. The new midibus was a direct challenger to the Dennis Dart, though featured air suspension and the option of ZF automatic transmission as well as Allison. Unlike the Dart it could be built to a full 2.5m width, and was also available with manual transmission as a small coach. It was to be built in Austria as the B6R, though after a few pre-production buses were built there all production moved to Irvine, and the name was changed to B6. Production began simultaneously with the Olympian and soon built up to reasonable volumes. The B6 had much in common with the bigger B10M, though the engine was a vertical 5.4litre TD63E mounted in-line at the rear with options of 180bhp or 210bhp.

Given the success of Volvo's products hitherto, it seemed likely that the B6 would quickly halt the runaway success of the Dennis Dart. Yet it was substantially heavier, not as refined — even with air suspension — and, despite its bigger bus technology and Volvo's usual reputation, quickly gained a poor reputation for reliability. Stagecoach was the first major customer, taking 200, and Volvo sold 550 in the first two years of production, for a time giving Volvo 40% of the midibus market. But operators, Stagecoach included, tended not to come back for more. Dennis surged ahead again.

Although Dennis had already announced its Dart

Right:
A Volvo B6 in service with Cambus. The Cambus B6s were the first to have the Marshall body derived from the original Duple design for the Dennis Dart.

Centre right:
An all-Scottish product of Henderson Travel, Lanark; a Volvo B6 with Alexander Dash bodywork.

Below:
For a time the Volvo B10M was built at Workington. Some of those built in Britain formed the basis of National Expressliners; this one was used on Caledonian Express services by Tayside Travel Services. The concept of the Expressliner was a standard National Express coach with Plaxton bodywork leased to operators on the National Express network through Plaxton's Roadlease subsidiary.
S. L. Render

Above:
A Northern Counties Palatine II-bodied Volvo Olympian for Bristol CityLine, used on Park-&-Ride work.

Below:
Alexander's 'de luxe' version of the R-type, the Royale, was originally built for Yorkshire Coastliner on Volvo Olympians. The first is seen here entering service at Leeds in 1993.

SLF, Volvo actually beat Dennis to producing a low-floor midibus. A new, low-entrance version of the B6, the B6LE with a deep-drop front beam axle, was first shown in March 1995. It had a new Wright body — despite the fact Wright never bodied the standard B6 — derived from the body on the Dennis Lance SLF and called the Crusader. Whereas the B6 had been available in 8.5m, 9m and 9.9m lengths, the B6LE

Above:
A Volvo Olympian with Alexander bodywork for London United. In its latter years the Volvo Olympian became almost the standard London double-decker.

Below:
East Lancs built bodywork to Alexander style on the Olympian; this one at Grimsby was for Road Car.
G. P. Senior

started at 9.9m, and the first built was the biggest midibus yet seen, at 10.6m. Items such as rear suspension and cooling were modified to sort out problems experienced with the standard model.

Again the B6LE was never destined to catch up with the Dart SLF in terms of sales, though Travel West Midlands adopted it as standard, with Wright bodywork. Indeed most B6LEs were bodied by Wright; at Coach & Bus '95 it was shown with the Plaxton Pointer body — though in practice most low-floor Pointers were built on Dennis — and Yorkshire Traction Group took a few with its favoured East Lancs bodywork. By 1999, combined production of B6 and B6LE had risen to just over 1,000; Dennis had built nearly six times as many Darts by this time. Thus, during 1999 another new version of the B6 was announced.

Volvo had already committed itself to producing low-floor buses with independent front suspension, as pioneered on the B10L and continued on the B10BLE, which combined the front end of the B10L with the less complex rear end of the B10B to create a lower-cost 12m low-floor single-decker for the British market. Although midibuses were detracting from the full-size market — especially as, with smaller wheels, they could come close to matching the capacity of a big bus in low-floor form, as reduced wheelarch intrusion created more passenger space — the Swedish-built B10BLE took a very respectable share of it. Once again, Wright bodywork (the Renown) was largely responsible for the B10BLE's success, though smaller numbers were bodied by Plaxton and Alexander.

Like the B10BLE, the new B6BLE had independent front suspension, and no longer offered a width of less than 2.5m. Three lengths were available, 9m, 9.6m and 10.5m, though Wright's body lengthened it by about 0.1m. Initial orders called for around 150, nearly all with Wright bodywork, including 60 for FirstGroup and 20 for Dublin Bus, but 15 with East Lancs bodywork entered service with London Traveller in September 1999 while 11 more were due for Yorkshire Terrier.

Volvo had announced in 1993 that, in addition to the Olympian and B6, the B10M would also be built at Irvine. The B10M is one of the most successful bus and coach chassis ever, with worldwide production now approaching 50,000. Building on the success of the earlier B58, which it began to replace from 1980, it is now one of the few mid-engined coach chassis still available. It is powered by a horizontal version of Volvo's 9.6litre engine, driving through (normally) a ZF synchromesh transmission, but also with the choice of Volvo's electronically-controlled Easy Gear Shift seven-speed 'box or ZF or Voith automatics. It differed from the B58 in having an all-welded chassis-frame (rather than bolted) and by offering air suspension as standard. With a fairly shallow engine in horizontal form, and with a chassis-frame dropped at the front

end, it made an excellent service bus as well as powerful premium coach chassis; used widely as a bus in Scandinavia it also became a standard bus type for Stagecoach until the move to low-floor buses rendered it no longer acceptable. With three shallow entrance steps and a completely flat floor inside, some would argue it is still well-suited to a service bus rôle, especially for interurban work.

Volvo's plan to move B10M production to Irvine came to fruition in August 1995, by which time the B10M was on to its Mk 4 model, the biggest difference from earlier models being the move of the radiator from the front to behind the nearside front wheel.

Although not subject to any further significant product development, the Olympian soldiered on. There was little significant double-deck competition for it; Dennis had virtually stopped building the Dominator, and its replacement, the in-line-engined Arrow, failed to catch on. Scania and DAF both nibbled away at the edges, the latter being offered with Northern Counties bodywork from 1994 as well as Optare. Yet the Olympian, the only double-decker on the market not derived from a single-decker, ruled supreme. London tenders specifying new double-deckers often went to the Olympian, and Stagecoach and FirstGroup bought it as standard. Even Arriva, which was not on the best of terms with Volvo and was DAF's UK importer, bought some, while other major buyers included Lothian Region Transport and Dublin Bus. Of all the major conurbations in the British Isles that operated double-deckers, West Midlands Travel alone did not buy the Olympian — and indeed, apart from a batch of 40 Scanias purchased in 1991, took no double-deckers following the end of MCW's production of the Metrobus until the low-floor era. Meanwhile, three-axle models continued to find their way to Hong Kong, where competition with Dennis was more on an equal footing.

Left:
Stagecoach standardised on the Olympian for its double-deckers until moving over to Dennis for low-floor ones. This Bluebird bus in Inverness has Northern Counties bodywork.
Paul Chancellor

Below:
FirstGroup also standardised on the Olympian for its corporate-style vehicles, using Alexander Royale bodywork in the main, as carried by this First Leeds bus, though others had Northern Counties.
Paul Chancellor

Only the move to low-floor buses was going to have any effect on the Olympian, and here it looked as if Volvo would score anyway. In most people's estimation, the star of the 1997 Coach & Bus Show was a new Volvo double-decker featuring a new Northern Counties-built Plaxton body, the President. Volvo was strangely tight-lipped about the chassis, leading to all sorts of wild speculation. Enough had leaked out or could be pieced together for most of us to know it was a low-floor chassis with an in-line 7litre vertical engine mounted in the nearside rear corner, and speculation that this was a derivative of a new low-floor single-deck chassis for worldwide use was also close to the mark. This was Volvo's new generation bus, the B7L, but no-one was prepared to admit it. The only thing that couldn't be worked out for sure was what the engine was — it was firmly locked away. It turned out to be a 7.3litre electronically-controlled derivative of the 7litre engine already offered in the new Swedish-built B7R rear-engined coach chassis, which had been launched the previous year.

DAF had a new, low-floor version of the DB250 chassis at the same show under an Optare Spectra for Travel West Midlands (as West Midlands Travel had become), but Volvo had obviously beaten Dennis in the race to produce a brand-new low-floor double-decker, and very nice it looked too. The Dennis Trident was at the show in three-axle export form, but so far the British version was only a drawing. Dennis was trailing because it had realised an in-line engine wouldn't work in a British-spec double-decker and had gone back to the drawing board . . .

In due course, Volvo found it had to do the same. It was another two years before the B7L emerged as a production double-decker, and this time Travel West Midlands was a significant customer; most of its order for 102 was delivered around the turn of 1999/2000, before any other orders were fulfilled, and was followed rapidly by a batch for London Central. By this time, Dennis was well and truly leading the double-deck market, having got production of its two-axle Trident going almost a year before Volvo and having turned them out as if there was no tomorrow during the rest of the year. With B6BLE sales not approaching those of the Dennis Dart, demand for 12m single-deckers and coaches being down, and having no suitable new-generation double-decker available, Volvo slipped to second place in the British market for the first time for many years, and was way behind Dennis.

The B7L is truly a worldwide low-floor model, though the transverse-engined version of it for double-deck use is a UK-market special. Production began at the Irvine factory, though the writing was already on the wall for British-built Volvos. It had already been announced that Irvine would close, with production switched to Sweden and to a new plant in Wroclaw, Poland. Irvine was due to close in mid-2000, ending the last of a long succession of British bus production with its roots in Leyland.

The B7L double-decker is available in 9.9m and 10.4m lengths, and is powered by a 7.3litre Volvo D7C engine. Nearly 450 were ordered off the drawing board, with major orders for Go-Ahead and FirstGroup in London following the 102 for Travel West Midlands, and 70 for London United, which had

Below:
A Solent Blue Line Volvo Olympian with East Lancs bodywork.

to keep elderly Metrobuses going while it waited for them.

The side-engined variant of the B7L is ultimately to replace Volvo's 12m low-floor single-deckers and the 18m articulated B10LA; while this is available as a complete vehicle in other markets, it remains to be seen whether Volvo will bring it in already bodied. A prototype B7LA had the first example of Wright's new Eclipse Fusion body when shown at Coach & Bus '99.

Meanwhile the Olympian lived on; home-market production was due to end in early 2000, with the final orders for Dublin and the last of all for Blazefield taking production of the model over the 10,000 mark. Nevertheless, a new export model, the Super Olympian, was developed, retaining the rear end of the

three-axle Olympian and marrying it up to a B10L front end to give a low floor. It retains the Volvo 9.6litre engine and is available in lengths of 10.6m, 11.3m and 12m. The first 100 are due to go to Kowloon Motor Bus (60) and New World First Bus (40).

The B10M coach chassis continued in production at Irvine, though a successor model is likely, as its 9.6litre horizontal engine looks unlikely to meet Euro 3 emission limits.

Although its days of UK production are numbered, Volvo continues to grow worldwide. In conjunction with Henlys it now owns Prevost, Novobus and Bluebird in the US, although, at the time of writing a proposed merger with Scania had been rejected by the European Union. Worldwide, Volvo is second only to Mercedes-Benz as a bus producer.

Above:
The first customer for the Volvo B6BLE was First Mainline; its vehicles have Wright bodywork.

Below:
Deliveries of the Volvo B7L finally commenced late in 1999. An early recipient was Go-Ahead Group, which had ordered the type in large numbers for its London operations. This London Central example is seen near Marble Arch on a route 12 Sunday working in March 2000.
Geoff Rixon